W9-AZT-897

AMERICAN HISTORY

RECONSTRUCTION TO THE PRESENT

Guided Reading Workbook

Copyright © by Houghton Mifflin Harcourt Publishing Company

All rights reserved. No part of this work may be reproduced or transmitted in any form or by any means, electronic or mechanical, including photocopying or recording, or by any information storage or retrieval system, without the prior written permission of the copyright owner unless such copying is expressly permitted by federal copyright law.

Permission is hereby granted to individuals using the corresponding student's textbook or kit as the major vehicle for regular classroom instruction to photocopy entire pages from this publication in classroom quantities for instructional use and not for resale. Requests for information on other matters regarding duplication of this work should be submitted through our Permissions website at https://customercare.hmhco.com/permission/Permissions.html or mailed to Houghton Mifflin Harcourt Publishing Company, Attn: Intellectual Property Licensing, 9400 Southpark Center Loop, Orlando, Florida 32819-8647.

Printed in the U.S.A.

ISBN 978-0-544-66908-6

11 12 13 14 15   0982   24 23 22 21 20

4500790182   B C D E F G

If you have received these materials as examination copies free of charge, Houghton Mifflin Harcourt Publishing Company retains title to the materials and they may not be resold. Resale of examination copies is strictly prohibited.

Possession of this publication in print format does not entitle users to convert this publication, or any portion of it, into electronic format.

Contents

© Houghton Mifflin Harcourt Publishing Company

HOW TO USE THIS BOOK

The purpose of this *Guided Reading Workbook* is to help you read and understand the content in *American History: Reconstruction to the Present*. You can use this *Guided Reading Workbook* in two ways.

1. Use the *Guided Reading Workbook* alongside the lessons in *American History: Reconstruction to the Present.*

• Refer to the *Guided Reading Workbook* while you are reading each lesson in *American History: Reconstruction to the Present*. All of the heads in the *Guided Reading Workbook* match the heads in the lessons.

• Use the *Guided Reading Workbook* to help you read and organize the information in each lesson.

2. Use the *Guided Reading Workbook* to study the material that will appear in the lesson tests.

• Reread the summary of every lesson.

• Review the definitions of the **Key Terms and People** in the *Guided Reading Workbook*.

• Review the graphic organizer that you created as you read the summaries.

• Review your answers to questions.

Strategy: Read the **Key Terms and People** and the definition of each. The **Key Terms and People** are in bold type.

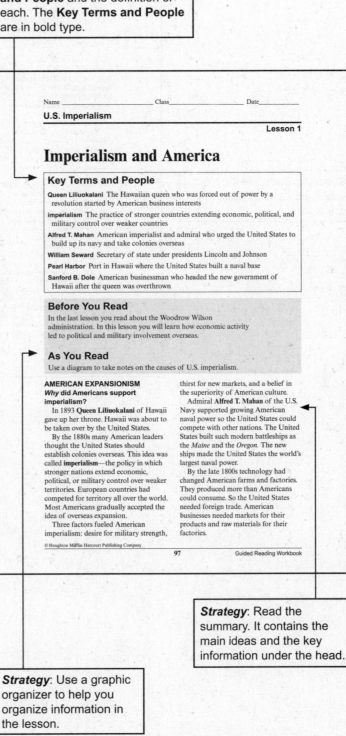

Name _____ Class_____ Date_____

U.S. Imperialism

Lesson 1

Imperialism and America

Key Terms and People

Queen Liliuokalani The Hawaiian queen who was forced out of power by a revolution started by American business interests

imperialism The practice of stronger countries extending economic, political, and military control over weaker countries

Alfred T. Mahan American imperialist and admiral who urged the United States to build up its navy and take colonies overseas

William Seward Secretary of state under presidents Lincoln and Johnson

Pearl Harbor Port in Hawaii where the United States built a naval base

Sanford B. Dole American businessman who headed the new government of Hawaii after the queen was overthrown

Before You Read

In the last lesson you read about the Woodrow Wilson administration. In this lesson you will learn how economic activity led to political and military involvement overseas.

As You Read

Use a diagram to take notes on the causes of U.S. imperialism.

AMERICAN EXPANSIONISM
***Why* did Americans support imperialism?**

In 1893 **Queen Liliuokalani** of Hawaii gave up her throne. Hawaii was about to be taken over by the United States.

By the 1880s many American leaders thought the United States should establish colonies overseas. This idea was called **imperialism**—the policy in which stronger nations extend economic, political, or military control over weaker territories. European countries had competed for territory all over the world. Most Americans gradually accepted the idea of overseas expansion.

Three factors fueled American imperialism: desire for military strength,

thirst for new markets, and a belief in the superiority of American culture.

Admiral **Alfred T. Mahan** of the U.S. Navy supported growing American naval power so the United States could compete with other nations. The United States built such modern battleships as the *Maine* and the *Oregon*. The new ships made the United States the world's largest naval power.

By the late 1800s technology had changed American farms and factories. They produced more than Americans could consume. So the United States needed foreign trade. American businesses needed markets for their products and raw materials for their factories.

© Houghton Mifflin Harcourt Publishing Company

97

Guided Reading Workbook

Strategy: Read the summary. It contains the main ideas and the key information under the head.

Strategy: Use a graphic organizer to help you organize information in the lesson.

Name _____ Class_____ Date_____
Lesson 1, *continued*

The third factor of American imperialism was a belief that the people of the United States were better than the people of other countries. This racist belief came from people's pride in their Anglo-Saxon (Northern European) heritage. People sometimes felt they had a duty to spread their culture and Christian religion among other people.

1. What were three reasons Americans supported imperialism?

_____

_____

THE UNITED STATES ACQUIRES ALASKA; THE UNITED STATES TAKES HAWAII
How did the Hawaiian Islands become a U.S. territory?

William Seward was secretary of state for presidents Lincoln and Andrew Johnson. In 1867 he purchased Alaska from Russia for $7.2 million. Some opponents in Congress made fun of the deal, calling it "Seward's Icebox" or "Seward's Folly."

The Hawaiian Islands, in the Pacific Ocean, had been important to the United States since the 1790s. Merchants had stopped there on their way to China and India. In the 1820s American missionaries founded Christian schools and churches on the islands.

A number of Americans had established sugar plantations in Hawaii. In the mid-1800s these large farms accounted for about three-quarters of the wealth in the islands. Plantation owners brought thousands of laborers to Hawaii from Japan, Portugal, and China. This weakened the influence of the native Hawaiians. By 1900 the foreign laborers outnumbered the Hawaiians three to one.

In 1875 the United States agreed to import Hawaiian sugar duty-free. Over the next 15 years, Hawaiian sugar production increased nine times. Then the McKinley Tariff in 1890 caused a crisis for Hawaiian sugar growers. With the duty on their sugar, Hawaiian growers faced stiff competition from other growers.

The powerful Hawaiian sugar growers called for the United States to annex Hawaii. The U.S. military had already understood the value of Hawaii. In 1887 the United States forced Hawaii to let it build a naval base at **Pearl Harbor,** Hawaii's best port. Also in that year, white business leaders forced Hawaii's King Kalakaua to amend Hawaii's constitution, limiting voting rights to only wealthy landowners. But when Kalakaua died in 1891, his sister became queen. Queen Liliuokalani wanted a new constitution that would give voting power back to ordinary Hawaiians. American business interests did not want this to happen.

American business groups organized a revolt against the queen. The U.S. ambassador John L. Stevens helped them. The planters took control of the island. They established a temporary government headed by American businessman **Sanford B. Dole.**

Stevens urged the U.S. government to annex the Hawaiian Islands. President Grover Cleveland refused to take over the islands unless a majority of Hawaiians favored that. In 1897, however, William McKinley became president. He favored annexation. In 1898 Hawaii became a U.S. territory.

2. How did Hawaiians lose control of their islands?

_____

© Houghton Mifflin Harcourt Publishing Company

98 Guided Reading Workbook

Strategy: Underline the main ideas and key information as you read.

Strategy: Answer the question at the end of each part.

© Houghton Mifflin Harcourt Publishing Company

The last page of each lesson of the *Guided Reading Workbook* ends
with a graphic organizer that will help you better understand the
information in the lesson. Use the graphic organizer to take notes as
you read. The notes can help you to prepare for the lesson and
module assessments.

Name _____ Class_____ Date_____

Lesson 1, *continued*

As you read this lesson, fill out the chart below by summarizing
reasons why the United States became an imperial power.

THE ROOTS OF AMERICAN IMPERIALISM		
1. Economic roots	2. Political and military roots	3. Racist roots

4. What did Admiral Mahan urge the United States to do to protect its interests?

For each year on the timeline below, identify one important event in the
history of U.S. involvement in Hawaii.

U.S. IMPERIALISM IN HAWAII	
1875	
1887	
1890	
1891	
1897	
1898	

© Houghton Mifflin Harcourt Publishing Company

99   Guided Reading Workbook

© Houghton Mifflin Harcourt Publishing Company

Prologue: American Beginnings

The Colonial Era

Key Terms and People

Christopher Columbus European explorer who believed he could reach Asia by sailing west across the Atlantic Ocean but reached the Americas instead

Juan Ponce de León Explorer who claimed what is now Florida for Spain

encomienda A system in which Native Americans were forced to work for Spanish settlers in the Americas

joint-stock companies Companies in which investors pooled their wealth with the hope of yielding a profit

Jamestown First permanent English settlement in North America

William Penn Founder of Pennsylvania

mercantilism Theory that a country's goal was self-sufficiency and that all countries were in a competition to acquire the most gold and silver

triangular trade The pattern of shipping trade across the Atlantic

Enlightenment Intellectual movement that started in Europe and applied reason and scientific methods to politics and social concerns

Great Awakening Religious revival movement in the colonies

French and Indian War War that gave the British control of North America

Before You Read

In this lesson you will learn about European exploration and settlement of the Americas.

As You Read

Use a chart to answer Who? What? Where? When? How? and Why? questions about the colonial era.

SPANISH COLONIES
What led the Spanish to claim land in the Americas?

In the 1400s new technology enabled Europeans to venture out over oceans. Ship captains tried new vessels called caravels and used the compass and astrolabe to plot direction at sea. Portugal was a leader in such ocean exploration, reaching the southern tip of Africa, and India as well.

Then Spain sponsored the voyage of **Christopher Columbus** as commander of the ships the *Niña,* the *Pinta,* and the *Santa María.* Searching for the Indies, he instead reached islands in the Americas. There he encountered a group of Native Americans called the Taino.

This introduction to the Americas led the Spanish to further explore and claim

© Houghton Mifflin Harcourt Publishing Company

the land. They believed it contained gold and silver. Explorer Hernándo Cortés conquered the Aztec to claim Mexico. Likewise, Francisco Pizarro defeated the Inca empire in South America. In 1513 **Juan Ponce de León** explored what is now Florida.

The Spanish established colonies in the lands they claimed. They forced Native Americans to work as slave labor in what is known as the *encomienda* system. In the mid-1500s the Spanish began to explore and settle the southwest and west regions of what is now the United States. In time, Spanish missions rose up as a way to convert Native Americans to Christianity.

1. What new technology allowed the Spanish and other Europeans to venture across the Atlantic Ocean?

_____

_____

ENGLISH COLONIES
Why were English colonies settled?

Spanish colonies were funded by the country's leader. In contrast, English colonies were often funded by **joint-stock companies.** These groups of investors were motivated by the desire to become rich. One such company, called the Virginia Company, sent colonists to settle in North America. John Smith and other colonists established the settlement of **Jamestown** in 1607. Smith convinced the colonists to farm rather than search for gold. After a shaky start, the Jamestown colony survived, partly through the help of the native Powhatan people.

A group of Puritans started a colony in New England for a different reason— the desire to have religious freedom. These Pilgrims founded the Plymouth Colony under the terms of the Mayflower Compact. This agreement was a first step toward establishing democracy in North America. The first New England settlement was not free of conflict. Roger Williams's differing beliefs about the rights of people led him to flee and start the colony of Rhode Island.

Meanwhile, the Dutch West India Company established the colony of New Netherland in their quest for trade goods. In time, the English peacefully took over the colony, renaming it New York. New Amsterdam, the colonial capital, became New York City.

William Penn soon established the English colony of Pennsylvania nearby. This colony became known for its support of the Quaker ideals of equality, cooperation, and religious toleration.

2. How did the reasons for the settlement for Jamestown and the Plymouth Colony differ?

_____

_____

COLONIAL ECONOMIES
How did the colonial economies of the North and South differ?

Thirteen British colonies had been founded by 1733. England benefited not only from the raw materials it gained from the colonies, but also from the sale of manufactured goods back to them. England wanted to increase its wealth and power through the economic system of **mercantilism.** In other words, England hoped to gain as much gold as possible and sell more goods than they bought. The English desire for trade helped both the English and the colonists.

© Houghton Mifflin Harcourt Publishing Company

The northern and southern colonies began to build very different economies. The southern economy was based on agriculture, and featured large plantations that focused on growing crops for sale. Slavery became an important way to fill labor needs. The sale of African people was part of a transatlantic network described as the **triangular trade.**

At the same time, the northern colonies concentrated on industries such as harvesting fish and building ships. Many immigrants arrived in the northern colonies to start new lives there.

3. Why was the triangular trade important to the southern colonies?

_____

_____

NEW SOCIAL MOVEMENTS
How did the Enlightenment and the Great Awakening affect the colonies?

During the Renaissance, Europeans had begun using reasoning to make discoveries about nature. These ideas about nature led to a movement called the **Enlightenment,** that applied reason and scientific methods to politics and social concerns.

Colonists, including Benjamin Franklin, embraced the idea of gaining truth through experimentation and reasoning. Franklin for example, flew his now-famous kite to demonstrate that lightning is a form of electrical power.

Enlightenment ideas also affected political thought. Thomas Jefferson and other colonists reasoned that human beings are born with natural rights that governments must respect.

Another movement called the **Great Awakening** brought back Puritan ideas about the importance of religion. The movement strengthened Christianity but also encouraged colonists to challenge the authority of established churches.

Both the Great Awakening and the Enlightenment caused people to question traditional authority. This, in turn, led colonists to question Britain's authority over their lives.

4. How did the Enlightenment affect the political attitudes of colonists?

_____

_____

THE FRENCH AND INDIAN WAR
What caused the French and Indian War and what were its effects?

At this same time British colonies in America were growing, the French had been establishing colonies in Canada and the Mississippi River valley. The colonists usually got along with Native Americans because they valued them as partners in the fur trade.

The **French and Indian War** was actually fought between the French and the British over disputes about who controlled the Ohio River valley region. Many Native Americans sided with the French, giving the war its name.

The British suffered early defeats but finally won the war. The war came to an end with the Treaty of Paris in 1763. Britain gained Canada and much of North America east of the Mississippi River. It also claimed Florida from Spain.

To help settle conflicts with Native Americans, the British prohibited colonists from settling west of the Appalachian Mountains with the Proclamation of 1763. Colonists ignored this and continued settling on Native American lands.

© Houghton Mifflin Harcourt Publishing Company

5. What were the effects of the French
and Indian War?

_____

_____

Answer these *Who? What? Where? When? How?* and *Why?* questions
about the colonial era.

SPANISH COLONIES	
1. **When** did Europeans begin using the oceans to reach other lands?	
2. **Why** did the Spanish want to claim land in the Americas?	
3. **Who** was the first European to explore Florida?	
ENGLISH COLONIES	
4. **What** Native American group helped the Jamestown settlers survive?	
5. **How** did the Mayflower Compact affect the future United States?	
COLONIAL ECONOMIES	
6. **What** did England hope to gain through mercantilism?	
7. **How** were the economies of the southern colonies and the northern colonies different?	
NEW SOCIAL MOVEMENTS	
8. **How** did Enlightenment ideas influence Thomas Jefferson?	
9. **What** effect did the Enlightenment and the Great Awakening have on the colonists' view of authority?	
THE FRENCH AND INDIAN WAR	
10. **What** two nations fought over territory during the French and Indian War?	
11. **Where** were colonists prohibited from settling under the Proclamation of 1763?	

© Houghton Mifflin Harcourt Publishing Company

Guided Reading Workbook

Prologue: American Beginnings

The American Revolution

Key Terms and People

Sugar Act Law passed by the British Parliament to raise tax money

Stamp Act Law passed by British Parliament to make colonists buy a stamp to place on items such as wills and newspapers

Boston Tea Party Protest against increased tea prices in which colonists dumped British tea into Boston Harbor

John Locke Enlightenment thinker who stated that people have natural rights to life, liberty, and property

Common Sense Pamphlet written by Thomas Paine that attacked the British monarchy

Thomas Jefferson Main author of the Declaration of Independence

Loyalists Colonists who were loyal to Britain

Patriots Colonists who wanted independence from Britain

Valley Forge Place where Washington's army spent the winter of 1777–1778

Charles Cornwallis British general who surrendered at the Battle of Yorktown

Yorktown Battle that gave Americans victory in the American Revolution

Treaty of Paris Treaty that officially ended the American Revolution

Before You Read

In the last lesson you learned about the colonial era. In this lesson you will learn how the American colonies gained freedom from Britain as a result of the American Revolution.

As You Read

Use a chart to describe people, places, items, and events related to the American Revolution.

THE ROAD TO REVOLUTION
What events led American colonists to fight for independence from Britain?

The British government needed to find a way to pay for the costs of the French and Indian War. In 1764 the government enacted the **Sugar Act,** which taxed the colonists for certain items they imported. The next year, they passed the **Stamp Act,** which placed a tax on documents and printed items.

These new taxes outraged the colonists. They did not believe Parliament should be able to tax colonists since the colonists were not represented in Parliament.

A colonial boycott of British goods

led Parliament to repeal the Stamp Act in 1766. However, it then passed the Declaratory Act, which stated that Parliament had total say over the colonies. They followed this act with the passing of the Townshend Acts, which taxed goods imported from Britain. The acts included a tax on tea, a popular drink in the colonies. Once again, the colonists boycotted British products.

The people of Boston were particularly angry. Some gathered at the Boston Customs House and harassed British soldiers. Their taunting led the British to open fire, killing five. One of the dead was Crispus Attucks. Aware of the growing tension in the colonies, Parliament repealed the Townshend Acts, except for the tax on tea.

Tensions did not decrease, however. Colonies began to set up committees of correspondence to exchange information about British threats to American freedoms.

More trouble erupted when Britain enacted the Tea Act, which allowed a British company to sell tea tax-free. This meant that its tea would cost less than tea from colonial sellers. Boston rebels disguised as Native Americans boarded the British company's ships and dumped its tea into Boston Harbor. The action became known as the **Boston Tea Party.**

An angry King George pressured Parliament to pass laws that became known as the Intolerable Acts. These acts closed Boston Harbor and allowed British soldiers to live in vacant colonial homes. Soon after, the committees of correspondence arranged the First Continental Congress. The delegates drew up a declaration of colonial rights. They stated that the colonies had a right to make their own decisions and could fight back if the British used force against them.

Preparing for a future fight, colonial minutemen—civilians who pledged to fight the British on a minute's notice—began storing guns and gunpowder in Concord, Massachusetts. The British made plans to seize the weapons, but Paul Revere and others warned colonists that the British were coming. The minutemen were ready for the approaching British soldiers, or "redcoats" as they became known. A brief fight took place in the town of Lexington and is remembered as the Battle of Lexington.

In May 1777 the Second Continental Congress met. They created the Continental army and made George Washington its commander. A fight at Breed's Hill led the Second Continental Congress to take further action. They asked Britain to agree to a request for peace called the Olive Branch Petition. King George promptly rejected it.

1. What British action led to the Boston Tea Party?

_____

_____

DECLARING INDEPENDENCE
Why did the American colonists declare independence?

More and more colonists began to think that war with Britain was the only solution to their problems. They thought carefully about the ideas of Enlightenment philosopher **John Locke.** He stated that people had natural rights to life, liberty, and property. In addition, he said that people have the right to resist and even overthrow a government that interferes with these basic rights.

The colonists were convinced that the various acts of Parliament violated their right as English citizens. Some of these

© Houghton Mifflin Harcourt Publishing Company

Guided Reading Workbook

rights included taxation only by consent, a presumption of innocence, and no quartering of troops in private homes.

In addition, colonists were moved by the words Thomas Paine had written in a pamphlet titled **Common Sense.** In it, Paine listed the benefits of independence.

The Continental Congress finally decided to form a new government. Virginia lawyer **Thomas Jefferson** was selected to prepare the final draft of a Declaration of Independence. The document declared that the rights of "Life, Liberty, and the pursuit of Happiness" were "unalienable," or could never be taken away. It also stated that people have a right to "alter or abolish" a government that denied citizens their basic rights. It continued with a list of British violations to this principle and declared the American colonies independent.

2. According to the Declaration, why was it necessary for the colonists to declare independence?

_____

_____

THE REVOLUTIONARY WAR
What events led the Americans to victory?

Americans found themselves divided about the issue of declaring independence. **Loyalists** opposed independence and remained loyal to the king. On the other hand, **Patriots** supported independence and thought it would help them both politically and economically.

Hoping to isolate New England, Britain fought Washington's Continental army to successfully capture New York City. Later they gained America's capital city, Philadelphia. Then the Americans met with success at Saratoga, where they surrounded British forces. This important victory convinced the French to support the Americans in their fight for freedom.

Low on food and supplies, Washington and his troops fought to stay alive at winter camp in **Valley Forge,** Pennsylvania. Many died, but those who stayed vowed to continue the fight. In fact, they learned new skills at Valley Forge. They also gained the assistance of the French Marquis de Lafayette. The Continental army was now an effective fighting force set to win victory.

Wives at home helped the war effort by managing farms and businesses. Some even washed and cooked for the troops. Some enslaved African Americans used the confusion of war to escape to freedom, and some fought for the Continental army. Most Native Americans remained apart from the war.

In 1778 the British won Savannah, Georgia. Then General **Charles Cornwallis** led British forces to capture Charles Town, South Carolina, in 1780. The next year, colonists fought hard to keep Cornwallis from taking the Carolinas. Moving into Virginia, Cornwallis stationed his army at **Yorktown.** There, French and American troops surrounded the British and forced Cornwallis to surrender. The war officially ended with the signing of the **Treaty of Paris** in 1783.

American society changed after the war. Distinctions between the rich and the average person began to fade. The idea of egalitarianism, or the belief in

© Houghton Mifflin Harcourt Publishing Company

Lesson 2, *continued*

the equality of all people, arose. Ability and effort became more important than personal wealth or family virtue. Still this idea of equality applied mainly to men and not to women and African Americans.

3. Why might the Battle of Saratoga be considered a turning point in the war?

_____

_____

Provide details about each person, place, item, or event related to the American Revolution.

THE ROAD TO REVOLUTION	
1. The French and Indian War	2. The Stamp Act
3. The Boston Tea Party	4. Battle of Lexington
DECLARING INDEPENDENCE	
5. John Locke	6. *Common Sense*
7. Thomas Jefferson	8. Continental Congress
THE REVOLUTIONARY WAR	
9. Loyalists	10. Valley Forge
11. Americans during the war	12. Yorktown

© Houghton Mifflin Harcourt Publishing Company

Prologue: American Beginnings

A New Nation

Key Terms and People

Federalists People who supported the Constitution

Antifederalists People who opposed the Constitution

Bill of Rights Constitutional amendments that protect the rights of citizens

cabinet The group of department heads who serve as the president's chief advisers

Alexander Hamilton The first secretary of the U.S. Treasury, who wanted to pay the nation's foreign debt immediately and gradually repay the full value of all bonds

sectionalism Placing the interest of a region ahead of the nation as a whole

nullification The idea that states had the right to nullify or void any law they deemed unconstitutional

Jeffersonian republicanism Thomas Jefferson's theory that the people should control the government and that a simple government best suited the needs of the people

Louisiana Purchase The purchase of Louisiana from France for $15 million, which roughly doubled the size of the United States

Missouri Compromise An agreement that settled the conflict over Missouri's application for statehood

Andrew Jackson The seventh president, who was said to speak for the common man

Trail of Tears An 800-mile forced march westward in which many Cherokee died

Before You Read

In the last lesson you learned about the American Revolution. In this lesson you will learn how the United States set up its new government.

As You Read

Use a chart to identify important events in early United States history.

© Houghton Mifflin Harcourt Publishing Company

Lesson 3, *continued*

FORMING A NEW GOVERNMENT
What important decisions did the Constitutional Convention make?

In 1781 the Second Continental Congress set up a plan for government called the Articles of Confederation. Under the plan, most governmental power was held by the states. However, each state had one vote in Congress, which decided large matters such as declaring war. The new nation faced many problems because the central government was so weak. It could not collect taxes, regulate trade, or easily pass and enforce laws.

Delegates called to the Constitutional Convention decided to abandon the Articles of Confederation and form a new government based on the Constitution.

Much debate took place over giving fair representation to both large and small states. Finally the Great Compromise promised a two-house Congress. Each state would be equally represented in the Senate, but representation in the House of Representatives would be based on population size. The Three-Fifths Compromise established that three-fifths of a state's slaves would be counted as part of the population.

The delegates went on to divide power between the states and the national government in a system called federalism. They created three branches of government—legislative, executive, and judicial—and established an amendment process for the Constitution.

Federalists supported the ratification of the Constitution because it balanced power between states and the national government. **Antifederalists** opposed having a strong government. Debate about ratification ended when

Federalists agreed to the Antifederalists' demand that a **Bill of Rights** be add to the Constitution.

1. What was the result of the Great Compromise?

_____

_____

SHAPING THE NEW NATION
What issues affected the early United States?

President George Washington and Congress now had to put the new plan into practice. Congress established executive departments such as the Department of State and the Department of the Treasury to assist the president. The leaders of these departments soon became part of the president's **cabinet,** or chief advisers.

Secretary of State **Alexander Hamilton** proposed the formation of a national bank. Opponents claimed that a bank could not be established since it was not mentioned in the Constitution. Cabinet members debated whether the Constitution should be strictly or loosely interpreted. The differing opinions gave rise to a two-party system. The Federalists wanted a strong central government, while the Democratic-Republicans wanted strong state governments.

The new government took action to raise much-needed money. For example, Congress passed a protective tariff, or import tax on goods produced overseas. A rebellion over a new tax on whiskey forced the government to assert its authority by sending in armed forces.

The presidential election of 1796 was a tricky one. Federalist John Adams won the presidency, but the Democratic-Republican candidate Thomas Jefferson

© Houghton Mifflin Harcourt Publishing Company

became the vice-president. Mainly northerners voted for Adams, while most southerners voted for Jefferson. This result showed the dangers of **sectionalism,** or placing the interest of a region ahead of the nation as a whole.

Adams's Federalist Party pushed through the Alien and Sedition Act, which resulted in Democratic-Republicans being punished for criticizing the government. The state of Kentucky asserted the principle of **nullification.** They said these acts of Congress were unconstitutional and would continue to be controversial.

2. Why did the two-party system form?

_____

_____

THE JEFFERSONIAN ERA
How did the United States change during Jefferson's presidency?

Thomas Jefferson narrowly defeated Adams for president in the 1800 election. Congress soon passed the Twelfth Amendment, which said that the president and vice-president must run together.

Jefferson practiced a theory of government that became known as **Jeffersonian republicanism.** He believed that a simple government best suited the needs of the people. Therefore, he worked to shrink the government and cut costs.

During this time, the Supreme Court struck down a law Congress had passed. In doing so, it established the principle of judicial review, which allows the court to declare a law unconstitutional.

Thomas Jefferson's presidency is perhaps best remembered for the **Louisiana Purchase.** Buying the Louisiana Territory from France nearly doubled the size of the United States. Jefferson then asked Meriwether Lewis and William Clark to explore the new territory and report their findings.

The next president, James Madison, saw the country through the War of 1812. After the war, Monroe helped the United States gain economic independence from Europe, established a protective tariff, and rechartered the national bank. During this time, the Federalist Party came to an end largely because it had opposed the war.

3. How did the Louisiana Purchase affect the United States?

_____

_____

NATIONALISM AND SECTIONALISM
What signs of nationalism and sectionalism became evident during the early 1800s?

Foreign affairs dominated the first term of President James Monroe, who was elected in 1816. His secretary of state, John Quincy Adams, based his foreign policy on nationalism, putting national interests ahead of regional issues.

During this time, the boundaries of the United States expanded. Its territory now included Florida and stretched to the Pacific Ocean. To deal with the rest of the world, President Monroe established what became known as the Monroe Doctrine. It warned European powers not to take part in Western Hemisphere issues. Likewise, the United States would not become involved in European affairs.

Meanwhile, the United States had become divided because of differing economies in the North and the South.

Industries thrived in northern states, while southern states depended on agriculture and slavery. Most northeasterners were pleased by new tariffs on European imports because they helped industry. However, people in the South and West did not think they were necessary.

Northerners and southerners also disagreed about admitting new states. Henry Clay's **Missouri Compromise** temporarily solved this problem by admitting Maine as a free state and Missouri as a slave state. The Louisiana Territory was divided in two: one part with slavery and one without.

4. What issues caused sectionalism in the early 1800s?

_____

_____

THE AGE OF JACKSON
On *what* issues did President Andrew Jackson hold strong views?

Andrew Jackson became president following John Quincy Adams's single term in office. Jackson won election with the promise to give common people greater political power. This idea became known as Jacksonian democracy. One way he did this was through the spoils system, which allowed him to fill government positions with friends and political allies.

Political power did not extend to Native Americans. With Jackson's approval, Congress passed the Indian Removal Act, which ordered Native Americans to move west. The Cherokee refused to leave their homes but eventually were forced west on the **Trail of Tears.**

In some ways, Jackson was a man of contradictions. For example, he defended federal powers in a nullification issue but wanted to decrease them when it came to the national bank.

5. On what main idea was Jacksonian democracy based?

_____

_____

Lesson 3, *continued*

Describe at least two events that took place during each time in history.

1. Time of the Constitutional Convention
2. George Washington's administration
3. Thomas Jefferson's administration
4. James Monroe's administration
5. Andrew Jackson's administration

© Houghton Mifflin Harcourt Publishing Company

Economic and Social Changes

Key Terms and People

free enterprise The freedom of private businesses to operate competitively for profit with little government regulation

entrepreneurs Business owners

Samuel F. B. Morse Inventor of the telegraph

Lowell textile mills Large facilities in Lowell, Massachusetts, that produced cloth in the early 1800s

strike Work stoppage

immigration The movement of people into another place, such as a country, to live permanently

Ralph Waldo Emerson Leading transcendental philosopher

abolition Movement to outlaw slavery

William Lloyd Garrison Abolitionist leader and newspaper editor

Frederick Douglass Escaped slave who became a noted abolitionist leader

Elizabeth Cady Stanton Leader in the abolitionist and women's rights movements

Seneca Falls Convention Convention held in 1848 to argue for women's rights

Before You Read

In the last lesson you learned about political changes in the early years of the nation. In this lesson you will learn about economic and social changes of the early 1800s.

As You Read

Complete a chart with facts about economic and social changes in the 1800s.

REGIONAL ECONOMIES
How did the economies of the North and South differ?

The economies of the different regions of the United States began to differ in the early 1800s. By this time, the Industrial Revolution that started in Britain had reached the United States. However, the use of new technology for large-scale production mainly impacted the North.

The first American industries rose up in New England. Soon, textile mills and other kinds of manufacturers dotted the North. Farmers in the North changed as well. They started to specialize in just one or two kinds of crops or livestock. They used the money they earned from the sale of their products to buy goods made in northern factories. The interconnection of agriculture and

© Houghton Mifflin Harcourt Publishing Company

manufacturing helped create a market economy.

Meanwhile, agriculture continued to support the southern economy. Eli Whitney's cotton gin allowed farmers in the South to grow cotton more profitably. Soon, cotton became the South's most important crop. Because many workers were needed to grow cotton, slavery expanded in the South.

1. How did the invention of the cotton gin affect the South?

_____

_____

THE MARKET REVOLUTION
How did the establishment of a market economy affect Americans?

America's market economy continued to spread. More and more people bought and sold goods rather than making them for themselves. **Free enterprise** had become a main driving force for economic growth. In this system, private businesses have freedom to compete to earn profits with little government regulation. **Entrepreneurs** invested their own money in new industries. They were willing to take risks to earn huge profits.

The early 1800s became a time of invention. Some inventions improved the ways people communicated. For example, **Samuel F. B. Morse** patented the telegraph, which sent messages quickly. Such inventions allowed businesses to communicate over long distances.

Better transportation systems improved how people and goods moved. Robert Fulton's steamboat became a main way to move freight on rivers. People even built canals to move products in places where there were

no waterways. Yet the introduction of railroads gave Americans an even better way to move goods.

American workers produced more and better goods than ever before. The products were more affordable for Americans and easier to get, even if they were made far away. By the 1840s improved transportation and communication had made America's regions more interdependent.

With the help of investors, the Northeast became the center of American commerce. The fertile soil of the Midwest led that area to excel at farming. The newly invented John Deere steel plow turned prairie land into farmland. Cyrus McCormick's reaper helped farmers harvest grain. The South continued to grow crops such as cotton and tobacco.

The market economy changed how Americans worked. Machines let unskilled workers do tasks once done only by skilled artisans. However, they needed to work in factories. This meant less time with families. Sometime, people moved to new communities built around factories.

Many women left family farms to find work in the **Lowell textile mills.** Factory owners welcomed women because they were paid less than men. Still, this work offered women better pay than sewing or other jobs open to them.

Factory workers often faced poor conditions, such as long hours and cramped workspaces. One way to protest this was by organizing a **strike,** or work stoppage. Striking workers hoped to force employers to make changes. Most strikes failed because employers could easily replace striking workers with newcomers to the country who needed jobs badly.

Between 1830 and 1860 European

immigration increased dramatically in the United States. Many Irish people came to escape the Great Potato Famine. These immigrants faced prejudice because they were poor and Roman Catholic. Also, some workers feared that the immigrants would take their jobs.

Unhappiness with working conditions led some workers to join together in trade unions to gain greater power. However, these new trade unions faced much opposition.

2. How did a market economy affect American life?

_____

_____

REFORMING AMERICAN SOCIETY
How **did Americans work to improve society?**

Besides working conditions, Americans faced many other problems. Religious and social reform movements formed to come up with solutions.

Many of the movements trace their beginnings to the Great Awakening. This Christian movement aimed at reviving religious feeling. It focused on individual responsibility for salvation and the improvement of society. Followers attended revival meetings where they listened to emotional sermons, studied the Bible, and reflected on their lives.

Writer **Ralph Waldo Emerson** led another kind of awakening known as transcendentalism. Transcendentalists believed that truth could be discovered by observing nature and relating it to one's own experience.

In the North, African American churches became political, cultural, and social centers. Slaves in the South did not have their own churches, but interpreted Bible stories they heard as promises of freedom. African Americans, along with some whites, envisioned an end to slavery.

Abolition, the movement to end slavery, became the most important reform movement of all. Editor **William Lloyd Garrison** strongly supported abolition and wrote about the subject. His efforts helped convince more people to work to end slavery. Former slave **Frederick Douglass** was well known for the eloquent speeches he gave about the evils of slavery.

Some slaves, such as Nat Turner, unsuccessfully tried to rebel against their condition. More northerners called for emancipation, while southerners called for tighter restrictions on African Americans.

Women of the early 1800s had limited economic or social opportunities. Still, they took part in many of the reform movements, especially abolition. Women also worked to end alcohol use and help the mentally disabled and the imprisoned.

Women made strides in gaining an education as well. Some new schools were started just for women, while others began accepting women for the first time. Often, improved education led to more opportunities for women. Elizabeth Blackwell became the first woman to graduate from medical college. African American women, though, continued to have little chance of gaining an education.

Participation of women in the various reform movements led to the women's rights movement. Its goal was to provide women with increased opportunities outside the home. Reformers **Elizabeth Cady Stanton** and Lucretia Mott were early leaders of the women's rights

Lesson 4, *continued*

movement. They and others worked hard to organize the **Seneca Falls Convention.** There, more than 300 women discussed issues such as gaining the right to vote.

3. What effect did working in reform movements have on women?

_____

_____

Fill in the chart about economic and social changes in the 1800s.

Describe the economies of the North and South during the early 1800s.	
1. North	2. South

Explain how the people and inventions helped expand the national market economy.	
3. Entrepreneurs	
4. Telegraph	
5. Steamboat and canals	
6. Steel plow and reaper	

Fill in details about each of the reform movements listed.		
Movement	**Key Leader(s)**	**Efforts Made on Behalf of the Movement**
7. Transcendentalism		
8. Abolition		
9. Women's Rights		

© Houghton Mifflin Harcourt Publishing Company

Westward Expansion

Key Terms and People

manifest destiny Belief that the United States was ordained to expand to the Pacific Ocean and into Mexican and Native American territory

Stephen F. Austin Established a colony in Texas

Sam Houston First president of Republic of Texas

Treaty of Guadalupe Hidalgo Treaty ending the War with Mexico

popular sovereignty The right of people in an area to decide issues for themselves, especially to settle the question of slavery

Stephen Douglas Senator from Illinois who worked to pass the Compromise of 1850

Underground Railroad Secret network of people who hid fugitive slaves as they traveled north to freedom

Harriet Tubman Famous "conductor" on the Underground Railroad

Dred Scott Slave who was briefly taken by his owner into free territory

Abraham Lincoln President during the Civil War

Confederacy "Confederate States of America," formed in 1861 by the southern states that seceded from the Union

Jefferson Davis President of the Confederate States of America

Before You Read

In the last lesson you learned about economic and social changes of the early 1800s. In this lesson you will learn about westward expansion, new territories in the West, the conflict over slavery, and secession.

As You Read

Use a chart to take notes on issues, events, and their outcomes.

MANIFEST DESTINY
Why did Americans move west?

In the 1840s American settlers began moving west. They thought they were helping fulfill the country's **manifest destiny** by expanding west.

Americans had other reasons for moving, such as available land and because of economic problems in the East. A religious group called the Mormons migrated to escape persecution for their beliefs. They settled near the Great Salt Lake, in what is now Utah.

Settlers used old Native American trails and new routes. The Santa Fe Trail

Lesson 5, *continued*

was one of the busiest trade routes. Another trail was the Oregon Trail.

Britain and the U.S. settled border disputes over the East and Midwest and continued "joint occupation" of the Oregon Territory. Then, in 1846 they agreed to extend the mainland boundary westward from the Rocky Mountains to Puget Sound, establishing the current border between the U.S. and Canada.

1. What were four reasons settlers moved west?

_____

_____

NEW TERRITORIES IN THE WEST
How did Texas, California, and other territories become part of the U.S.?

After Mexico won independence from Spain, the Mexican government wanted Americans to settle in Texas. Soon there were more Anglo, or English-speaking, settlers than Tejanos, or Mexican settlers, in Texas.

In 1821 **Stephen F. Austin** established a colony in Texas. Cultural differences were a problem. The Protestant Anglo settlers spoke English. Also, many settlers were southerners who had brought slaves with them. Mexico had ended slavery in 1829 and insisted, in vain, that Texans free their slaves.

Austin went to Mexico to ask the president, Santa Anna, for more self-government for Texas. Santa Anna put Austin in prison. When he was freed, Austin thought war was necessary. Santa Anna, determined to make Texas obey Mexican law, marched his army to San Antonio, and the Texas Revolution began.

The commander of the mission and fort at the Alamo in San Antonio

thought his troops could stop Santa Anna. But Santa Anna and his troops attacked the Alamo. After 13 days, the Mexicans captured the mission after killing all 187 Anglos.

Six weeks later, Texans defeated Santa Anna near the San Jacinto River. **Sam Houston** led the Americans as they shouted "Remember the Alamo!" They captured Santa Anna, but set him free when he granted Texas independence. Houston was elected president of the new Republic of Texas in 1836.

Most Texans wanted to be annexed by the United States. Southerners wanted Texas because it had slavery. Northerners feared another slave territory would tip the balance in the Senate in favor of slave states. When James K. Polk became president in 1844, he favored annexation. Texas entered the Union in 1845.

President Polk thought a war with Mexico would bring California and New Mexico into the Union. So he supported Texan claims that its southern border extended to the Rio Grande.

Polk tried to purchase California and New Mexico and negotiate the boundary dispute. Mexico's officials refused to discuss it. Polk ordered U.S. troops into the area claimed by the United States.

Then Americans sent an exploration party into California in 1845, which violated Mexico's rights. Mexican troops crossed the Rio Grande into Texas and killed 11 U.S. soldiers. Polk asked Congress to declare war, and it did.

Some Americans in California had already declared their independence, and they set up the Republic of California. Mexican troops fought this but did not win.

Generals Zachary Taylor and

© Houghton Mifflin Harcourt Publishing Company

Winfield Scott won one victory after another until Mexico was defeated. In 1848 Mexico and the United States signed the **Treaty of Guadalupe Hidalgo,** ending the war. Mexico agreed to the Rio Grande as the border between the United States and Mexico. It also ceded New Mexico and California for $15 million. The area included present-day California, Nevada, New Mexico, Utah, most of Arizona, and parts of Colorado and Wyoming.

In 1853 the U.S. paid Mexico another $10 million to secure a southern railroad route to the Pacific Ocean. Known as the Gadsden Purchase, it set the current borders of the contiguous 48 states.

Then, in 1848 gold was discovered near Sutter's Mill in the Sierra Nevada. People raced to Sacramento to pan for gold. By the end of 1849, California's population was over 100,000. The discovery of gold helped California's economy.

2. Why were southerners in favor of Texas annexation and northerners opposed to it?

_____

_____

THE CONFLICT OVER SLAVERY; PROTEST, RESISTANCE, AND VIOLENCE
Why was slavery a major issue?

Although the North and South were different culturally and economically, it was slavery that led to conflict. The southern plantation economy needed enslaved labor. The North was industrialized and opposed it. As new states and territories came into the Union, supporters wanted more slave states, while opponents did not want it to spread.

The issue of slavery in California and western territories was a problem for the 31st Congress in December 1849. It had to deal with statehood for California, and a border dispute between Texas and part of New Mexico Territory. Senator Henry Clay presented a compromise. To please the North, the compromise said that California would be admitted as a free state. To please the South, the compromise called for a stricter fugitive slave law. To make both sides happy, he called for **popular sovereignty** in New Mexico and Utah so they could decide whether to be a slave or free state.

The Senate rejected the compromise. **Stephen Douglas** of Illinois then reintroduced each part one at a time. When President Zachary Taylor died, Millard Fillmore, his successor, supported the compromise. The Compromise of 1850 became law.

The Fugitive Slave Act denied fugitive slaves a jury trial and said that people found guilty of helping a fugitive could be fined or imprisoned. Northerners resisted the law and organized committees to send endangered African Americans to safety in Canada, which was dangerous.

Free African Americans and white abolitionists developed a secret network of people who would hide fugitive slaves. The escape routes were called the **Underground Railroad. Harriet Tubman** was a famous conductor on the Underground Railroad. She made 19 trips back to the South and helped about 300 slaves flee to freedom.

In 1852 Harriet Beecher Stowe published *Uncle Tom's Cabin,* which showed the horrors of slavery. It stirred abolitionists to increase their protests against the Fugitive Slave Act. Southerners criticized the book as an attack on the South.

The debate over slavery in the West continued with the Nebraska and Kansas territories, which were north of the Missouri Compromise line, and therefore closed to slavery. Stephen Douglas wanted to divide the area into Nebraska in the north and Kansas in the south. His bill would repeal the Missouri Compromise and allow popular sovereignty. After bitter debate, the Kansas-Nebraska Act passed.

Supporters and opponents of slavery rushed to Kansas to vote on slavery. Thousands of "border ruffians" from Missouri went into Kansas to vote illegally. Violence occurred, and the territory got the name "Bleeding Kansas."

3. How did the Compromise of 1850 attempt to solve U.S. problems?

_____

_____

CONFLICT LEADS TO SECESSION
What **events led to secession?**

Conflicts continued about slavery. A Supreme Court case in 1857 involved a slave, **Dred Scott,** whose owner took him from the slave state of Missouri to free territory in Illinois and Wisconsin and then back to Missouri. Scott appealed to the Supreme Court for his freedom since he had lived in free territory for several years. The Supreme Court said that Dred Scott could not sue in federal court because he was not a citizen. The Court said that being in a free territory did not make a slave free and that slaves were property and the Fifth Amendment protected people from losing property. It also said that territories could not deprive slaveholders of their property by excluding slavery.

In 1858 the race for the U.S. Senate between Democratic incumbent Stephen Douglas and Republican **Abraham Lincoln** started. Lincoln challenged Douglas to a series of debates about slavery in the territories. Douglas opposed slavery but was in favor of popular sovereignty. Lincoln thought slavery was immoral. He did not think people would give it up unless a constitutional amendment abolished it.

In their second debate, Lincoln asked if the settlers of a territory could vote to exclude slavery before it became a state. The *Dred Scott* decision said no, so popular sovereignty did not mean anything. Douglas then said that the people of a territory could get around the Dred Scott decision by electing representatives who would not enforce slave property laws. Douglas won the Senate seat.

Abolitionist John Brown decided to take action. In October 1859 he led a band of 21 followers to Harpers Ferry, Virginia. He planned to seize the federal arsenal there and start a slave uprising. Instead, troops ended the rebellion. Brown was tried and executed. Reaction was intense in both sections of the country. The North denounced the South, while southerners assaulted whites suspected of antislavery views.

Lincoln won the 1860 presidential election. He had pledged to halt the spread of slavery, but said he would not abolish it. He received no electoral votes from the South. His victory convinced southerners that they had lost their political voice in the national government. Some southern states began seceding from the Union. South Carolina seceded on December 20, 1860. Then Mississippi, Florida, Alabama, Georgia, Louisiana, and Texas seceded,

© Houghton Mifflin Harcourt Publishing Company

too. Together, they formed the Confederate States of America, or **Confederacy.** They elected **Jefferson Davis** president. People wondered if the North would allow the South to secede without a fight.

4. Why did the South secede?

_____

_____

Identify the outcomes of each issue or event.

Issues or Events	Outcomes
1. What was the effect of manifest destiny?	
2. What brought American settlers into conflict with the Mexican government?	
3. Why was the United States at first reluctant to annex Texas?	
4. How did the war with Mexico end?	
5. How did California's statehood affect the U.S.?	
6. What were the terms of the Compromise of 1850?	
7. How did the Kansas-Nebraska Act propose to deal with the issue of slavery?	
8. How did the *Dred Scott* case affect slavery?	
9. What was the effect of the raid on Harpers Ferry and John Brown's execution?	
10. What did Lincoln's election lead to?	

© Houghton Mifflin Harcourt Publishing Company

Prologue: American Beginnings

The Civil War

Key Terms and People

Stonewall Jackson Confederate general

Ulysses S. Grant Union general

Robert E. Lee Confederate general

Emancipation Proclamation Order issued by Lincoln freeing slaves behind Confederate lines

conscription Drafting of men to serve in the army

income tax Tax that takes a percentage of an individual's income

Gettysburg Most decisive battle of the war

William Tecumseh Sherman Commander of Union troops in Georgia and South Carolina

Appomattox Courthouse Site of the Confederate surrender

Thirteenth Amendment Abolished slavery everywhere in the United States

John Wilkes Booth Assassin of President Lincoln

Before You Read

In the last lesson you learned about westward expansion. In this lesson you will learn about the Civil War and its effects on the people of the North and the South.

As You Read

Use a chart to take notes on the causes and effects of different situations related to the Civil War.

THE WAR BEGINS
What made the Union stronger than the Confederacy?

Soon after the Confederacy was formed, Confederate soldiers attacked Fort Sumter. The next day, Union forces defending the fort surrendered.

The North became united after its loss of Fort Sumter. When Lincoln asked for volunteers for the Union army, the response was overwhelming. In the South, Virginia, North Carolina,

Arkansas, and Tennessee seceded. So 11 states were now in the Confederacy. People in western Virginia opposed slavery, so they seceded from Virginia and joined the Union as West Virginia. The four slave states of Maryland, Kentucky, Delaware, and Missouri stayed in the Union.

The North had advantages over the South such as a larger population, more factories, more food production, and better railroads. The South had cotton,

© Houghton Mifflin Harcourt Publishing Company

Guided Reading Workbook

Lesson 6, *continued*

better generals, and motivated soldiers.

The North had to conquer the South to win. Its plan was to blockade southern ports to keep out supplies, to split the Confederacy in two at the Mississippi River, and to capture the Confederate capital of Richmond, Virginia. The Confederacy's strategy was mostly defensive, although southern leaders encouraged their generals to attack the North if the opportunity arose.

Confederates won the first battle of the war, Bull Run. The winning general was **Stonewall Jackson.** He earned his nickname because of his strong defense.

General **Ulysses S. Grant** invaded western Tennessee Confederate forts and pushed on toward the Mississippi River. Meanwhile, the navy, commanded by David C. Farragut, captured the port of New Orleans. Grant and Farragut had almost cut the Confederacy in two.

Confederate general **Robert E. Lee** and his troops crossed the Potomac River into Maryland. Union general McClellan ordered his troops to pursue Lee. The two sides fought near Antietam. Lee retreated. However, Union troops did not chase Lee's troops. If they had, the war might have ended then. Lincoln fired McClellan.

The South had supplied Britain with much of its cotton. When the Civil War broke out, the South hoped that Britain would provide support and recognize it as an independent nation. But Britain had a large supply of cotton and did not depend on the South. Britain remained neutral.

Abolitionists in the North felt that slavery should be abolished. Eventually, Lincoln issued the **Emancipation Proclamation.** The proclamation freed all slaves behind Confederate lines.

Both the Union and Confederate governments had to figure out what to do about dissent. Both Davis and Lincoln expanded their presidential power to keep order and to put down opposition. They suspended the writ of *habeas corpus,* which prevents the government from holding citizens without formally charging them.

1. How did the Union hope to defeat the Confederacy?

_____

_____

LIFE DURING WARTIME
Why were many men forced to serve in the army?

As the war continued, there were many casualties and desertions. So both sides turned to **conscription,** a draft that forced men to serve in the army.

Some African Americans fought for the Union. In fact, by the end of the war, African Americans made up 10 percent of the Union army. However, they faced discrimination. They served in separate regiments and were paid less than whites.

Women did not fight, but they made contributions by serving as army nurses. Clara Barton was one of these nurses. She later founded the American Red Cross.

The war hurt the South's economy as food prices and inflation rose. However, the war expanded the North's economy. Industries grew, but wages did not keep up with prices. The Union needed money to pay for the war, so Congress began the nation's first **income tax.**

2. What was being in the army like for African Americans?

_____

_____

Lesson 6, *continued*

THE NORTH TAKES CHARGE
How did Union forces wear down the South?

Lee's army defeated the Union army at Fredericksburg, Virginia, in 1862 and at Chancellorsville, Virginia, in 1863. Lee decided to invade the North.

The most decisive battle of the war was near **Gettysburg,** Pennsylvania. The Union army defeated Lee's troops after three days of vicious fighting.

In November 1863 a cemetery was dedicated at Gettysburg. President Lincoln gave a speech, the Gettysburg Address. His words helped the country see that it was not just a group of individual states but rather a unified nation.

Meanwhile, General Grant fought to take Vicksburg, a Confederate stronghold on the Mississippi River. Grant tried several times with no success. Then, in May 1863 his troops began shelling the city from the river and from land. Food supplies ran low and civilians were forced into caves. The Vicksburg command asked Grant for terms of surrender. The defeats at Gettysburg and Vicksburg caused the South to lose much of its army.

Meanwhile, Lincoln made Grant commander of all Union armies. Grant made **William Tecumseh Sherman** commander of the military division of the Mississippi. Both generals wanted to wage total war. They believed that if the Union could destroy the southern people's will to fight, the Confederacy would collapse.

Grant set out to destroy Lee's army in Virginia. Even if his casualties ran twice as high as those of Lee, the North could afford it. The South could not. In 1864 Sherman began his march through Georgia to the sea. His troops destroyed houses, railroads, and everything in its path.

Back in Washington, Lincoln feared he would not be reelected in 1864. Many northerners thought the war had lasted too long. But news of Sherman's victories helped Lincoln win a second term.

On April 9, 1865, generals Lee and Grant met at **Appomattox Courthouse** and arranged the Confederate surrender. Grant paroled Lee's soldiers and sent them home with their personal possessions, horses, and three days' worth of rations. After four years, the Civil War was over.

3. What did the Gettysburg Address help Americans to realize?

_____

_____

LEGACY OF THE CIVIL WAR
How was the nation changed by the Civil War?

The Civil War increased the federal government's power and authority. Also, no state ever threatened secession again.

The war widened the economic gap between North and South. The northern economy boomed. The southern economy was devastated. The war ended slavery as a labor system but also ruined southern industry and farms. The gap between the regions did not end until the 20th century.

After the war, African Americans began to experience change. In 1865 the **Thirteenth Amendment** was ratified. It ended slavery in the United States.

Lincoln's plans to reunify the country after the war never happened because only five days after Lee surrendered to Grant, Lincoln was shot. The assassin

© Houghton Mifflin Harcourt Publishing Company

was **John Wilkes Booth.** The president died the next day. It was the first time a president of the United States had been assassinated.

4. How did the war widen the economic gap between the North and South?

_____

_____

Write the causes or effects (depending on which is missing) of each situation.

Causes	Effects
1. The South wins at Fort Sumter.	
2. General Grant invades western Tennessee Confederate forts and pushes on toward the Mississippi River. Commander Farragut of the navy captures the port of New Orleans.	
3.	Britain remains neutral.
4. There are heavy casualties and desertions on both sides.	
5. African Americans in the Union army face discrimination.	
6. The South is defeated at Gettysburg and Vicksburg.	
7.	The Union realizes that it is a unified nation.
8. Grant and Sherman believe that if they can destroy the South's will to fight, the Confederacy will collapse.	
9. News of Sherman's victories reach Washington, DC.	
10.	Slavery ends in the U.S.
11.	Lincoln's plans to reunify the country after the war never happen.

© Houghton Mifflin Harcourt Publishing Company

Prologue: American Beginnings

Reconstruction

Key Terms and People

Andrew Johnson President after Lincoln

Reconstruction Period of rebuilding the United States after the Civil War

Radical Republicans Congressional Republicans who wanted to destroy the political power of slaveholders and give African Americans citizenship and the right to vote

Freedmen's Bureau Government agency that helped former slaves and poor whites by giving out food and clothing and by setting up schools and hospitals

black codes Laws that restricted African Americans' lives

Fourteenth Amendment Prevented states from denying rights and privileges to any U.S. citizen, now defined as "all persons born or naturalized in the United States"

Fifteenth Amendment Banned states from denying African Americans the right to vote

carpetbaggers Northerners who moved to the South after the war

scalawags White southerners who joined the Republican Party to have greater political opportunities

Hiram Revels First African American senator

sharecropping System in which landowners leased a few acres of land to farmworkers in return for a portion of their crops

Ku Klux Klan (KKK) Southern vigilante group who used violence to intimidate African Americans

Before You Read

In the last lesson you learned about the Civil War and its effects on the people of the North and the South. In this lesson you will learn about Reconstruction, how it affected society, and how it ended.

As You Read

Complete a timeline by providing details about Reconstruction, its results, and its ending.

© Houghton Mifflin Harcourt Publishing Company

Guided Reading Workbook

Lesson 7, *continued*

THE POLITICS OF RECONSTRUCTION
What was Reconstruction?

After Lincoln's assassination, **Andrew Johnson** became president. This time was called **Reconstruction.** It was the period of rebuilding after the Civil War and the process of readmitting Confederate states to the Union. It lasted from 1865 to 1877. People had different ideas about how it should work.

During the war, Lincoln had announced the Ten-Percent Plan, whereby the government would pardon Confederates (except high-ranking officials) who would swear allegiance to the Union. A state would be readmitted as soon as 10 percent of its voters took the oath of allegiance.

Radical Republicans, a minority of Republicans, were angry over the plan. They wanted to end the political power of former slaveholders and make African Americans citizens.

Lincoln was assassinated before his plan was fully implemented, but Johnson's plan was similar. Many states met the plan's terms and were readmitted to the Union. In December 1865 southern congressional members began arriving in Washington. Radical Republicans refused to admit them. Then Congress enlarged the **Freedmen's Bureau,** which gave food and clothing to former slaves and set up hospitals and schools. It also passed the Civil Rights Act of 1866, which banned **black codes.** These were laws that discriminated against African Americans. Johnson thought the two bills gave the federal government too much power, so he vetoed them.

Republicans were angry over Johnson's actions, and they overrode his vetoes. Congress also passed the

Fourteenth Amendment, which prevented states from denying rights and privileges to any U.S. citizen, including African Americans.

The Radical Republicans took control of Congress in 1866. The Reconstruction Act of 1867 was passed, which did not recognize state governments created under Lincoln and Johnson's plan. It put the former Confederate states under military control and said that no state could reenter the Union until it approved the Fourteenth Amendment and allowed African Americans to vote. Johnson vetoed the bill; Congress overrode it.

Congress wanted to impeach President Johnson since its members thought he was blocking Reconstruction. When Johnson removed a cabinet member from office, Congress said his actions were illegal. The House voted to impeach him, but the Senate voted not to convict.

In 1868 Civil War hero Ulysses S. Grant was elected president. African American votes in the South helped him win. After the election, the Radicals introduced the **Fifteenth Amendment.** It said that no one could be kept from voting because of "race, color, or previous condition of servitude."

1. Why were the Fourteenth and Fifteenth Amendments passed?

   _____

   _____

RECONSTRUCTING SOCIETY
How did conditions change in the South during Reconstruction?

By 1870 all former Confederate states had elected Republican-dominated governments. Republicans wanted to

© Houghton Mifflin Harcourt Publishing Company

Lesson 7, *continued*

make economic changes in the South. Plantations and small farms were ruined, and the region's population had been devastated. So governments began public programs to fix the physical damage and to provide social services.

Three groups made up the South's Republican Party. **Carpetbaggers** were northerners who had moved to the South after the war. **Scalawags** were white southerners who joined the Republican Party for political opportunities. Many were small farmers who did not want wealthy planters to regain power. The third group was African Americans eager to vote and take part in politics.

The alliance of these groups was an uneasy one. They did not always agree on issues. Also, African Americans' new status meant southern white attitudes had to change. Many white southerners refused to accept equal rights for African Americans.

During Reconstruction, African Americans founded their own churches, and their ministers often became important community leaders. Since 95 percent of former slaves were illiterate, they needed an education to become economically self-sufficient. Reconstruction governments, African American churches, and the Freedmen's Bureau started and ran schools, including universities.

African Americans became active in government. They voted and held office. However, those in office were in the minority. Out of 125 southerners elected to Congress, only 16 were African Americans. Among these was the first African American senator, **Hiram Revels.**

Since most Republicans thought that private property was a basic right, they would not give away land owned by plantation owners. So African Americans and poor white farmers could not grow crops to sell or to use to feed their families. Many had to take part in **sharecropping,** a system in which landowners divide land and assign each worker a few acres. Sharecroppers keep part of the crop and give the rest to landowners.

2. What groups made up the Republican Party after the war?

_____

_____

THE COLLAPSE OF RECONSTRUCTION
What caused the end of Reconstruction?

Southerners reacted differently to African American suffrage and participation in government. Some just swallowed their resentment. Others did not register to vote. Others became frustrated and formed vigilante groups and used violence to intimidate African Americans.

The most notorious and widespread vigilante group was the **Ku Klux Klan.** The Klan wanted to destroy the Republican Party, end Reconstruction governments, aid the planters, and prevent African Americans from taking part in politics.

To stop Klan violence, Congress passed acts in 1870 and 1871 to supervise southern elections and to give the president power to use federal troops where the Klan was. Congress also passed laws that weakened the Republican Party's power in the South such as the Amnesty Act in 1872. It allowed many former Confederates to

Lesson 7, *continued*

vote and to hold office. Congress also allowed the Freedmen's Bureau to expire. Southern Democrats began to regain power.

Support for Reconstruction started to weaken. The Republicans were less united, so Radicals could not impose their plan. Bank failures led to a depression, and northerners focused on that problem. Also, the Supreme Court began undoing some social and political changes.

Southern Democrats began to regain control. In the 1876 election, the Democratic candidate Samuel Tilden

won the popular vote, but was one vote short of the electoral victory. Congress appointed a commission to award the votes, which voted along party lines. The Republican Rutherford B. Hayes won. To avoid conflict, Democrats allowed Hayes to become president and Republicans agreed to withdraw federal troops from the South. Reconstruction was over.

3. How did southerners react to Reconstruction?

_____

_____

© Houghton Mifflin Harcourt Publishing Company

Guided Reading Workbook

Complete the timeline by providing details about Reconstruction, its results, and its ending.

1865 Reconstruction begins. → Radical Republicans refuse to admit elected southerners.	1. Why were Radical Republicans angry over Lincoln and Johnson's Reconstruction plans?
1866 Congress votes to continue and expand the Freedmen's Bureau. Congress passes the Civil Rights Act of 1866. Johnson vetoes the Freedmen's Bureau Bill and the Civil Rights Act. Congress overrides the vetoes and adopts the Fourteenth Amendment.	2. What was the purpose of the Freedmen's Bureau? 3. What was accomplished by the Civil Rights Act? Why did Johnson override both the Civil Rights Act and the expanded Freedmen's Bureau? 4. What were the main provisions of the Fourteenth Amendment?
1867 Congress passes the Reconstruction Act. Johnson vetoes it. Congress overrides the veto and wants to impeach Johnson.	5. What were the main features of the Reconstruction Act?
1868 Grant is elected president. Congress adopts the Fifteenth Amendment.	6. What did the Fifteenth Amendment guarantee?
1870 All former Confederate states elect Republican-dominated governments. Hiram Revels becomes the first African American elected to the U.S. Senate.	7. Why was it hard for carpetbaggers, scalawags, and African Americans to have a strong political alliance? 8. How many African Americans were elected to Congress during this time?
1872 Congress passes acts to stop Ku Klux Klan violence. Congress passes Amnesty Act.	9. What restrictions did the acts Congress passed in 1870 and 1871 place on the South? 10. What did the Amnesty Act do?
1876 Reconstruction starts to weaken. Rutherford B. Hayes is elected president.	11. What events led to the end of Reconstruction?

© Houghton Mifflin Harcourt Publishing Company

Westward Expansion

Cultures Clash on the Prairie

Key Terms and People

Great Plains The grassland region of the United States

Treaty of Fort Laramie 1868 treaty in which the Sioux agreed to live on a reservation

Sitting Bull Leader of Hunkpapa Sioux

George A. Custer Colonel in U.S. Cavalry

assimilation Name of plan to make Native Americans part of white culture

Dawes Act Law that broke up Native American reservations

Battle of Wounded Knee U.S. massacre of Sioux at Wounded Knee Creek, South Dakota

Before You Read

In the last lesson you read about Reconstruction and its effects on the nation. In this lesson you will read how Americans began settling the West in the years following Reconstruction, and the effects on Native Americans.

As You Read

Use a timeline to take notes about the events that occurred on the Great Plains.

THE CULTURE OF THE PLAINS INDIANS
How did the Plains Indians live?

Native Americans lived on the **Great Plains,** the grasslands in the west-central portion of the United States. They followed a way of life that centered on the horse and buffalo. The horse allowed them to hunt more easily and to travel farther. The buffalo provided food, clothing, shelter, and other important items. By the 1700s most Great Plains nations had left their farms to roam the plains and hunt.

The Indians of the Great Plains lived in small extended family groups. The men hunted for food. The women helped butcher the game and prepare the buffalo hides that the men brought back to camp. Children learned the skills they would need as adults.

1. What were the responsibilities of the different members of Plains Indian families?

_____

_____

THE GOVERNMENT RESTRICTS NATIVE AMERICANS; BLOODY BATTLES CONTINUE
Why did Indians and settlers fight each other?

After the Civil War, thousands of white settlers moved to the Great Plains. Settlers argued that because Native Americans had not settled down to "improve" the land, white settlers could stake their claim.

Railroad expansion made it possible for more settlers to move westward and had an effect on the government's policy toward Native Americans living on the Great Plains. First, the government treated the Great Plains as a giant reservation. When it needed more land for railroads, it created treaties that defined boundaries for nations. However, Native Americans ignored the treaties, hunted on their lands, and fought with settlers and miners.

One of the more tragic clashes occurred in 1864. The Cheyenne were returning home to Colorado's Sand Creek Reserve for the winter. An army commander sent a telegram to a militia colonel telling him to attack the Native Americans. The colonel and his troops attacked and killed more than 150 Cheyenne in an incident known as the Sand Creek Massacre.

Fighting continued. In the **Treaty of Fort Laramie,** which was forced on Sioux leaders, the Sioux agreed to live on a reservation. But **Sitting Bull,** an important Sioux leader, never signed the treaty.

Then four years after the Treaty of Fort Laramie, miners started searching for gold in the Black Hills. Native American nations protested this invasion. By 1874 a gold rush was on in the area. Appeals by Native Americans to the government yielded no results.

Then, in 1876 Sitting Bull and other Native Americans defeated army troops led by **George A. Custer,** at the Little Bighorn River. The Sioux won decisively, killing Custer and all his soldiers. The battle became known as Custer's Last Stand. The army recovered, however. Within months, the army defeated the Sioux.

2. What were the reasons for the clashes between the U.S. government and the Sioux?

_____

_____

THE GOVERNMENT SUPPORTS ASSIMILATION; THE BATTLE OF WOUNDED KNEE
Why did assimilation fail?

To deal with the Native American problem, the U.S. government adopted a plan of **assimilation.** In this plan, Native Americans would give up their beliefs and culture and become part of white culture.

Another blow to tribal life was the destruction of the buffalo. Tourists and fur traders shot buffalo for sport. With the buffalo gone, the Plains Indians' source of food, clothing, shelter, and fuel was gone. Native Americans began to roam greater distances looking for food. This meant that reservations could not meet their needs. So the government decided to make Native Americans farmers. Congress passed the **Dawes Act** in 1887. The act broke up reservations and gave some of the land to each Native American family for farming. The plan, however, failed mainly because Native Americans did not understand the terms of the Dawes Act. They were not used to the idea of private land ownership.

© Houghton Mifflin Harcourt Publishing Company

Lesson 1, *continued*

The Sioux suffered poverty and disease. They adopted a ritual called the Ghost Dance, which they hoped would restore their lands and way of life. Military leaders were bothered by this and decided to arrest Sitting Bull. He was killed. Shortly after, army troops rounded up a Sioux group and took them to a camp at Wounded Knee Creek in South Dakota. The soldiers demanded the Native Americans give up all their weapons. As many as 300 Sioux were slaughtered. Their corpses were left to freeze. This event was known as the **Battle of Wounded Knee.** It marked the end of the Indian wars.

3. What were two reasons why assimilation failed?

_____

_____

Answer questions related to the timeline below.

1864 Sand Creek Massacre	→	1. What happened at Sand Creek?
1868 Treaty of Fort Laramie	→	2. What were the terms of the Treaty of Fort Laramie?
1874 Invasion by gold miners of the Sioux's sacred Black Hills		
1876 George A. Custer's Last Stand	→	3. What happened at the Battle of Little Bighorn?
1887 The policy of assimilation formalized in the Dawes Act	→	4. What was the purpose of the Dawes Act?
1890 The Spread of the Ghost Dance movement; Death of Sitting Bull; Battle of Wounded Knee	→	5. What happened at Wounded Knee Creek?

© Houghton Mifflin Harcourt Publishing Company

Westward Expansion

Mining and Ranching

Key Terms and People

Comstock Lode Mine in present-day Nevada where prospectors found silver

placer mining Method of extracting gold from loose sand and gravel by panning or sluicing

hydraulic mining Method of extracting gold by using water under high pressure to blast away dirt and expose minerals

hard-rock mining Method of extracting gold that involved digging tunnels and breaking up the ore

longhorn Sturdy cattle accustomed to dry grasslands

Chisholm Trail Major cattle route from San Antonio, Texas, through Oklahoma to Kansas

long drive Three-month-long overland transport of cattle

Before You Read

In the last lesson you read how settlement in the West affected Native Americans. In this lesson you will read about the mining and cattle booms of the American West.

As You Read

Use a chart to take notes about mining and ranching.

THE LURE OF SILVER AND GOLD
What **effect did the discovery of gold and silver have on people in the West?**

People were drawn to the West because they thought they might strike it rich by finding gold. After the California gold rush, tens of thousands of miners flocked to areas where they heard about gold discovery. In the Carson River valley of what is now Nevada, miners found silver in a mine. It became known as the **Comstock Lode,** and miners took about $500 million from it over a 20-year period.

Some mining camps grew into towns. Women and children came to join the men. Families made the towns into respectable communities with churches, schools, and other buildings. While some gold rush towns disappeared, others became full-fledged cities.

Mining was hard work. **Placer mining** involved minerals found in loose sand and gravel. Extracting the gold was tedious. Since most gold was in veins in underground rock, miners needed equipment to extract it. Mining companies used two methods. **Hydraulic mining** used water under high pressure to blast away dirt and expose the minerals. **Hard-rock mining** involved digging tunnels and breaking up the ore.

By the 1880s large companies were in charge of mining. Miners worked for them. The risks of mining were great, and thousands of people died while digging for gold and silver.

Danger also existed in the mining camps. Competition for gold led to violence. Many immigrants were wrongly blamed for crimes and faced vigilante justice.

1. What was the significance of the Comstock Lode?

_____

_____

CATTLE BECOMES BIG BUSINESS
What caused the cattle business to grow?

Cattle ranching became a big business as the herds of buffalo disappeared and Native Americans were forced onto reservations. Fewer buffalo meant that grass was abundant. Ranchers raised **longhorns,** a sturdy breed first brought to the Americas by the Spanish. Unlike other breeds, longhorns were hardy, could travel long distances without much water, and could live on grass alone. They were well suited to life on the Plains. American cowboys learned the skills necessary for managing cattle from vaqueros, the first cowboys who worked on Spanish ranches in Mexico.

Although there were plentiful herds of cattle, cowboys were not in much demand until the railroads reached the Great Plains. Then after the Civil War, there was a huge demand for beef fueled by rapidly growing cities. Texas ranchers shipped their cattle to Chicago and to the East. Cattle ranchers also drove their

cattle over the **Chisholm Trail** from San Antonio, Texas, to Kansas, where they were shipped by rail to Chicago.

2. What are two factors that helped the cattle business to grow?

_____

_____

A DAY IN THE LIFE OF A COWBOY; THE END OF THE OPEN RANGE
Why was life difficult for cowboys?

When the Chisholm Trail and the railroad met in Abilene, Kansas, it brought about the rise of the cowboy. Between 1866 and 1885 about 55,000 cowboys worked the plains. About 12 percent of these cowboys were Mexican. About 25 percent were African American.

A cowboy's life was difficult. Cowboys worked between 10 and 14 hours a day in all kinds of weather. They worked hard all spring and summer. In the winter, they lived off their savings or went from ranch to ranch and looked for odd jobs. In the spring, cowboys rounded up their cattle and headed them out on the **long drive.** This was the journey from the plains to the shipping yards in Abilene, Kansas. The days of the open range and cattle drive did not last long. Bad weather in the 1880s wiped out many ranchers. Others started using barbed wire to fence in their ranches.

3. What factor brought about the rise of the cowboy?

_____

_____

Lesson 2, *continued*

Answer questions about mining and ranching.

1. What drew people to the West?	2. What caused some mining camps to grow into towns or cities?
3. How are placer mining, hydraulic mining, and hard-rock mining different?	4. What effect did the railroads have on the development of cattle ranching on the Great Plains?
5. Some people say that western cattlemen found their own version of gold on the Great Plains. What do you think this means?	6. Why were longhorns able to survive the Great Plains?

© Houghton Mifflin Harcourt Publishing Company

Westward Expansion

Settling on the Great Plains

Key Terms and People

Homestead Act Act that offered free land to western settlers

exoduster African American settler in the West

soddy A frontier home, usually dug into a hill or made from sod

Morrill Act Act that helped establish agricultural colleges

bonanza farm A large, single-crop farm

Before You Read

In the last lesson you read about the growth of the mining and cattle
industry. In this lesson you will read about life on the Great Plains
for the men and women who settled there in search of land and
prosperity.

As You Read

Use a chart to make notes on the causes and effects of events that
shaped the settling of the Great Plains.

SETTLERS MOVE WESTWARD TO FARM
How did the U.S. government get people to go West?

More and more people migrated to
the Great Plains with the building of the
railroads. From 1850 to 1871 the federal
government gave huge tracts of land to
companies ready to lay tracks through
the West.

In 1867 the Central Pacific company
began laying tracks east from
Sacramento, California. Another
railroad company, the Union Pacific,
began laying tracks west from Omaha,
Nebraska. Much of the work was
done by African Americans, Irish and
Chinese immigrants, and Mexican
Americans. In 1869 the two routes met
in Utah. America's first transcontinental
railroad was finished.

The railroad companies sold some
of their land at low prices to settlers
willing to farm it. Some companies even
recruited people from Europe to settle
on the land.

In addition, a growing number of
people were responding to the
Homestead Act of 1862. Under this
act, the government offered 160 acres of
free land to anyone who would build a
home, make improvements, and farm
the land for five years. By 1900 the
Great Plains was filled with more than
600,000 homesteaders, or settlers on
this free land.

Several thousand settlers were
exodusters. They were African Americans
who moved from the post-Reconstruction
South to Kansas. With the Homestead
Act, African Americans could own their
own land and start new lives in the West.

© Houghton Mifflin Harcourt Publishing Company

But the law did not always work as the government had planned. Only about 10 percent of the land was settled by the families for whom it was intended. Cattlemen and miners claimed much of the rest.

The government continued to pass other laws to encourage people to settle the West. In 1889 Oklahoma offered a major land giveaway. This led thousands of settlers to claim 2 million acres in less than 24 hours.

As more and more settlers gobbled up land in the West, the government took action to preserve some wilderness. In 1872 the government set aside land in Wyoming to create Yellowstone National Park. Millions of acres more were set aside later.

1. How did the government and the railroads encourage settlement of the West?

_____

_____

SETTLERS MEET THE CHALLENGES OF THE PLAINS
What was life like for settlers of the West?

From 1850 to 1900 the number of people living west of the Mississippi River grew from 1 percent of the nation's population to almost 30 percent. These settlers had to endure many hardships including blizzards, heat, tornadoes, locusts, and dangers of raids by outlaws and Native Americans.

The Great Plains did not have many trees. As a result, people built **soddies.** These homes were dug into the side of hills or made from sod. A soddy was warm in winter and cool in summer. However, it offered little light or air.

Homesteaders were largely isolated from one another. They had to make nearly everything they needed. Women worked in the fields alongside men. Women in the West were also allowed to vote and hold elected office. These rights were granted 50 years before the 19th Amendment was passed guaranteeing the right for all women to vote.

Farming the Great Plains was difficult work. But several inventions helped make the task easier. The steel plow helped break up the prairie's tough soil. A new reaper cut wheat even faster. Other inventions made it possible for farmers to work faster and with less effort. Inventions made more grain available for more people.

The government also helped in the effort to improve farming techniques. The **Morrill Act** of 1862 and 1890 helped establish agricultural colleges. The government also established experiment stations on the Great Plains. Researchers there developed new types of crops as well as new growing techniques.

Seasonal lack of rain and extended droughts were a constant problem for farmers, so many learned how to use dry farming methods to raise crops in dry years. These ideas helped the plains to flourish.

To buy much of the new farming machinery, farmers often went into debt. When crop prices fell, farmers lost money, which meant they could not repay their loans. To make more money, they often had to raise more crops. This in turn led to the growth of **bonanza farms.** These were huge single-crop farms.

By 1900 the average farmer had nearly 150 acres under cultivation. However, when a drought hit the plains

© Houghton Mifflin Harcourt Publishing Company

Lesson 3, *continued*

between 1885 and 1890, many bonanza farms folded. They could not compete with the smaller farmers, who were more flexible in the crops they grew. The high price of shipping their crops also added to farmers' debt.

2. Name at least one social and one economic hardship settlers faced.

_____

_____

Complete the chart by identifying the effects for each of the causes listed. Then describe some of the hardships faced by settlers.

Causes	Effects
1. Land grants given to the railroads	
2. The Homestead Act	
3. Inventions and improvements in farm technology	
4. The Morrill Land Grant Act	
5. What were some hardships faced by frontier farmers? (Note: one hardship per box)	

© Houghton Mifflin Harcourt Publishing Company

Westward Expansion

Farmers and the Populist Movement

Key Terms and People

Oliver Hudson Kelley Farmer who founded the Grange

Grange Organization that fought for farmers' rights

Farmers' Alliances Groups of farm organizations

Populism Political movement that sought advancement for farmers and laborers

bimetallism Backing money with silver and gold

gold standard Backing dollars solely with gold

William McKinley 1896 Republican presidential nominee

William Jennings Bryan 1896 Populist/Democratic presidential nominee

Before You Read

In the last lesson you read about life for thousands of farmers trying to make a living on the Great Plains. In this lesson you will read how these farmers organized and fought to improve their conditions.

As You Read

Use a chart to take notes about farmers, Populists, and the People's Party.

FARMERS UNITE TO ADDRESS COMMON PROBLEMS
How did farmers fight back?

Farmers faced serious problems after the Civil War. The prices they could sell their crops for kept going down. This was because the United States was retiring greenbacks, or money printed for the Civil War, from circulation. The decline in prices also meant that farmers had to pay back their loans in money that was worth more than when they borrowed it. Farmers urged the government to increase the money supply, but to no avail.

Meanwhile, farmers continued to pay high prices to railroads to transport grain. Often they paid as much to ship their crops as they received for them.

Also, railroads made secret agreements with grain brokers that allowed the railroads to control prices. Many farmers had to mortgage their farms and buy seed and supplies on credit. Suppliers charged high interest rates.

Many farmers pushed for reform. In 1867 a farmer named **Oliver Hudson Kelley** started an organization that became known as the **Grange.** Its original purpose was to provide a place for farm families to discuss social and educational issues. By the 1870s, however, Grange members spent most of their time and energy fighting the railroads.

The Grange led to other organizations. They included the **Farmers' Alliances,** organizations that included people who

Lesson 4, *continued*

sympathized with farmers. Alliance members traveled throughout the Great Plains educating farmers about issues, including how to obtain lower interest rates and ways to protest the railroads.

1. What steps did farmers take to address their concerns?

   _____

   _____

THE RISE AND FALL OF POPULISM
What did the Populist movement hope to achieve?

Farmers' Alliance leaders knew that they needed political power. In 1892 they created the Populist Party, or People's Party. This party was the beginning of **Populism,** a movement to gain more political and economic power for common people.

The Populist Party wanted reforms for farmers. It called for an increase in the money supply, bank regulation, and income tax changes. It wanted the government to own and regulate railroad companies. It called for reforms to make government more democratic, including the election of senators by popular vote and a secret ballot to stop voter cheating. It also wanted an eight-hour workday and immigration restrictions.

Most Americans thought the Populists' beliefs too radical. However, struggling farmers and laborers liked it. In 1892 the Populist presidential candidate won almost 10 percent of the total vote. In the West, Populist candidates won many local elections. It was not as strong as the two major parties, but it had become a political force.

Then, in 1893 the nation faced an economic crisis called the Panic of 1893. Its causes started in the 1880s when many companies and individuals borrowed too

much money. Then, in 1893 many of these companies went bankrupt. They could not pay back their loans. Many people lost their jobs.

The panic continued into 1895. As political parties began to choose candidates for the 1896 presidential election, the central issue of the campaign was which metal would be the basis of the nation's monetary system. On one side were the "silverites," many of whom were farmers, who favored **bimetallism,** a monetary system in which the government would give people either gold or silver in exchange for paper currency or checks. On the other side were the "gold bugs," who favored the **gold standard,** or backing dollars solely with gold.

"Gold bugs" favored gold because using the gold standard would keep prices from rising. Silverites favored bimetallism because it would make more dollars available, and therefore prices and wages would rise.

Republicans were "gold bugs." They nominated **William McKinley** for president. The Democrats and the Populists both favored bimetallism. Both parties nominated **William Jennings Bryan,** who supported bimetallism.

But on Election Day, McKinley won. McKinley's election brought an end to Populism. The movement left two powerful legacies: a message that poor people and less powerful groups in society could organize and have a political impact, and an agenda of reforms, many of which would be enacted in the 20th century.

2. Which groups did the Populist Party appeal to most?

   _____

   _____

© Houghton Mifflin Harcourt Publishing Company

Lesson 4, *continued*

Answer questions about farmers, Populists, and the People's Party.

In the late 1800s, farmers faced increasing costs and decreasing crop prices.	
1. Why had farming become unprofitable during this period?	2. Why did farmers support bimetallism?

In 1892 farmers and farm organizations, such as the Grange, found support in Populism and the People's Party.	
3. What economic reforms did the Populist Party call for?	4. What political reforms did the Populist Party call for?

In 1896 the Populists supported presidential candidate William Jennings Bryan.	
5. Who were the "gold bugs"? Who was their candidate for president?	6. Which parties favored bimetallism? Who was their candidate?
7. What effect did Populism have on the future?	

© Houghton Mifflin Harcourt Publishing Company

Industrialization

The Expansion of Industry

Key Terms and People

Edwin L. Drake First person to use steam engine to drill for oil

Bessemer process Technique used to make steel from iron

Thomas Alva Edison Inventor of the light bulb

Lewis H. Latimer African American inventor of the carbon filament

Christopher Sholes Inventor of the typewriter

Alexander Graham Bell Inventor of the telephone

Before You Read

In the last lesson you read about the growth of the Populist movement. In this lesson you will read how Americans used their natural resources and technological breakthroughs to begin building an industrialized society.

As You Read

Use a chart to identify the resources and inventions that affected the expansion of industry and how each contributed to industrialization.

NATURAL RESOURCES FUEL INDUSTRIALIZATION
What were America's important natural resources?

In the years after the Civil War, advances in technology began to change the nation. There were three causes of these advances: a large supply of natural resources, government support for businesses and inventions, and a growing city population that wanted the new products.

One of the more important natural resources was oil. In 1840 a Canadian geologist discovered that kerosene could be used to light lamps. Kerosene was produced from oil. This increased Americans' demand for oil.

In 1859 **Edwin L. Drake** used a steam engine to drill for oil. This technological breakthrough helped start an oil boom in Kentucky, Ohio, Illinois, Indiana, and Texas. Oil-refining industries started in Cleveland and Pittsburgh, and entrepreneurs began turning oil into kerosene.

Oil produced yet another product—gasoline. At first, gasoline was thrown away. However, when the automobile became popular, gasoline was in great demand.

In addition to oil, Americans discovered that their nation was rich in coal and iron. In 1887 explorers found large amounts of iron in Minnesota. At the same time, coal production increased from 33 million tons in 1870 to more than 250 million tons in 1900.

© Houghton Mifflin Harcourt Publishing Company

Lesson 1, *continued*

Iron is a strong metal. However, it is heavy and tends to break and rust. Researchers eventually removed the element carbon from iron. This produced a lighter, more flexible metal that does not rust. It became known as steel. The **Bessemer process,** named after British manufacturer Henry Bessemer, provided a useful way to turn iron into steel.

Americans quickly found many uses for steel. The railroads, with thousands of miles of track, bought large amounts of the new metal. Steel was also used to improve farm tools such as the plow and reaper. Engineers used steel to build bridges. One of the most remarkable bridges was the Brooklyn Bridge. Steel also was used to build skyscrapers, such as the Home Insurance Building in Chicago.

1. Name two ways Americans used steel.

   _____

   _____

INVENTIONS PROMOTE CHANGE
How **did the new inventions change Americans' way of life?**

Beginning in the late 1800s, inventors produced items that changed the way people lived and worked. In 1876 **Thomas Alva Edison** established the world's first research laboratory in Menlo Park, New Jersey. He used the lab to develop new inventions. Edison perfected an early light bulb there. Then, **Lewis H. Latimer** helped Edison improve the light bulb with his invention of a carbon filament. This filament lasted longer than those in the past. Later, Edison worked to establish power plants to generate and distribute electricity.

Another inventor, George Westinghouse, developed ways to make electricity safer and less expensive.

The use of electricity changed America. By 1890 electricity ran machines such as fans and printing presses. Electricity soon became available in homes. This led to the invention of many appliances. Cities built electric streetcars that made travel cheaper and easier. This led to the spread of urban areas. In addition, electricity made it possible for businesses to have greater flexibility in the location of their plants. They could locate their companies in areas with large populations, where there were many natural resources, or where there was easy access to rail and water shipping routes. This flexibility helped industries to grow.

In 1867 **Christopher Sholes** invented the typewriter. This led to dramatic changes in the workplace. Almost ten years later, in 1876, **Alexander Graham Bell** and Thomas Watson invented the telephone.

Both these inventions had an impact on office work and led to the creation of jobs for women. By 1910 women made up about 40 percent of the nation's office work force. In addition, work that had been done at home—such as sewing clothes—was now done in factories. With so much clothing being mass-produced in factories, more garment workers were needed. Many of these workers were women.

Inventions had several positive effects. Machines allowed employees to work faster, which led to a shorter workweek. Inventions improved the standard of living in the country, too. This attracted new immigrants looking for a better life. In turn, this created a larger work force and more consumers.

© Houghton Mifflin Harcourt Publishing Company

2. Name two ways in which electricity
   changed people's life.

   _____

   _____

Answer the questions to identify the resources and inventions that
affected the expansion of industry and how each contributed to
industrialization.

1.	Which resources played crucial roles in industrialization?	
2.	How did Edwin L. Drake help industry to acquire larger quantities of oil?	
3.	How did the Bessemer process allow better use of iron?	
4.	What new uses for steel were developed at this time?	
5.	How did Thomas Alva Edison contribute to this development?	
6.	How did George Westinghouse contribute to it?	
7.	How did Christopher Sholes contribute?	
8.	How did Alexander Graham Bell contribute?	

© Houghton Mifflin Harcourt Publishing Company

Industrialization

Lesson 2

The Age of the Railroads

Key Terms and People

transcontinental railroad A railroad that crosses the entire country

Cornelius Vanderbilt Major figure in the expansion of regional railroads

George M. Pullman Inventor of the sleeping car

Crédit Mobilier Name of company involved in stealing of railroad money

Munn v. *Illinois* Court case that gave government right to regulate private industry

Interstate Commerce Act Law granting Congress authority to regulate railroad activities

---

Before You Read

In the last lesson you read about how Americans used natural resources and inventions to begin changing society. In this lesson you will read about the growth of the railroad industry and its effect on the nation.

As You Read

Use a chart to take notes on the positive and negative effects of railroads.

RAILROADS SPAN TIME AND SPACE

How did the railroads change the way Americans told time?

Before and after the Civil War, railroads extended throughout the United States. In 1869 the nation completed work on its first **transcontinental railroad**—a railroad that crossed the entire continent. By 1890 more than 200,000 miles of rail lines zigzagged across the United States. A major figure in the expansion of regional railroads was **Cornelius Vanderbilt.** He linked small railroads into a larger network, connecting New York to the Midwest.

Railroads made long-distance travel a possibility for many Americans. However, building and running the railroads was difficult and dangerous work. Those who did most of the work were Chinese and Irish immigrants and desperate out-of-work Civil War veterans. Accidents and diseases affected railroad builders. By 1888 more than 2,000 workers had died. Another 20,000 workers had been injured.

Railroads eventually linked the many different regions of the United States. However, railroad schedules proved hard to keep because each community set its own times—based mainly on the movement of the sun. The time in Boston, for example, was almost 12 minutes later than the time in New York.

To fix this problem, officials devised a plan to divide the earth's surface into 24 time zones, one for each hour of the day. Under this plan, the United States would contain four time zones: Eastern, Central, Mountain, and Pacific. Everyone living in a particular zone would follow the same time. The railroad companies supported this plan. Many communities did too.

1. How did time zones first come about?

_____

_____

OPPORTUNITIES AND OPPORTUNISTS
How did the growth of the railroads affect the nation?

Railroads made it easier for people to travel long distances and helped many industries grow. The iron, steel, coal, lumber, and glass industries all grew partly because the railroads needed their products. Railroads also increased trade among cities and towns. This allowed many communities to grow and prosper.

Railroads brought about new towns. In 1880 **George M. Pullman** built a factory on the prairie outside Chicago. Workers made the sleeping cars Pullman invented for trains. As demand for his cars rose, Pullman built a large town to house his workers. The housing was high quality, but he tried to control workers' lives. Eventually, they rebelled.

The railroad industry offered people the chance to become rich, so it attracted many corrupt individuals. A well-known case of corruption occurred in 1864, when some stockholders in the Union Pacific Railroad formed a construction company called **Crédit Mobilier.** They gave this company a contract to lay railroad track at two to three times the actual cost. They kept all profits. To prevent the government from interfering, they gave shares of stock to some members of Congress. Eventually, authorities uncovered the scheme.

2. What was one positive and one negative effect of the growth of railroads?

_____

_____

THE GRANGE AND THE RAILROADS
Why did the farmers fight the railroads?

One group angered by corruption in the railroad industry was farmers. Farmers were upset for a number of reasons. First, they claimed that railroads sold government land grants to businesses rather than to families. They also accused the railroad industry of setting high shipping prices to keep farmers in debt. They said railroads charged customers different prices.

In response to these abuses, the Grangers took political action. They convinced some states to pass laws regulating railroad activity. Members of the railroad companies challenged the states' rights to regulate them.

The battle reached the Supreme Court in 1877. In the case of *Munn* v. *Illinois,* the Court declared that government could regulate private industries to protect the public interest. The railroads had lost their fight.

A decade later, Congress passed the **Interstate Commerce Act.** The act gave the federal government the right to supervise railroad activities and other controls. The railroad companies, however, continued to resist all

© Houghton Mifflin Harcourt Publishing Company

government intervention.

Beginning in 1893 an economic depression struck the country. It affected numerous institutions—including the railroads. Many railroad companies failed. As a result, they were taken over by financial firms. By 1900, seven companies owned most of the nation's railways.

3. Give two reasons why farmers were upset with the railroad companies.

_____

_____

Answer the questions to explain the positive and negative effects of the railroad industry.

Positive Effects of the Railroads	Negative Effects of the Railroads
1. Why was a transcontinental railroad important to the United States?	2. What problems did employees of the railroad companies face?
3. How did the creation of time zones aid the railroad as well as different parts of the United States?	4. Who was involved in Crédit Mobilier, and what was the purpose of this company?
5. Why did railroads help industries and cities to grow?	6. In what ways did the railroad companies use their power to hurt farmers?

© Houghton Mifflin Harcourt Publishing Company

Industrialization

Lesson 3

Big Business

Key Terms and People

laissez-faire Capitalism that allows companies to conduct business without government intervention

Social Darwinism Theory that taught only the strong survived

Andrew Carnegie Scottish immigrant who became a giant in the steel industry

vertical integration Process in which a company buys out its suppliers

horizontal integration Process in which companies producing similar products merge

J.P. Morgan Banker who made his money by taking over and merging other businesses

John D. Rockefeller Head of the Standard Oil Company

trust Group of businesses owned by competing companies that is controlled by a single group of trustees

monopoly Complete control over an industry's production, wages, and prices

Sherman Antitrust Act Made it illegal to form a trust that interfered with free trade

Before You Read

In the last lesson you read about the growth of the railroad industry in the United States. In this lesson you will read about the growth and power of big business in America.

As You Read

Use a chart to take notes on the causes and effects of business practices and government regulation.

A FAVORABLE CLIMATE
How did Social Darwinism justify the idea of laissez-faire capitalism?

The late 1800s was perfect for people who wanted to build huge companies and gain great wealth. With free enterprise, individuals and private businesses ran most industries. By the late 1800s many business leaders followed **laissez-faire** capitalism. They did not want the government destroying their independence, reducing profits, or hurting the economy. They wanted the government to stay out of business.

Some business leaders believed in the theory of **Social Darwinism.** This theory, based on the ideas of biologist Charles Darwin, said that *"natural selection"* enabled the best-suited people to survive and succeed. Social Darwinism supported the ideas of competition, hard work, and responsibility. The

© Houghton Mifflin Harcourt Publishing Company

Lesson 3, *continued*

wealthy found this theory sensible; however, others did not.

1. Why would business leaders favor laissez-faire capitalism and Social Darwinism?

_____

_____

NEW BUSINESS STRATEGIES
How did entrepreneurs try to control competition?

Most entrepreneurs were willing to do whatever was necessary to gain control of their industry. **Andrew Carnegie** entered the steel industry in 1873, and by 1899 he was determined to control the entire steel industry. Through **vertical integration,** he bought companies that supplied his raw materials such as iron and coal, and railroads to transport the steel. He used **horizontal integration** by buying out or merging with other steel companies.

Some entrepreneurs tried to control competition. Banker **J.P. Morgan,** for example, did this by taking over and merging other people's businesses. He created companies that did nothing but buy out the stock of other companies. So he gained control of the railroad, steel, and farm equipment industries. Eventually, he merged the Carnegie Steel and other steel companies to form the United States Steel Corporation.

John D. Rockefeller had another approach to mergers. He formed **trusts** in which competing companies put control of their businesses under a single group of trustees. He used the Standard Oil trust to almost completely control the oil industry. Rockefeller's ruthless business practices earned him huge profits.

Carnegie, Morgan, and Rockefeller each created a **monopoly,** or complete control over their industry's production, wages, and prices. Consumers had fewer choices and were forced to pay whatever price stated for products. Workers had fewer choices, too. They were stuck with the wages companies offered because they could not easily find another job.

While Carnegie and other wealthy business owners made charitable contributions, some Americans thought of them as robber barons because they took advantage of workers and consumers.

2. What problems were caused by monopolies?

_____

_____

GOVERNMENT AND BUSINESS
What was the purpose of the Sherman Antitrust Act?

As the power of giant corporations grew, the government became concerned that there was a lack of free competition. In 1890 the **Sherman Antitrust Act** made it illegal to form a trust and prohibited monopolies and other activities that prevented competition.

However, this was a difficult act to enforce. First, the definitions of a trust and monopoly were not clear. Second, large companies that were pressured by the government reorganized into a single corporation to avoid prosecution. Even the Supreme Court threw out cases the federal government brought against trusts.

While the North was experiencing industrial growth, the South was experiencing difficult times as it tried to recover from the Civil War. There was little money for investment. So the South stayed mainly agricultural.

© Houghton Mifflin Harcourt Publishing Company

Entrepreneurs there had to deal with high transportation costs, high tariffs, and lack of skilled workers. The business boom in the United States bypassed the South, which continued to suffer economic stagnation.

3. What made the Sherman Antitrust Act so ineffective?

_____

_____

Answer the questions to identify causes and effects of business practices and government regulation.

Cause	Effect
1. Why were big businesses able to thrive during the late 1800s?	2. What were the effects of laissez-faire capitalism?
3. What did Andrew Carnegie want to gain control of?	4. How did Andrew Carnegie reach his goal?
5. Why was J.P. Morgan able to control his competition?	6. What was the result of his controlling the competition?
7. What was the purpose of trusts?	8. How did forming trusts help John D. Rockefeller?
9. Why did monopolies come about?	10. What problems did monopolies create?
11. Why did the government pass the Sherman Antitrust Act?	12. What were the results of the Sherman Antitrust Act?

© Houghton Mifflin Harcourt Publishing Company

Guided Reading Workbook

Industrialization

The Rise of the Labor Movement

Key Terms and People

collective bargaining Negotiations between labor and management to win higher wages and shorter workweeks

Samuel Gompers Union leader

American Federation of Labor (AFL) Name of union led by Gompers

Eugene V. Debs Leader of the American Railway Union, an industrial union

Industrial Workers of the World (IWW) Union of radicals and socialists nicknamed the Wobblies

Mary Harris Jones Organizer for United Mine Workers

Before You Read

In the last lesson you read about the growth and power of big business. In this lesson you will read about how workers united to improve conditions in growing industries.

As You Read

Use a chart to take notes on the unions, strikes, and government policies.

LABOR UNIONS EMERGE; UNION MOVEMENTS DIVERGE
Why were unions able to help workers?

Business leaders merged and so did workers. They responded to business consolidation by forming labor unions. Many workers worked long hours under dangerous conditions for low wages. There was no vacation time or sick leave. Women, children, and workers in sweatshops worked under especially harsh conditions. They were paid the lowest wages too.

The National Labor Union (NLU) was an early labor union formed in 1866. Two years later, it persuaded Congress to legalize an eight-hour day

for government workers. The NLU excluded African American workers, who formed the Colored National Labor Union (CNLU). The Knights of Labor also enjoyed success but declined after the failure of a series of strikes.

More and more workers joined unions, which meant unions were able to get some benefits for workers. Union leaders negotiated using **collective bargaining**—negotiations between labor and management to win higher wages and shorter workweeks. If the talks failed, the workers might strike. As unions became more powerful, they began to exert influence over politics. Some politicians tried to pass laws to help labor, and unions raised money for their favorite candidates.

Two major types of unions made great gains. One was craft unions. **Samuel Gompers** formed the **American Federation of Labor (AFL)** in 1886. Gompers used strikes and collective bargaining. **Eugene V. Debs** believed in industrial unionism—a union of all workers, both skilled and unskilled in a single industry. He formed the American Railway Union (ARU). Debs and other workers turned to socialism. In 1905 a union of radicals and socialists was formed called the **Industrial Workers of the World (IWW),** or the Wobblies. In the West, Japanese and Mexican farm workers formed a union to improve conditions.

1. How did collective bargaining benefit workers?

_____

_____

STRIKES TURN VIOLENT
What was the effect of strikes on businesses and workers?

Unions used strikes to try to improve conditions. In 1877 workers for the Baltimore and Ohio Railroad went out on strike over reduced wages. The Great Strike of 1877 caused most freight and some passenger trains to be stopped for more than a week. The strike was broken up by federal troops.

Later strikes turned violent. The Haymarket Affair took place in 1886. A bomb exploded at a demonstration in Chicago's Haymarket Square in support of striking workers. Several people were killed. Labor leaders were charged with inciting a riot and four were hanged, although no one knows who actually set off the bomb. In 1892 steelworkers were angry when the head of a steel plant in Homestead, Pennsylvania, near

Pittsburgh, said wages were going to be cut. Workers called a strike and fought a battle with Pinkerton Guards that left dead on both sides. This strike was the Homestead Strike. Two years later, a strike over the layoff of thousands of workers and reduced wages was held against the Pullman Company. Led by Eugene Debs and his American Railway Union, the strike turned violent, and federal troops were called out to break the strike.

Women were kept out of most unions; however, they united behind leaders such as **Mary Harris Jones,** known as Mother Jones. She was an organizer for the United Mine Workers, who exposed abuses of working children and helped change child labor laws.

In 1911 a tragedy occurred that made the public aware of the terrible working conditions in factories. The Triangle Shirtwaist factory in New York caught fire. Workers, mostly female, could not escape because the company had locked all but one door. The public was outraged, but factory owners were never punished.

Unions gained greater power, and businesses feared them. They tried to stop workers from joining unions and even hired prison laborers. The government helped management. Courts even used federal law, the Sherman Antitrust Act, against the workers. A business just had to say that a strike would harm interstate trade, and the government would stop the labor action. However, none of these actions kept unions from growing.

2. Why were there so many strikes between the 1870s and the 1890s?

_____

_____

© Houghton Mifflin Harcourt Publishing Company

Lesson 4, *continued*

Answer questions about unions, strikes, and government policies.

	What it was	How it aided or harmed workers
1. National Labor Union		
2. Collective bargaining		
3. The Great Strike of 1877		
4. Triangle Shirtwaist factory fire		
5. Sherman Antitrust Act		

© Houghton Mifflin Harcourt Publishing Company

Immigration and Urbanization

The New Immigrants

Key Terms and People

Ellis Island Inspection station for immigrants arriving on the East Coast

Angel Island Inspection station for immigrants arriving on the West Coast

melting pot A mixture of different cultures and races who blended together

nativism Obvious favoritism toward native-born Americans

Chinese Exclusion Act Act that limited Chinese immigration

Gentlemen's Agreement Agreement in which Japan agreed to limit unskilled workers from emigrating to the U.S. if U.S. repealed the San Francisco segregation order

Before You Read

In the last lesson you read about the nation's labor movement. In this lesson you will read about the immigrants who entered the U.S., how their lives changed, and how they affected the U.S.

As You Read

Use a chart to take notes on where immigrants came from, why they came, where they entered the U.S., and the differences between immigrants and native-born Americans.

THROUGH THE "GOLDEN DOOR"
***Where* did the immigrants come from?**

Between 1870 and 1920 about 20 million Europeans immigrated to the United States. Many of them came from eastern and southern European countries such as Germany, Italy, Poland, and Russia.

Some immigrants came to escape religious persecution. Others left because of rising populations and to overcome poverty and improve their economic situation. Still others came to experience greater freedom in the United States.

A smaller number of immigrants came from Asia. About 200,000 Chinese

immigrants came from 1851 to 1883. They came to get rich during the gold rush. Many Chinese immigrants helped build the nation's first transcontinental railroad. When the United States annexed Hawaii in 1898, several thousand Japanese immigrants came to the United States.

From 1880 to 1920 about 260,000 immigrants arrived from various islands in the Caribbean Sea. They came from Jamaica, Cuba, Puerto Rico, and other islands. Many left their homelands because jobs were scarce.

Many Mexicans came to the United States as well. Some became U.S. citizens when the nation acquired

© Houghton Mifflin Harcourt Publishing Company

Mexican territory in 1848 as a result of the Mexican War. About 700,000 Mexicans arrived from 1910 to 1930 to escape turmoil in their country.

1. Name two regions of the world where immigrants to the United States came from.

_____

_____

A DIFFICULT JOURNEY; LIFE IN THE NEW LAND
How did immigrants cope in America?

Many immigrants traveled to the United States by steamship. On board the ship, they shared a cramped, unsanitary space. Under these harsh conditions, disease spread quickly. As a result, some immigrants died before they reached America.

Most European immigrants to the United States arrived in New York. There, they had to pass through an immigration station located on **Ellis Island** in New York harbor. Officials at the station decided whether the immigrants could enter the country or had to return. Any immigrant with serious health problems or a contagious disease was sent home. Inspectors also made sure that immigrants met the legal requirements for entering the United States.

Asian immigrants arriving on the West Coast went through **Angel Island** in San Francisco. The inspection process on Angel Island was more difficult than on Ellis Island. Other immigrants, from the West Indies and Mexico, arrived in the eastern, southeastern, and western U.S.

Getting along in a new country with a different language and culture was a great challenge for new immigrants.

Many immigrants settled in communities with other immigrants from the same country. This made them feel more at home, and they could practice their customs and speak their native language. These ethnic neighborhoods provided support and a connection. People built churches or synagogues, ate ethnic foods, and set up businesses. Immigrants also wanted to fit in, but native-born people often disliked immigrants' customs and languages.

2. Name two ways immigrants dealt with adjusting to life in the United States.

_____

_____

IMMIGRATION RESTRICTIONS
How did some Americans react to immigration?

By the turn of the century, some people thought of America as a **melting pot.** This term described the blending together of different cultures and races by giving up their native languages and customs.

However, many new immigrants refused to give up their culture and language. This led some Americans to have strong feelings against immigrants. Also, since many Americans were Protestants, they resented that some immigrants were Catholic or Jewish. These feelings led to **nativism,** an obvious preference for native-born Americans. Nativism gave rise to anti-immigrant groups and a demand for immigration restrictions.

On the West Coast, prejudice against Asians was first directed at the Chinese. During the 1870s depression, many Chinese immigrants worked for low

© Houghton Mifflin Harcourt Publishing Company

Lesson 1, *continued*

wages. American workers feared they would lose their jobs. As a result, labor groups pressured politicians to restrict Asian immigration. In 1882 Congress passed the **Chinese Exclusion Act,** which banned all but a few Chinese immigrants. The ban was not lifted until 1943.

Americans showed prejudice against Japanese immigrants, too. In San Francisco, the local school board put all Asian children in separate schools. Japan protested the action. President

Theodore Roosevelt persuaded San Francisco officials to stop their separation policy. Then, Japan agreed to limit emigration of unskilled workers to the United States under the **Gentlemen's Agreement** of 1907–1908.

3. Give two examples of anti-immigration measures in the U.S.

_____

_____

Answer the questions about immigration in the United States during the late 19th and early 20th centuries. In the fourth column, mark an X in each box that applies.

Immigrants from . . .	From where did immigrants come?	What reasons did they often have for coming to the U.S.?	Where did they often enter the U.S.?
1. Southern and Eastern Europe			❑ Ellis Island ❑ Angel Island ❑ Southeastern U.S. ❑ Southwestern U.S.
2. Asia			❑ Ellis Island ❑ Angel Island ❑ Southeastern U.S. ❑ Southwestern U.S.
3. West Indies and Mexico			❑ Eastern U.S. ❑ Angel Island ❑ Southeastern U.S. ❑ Western U.S.
What was an important difference between native-born Americans and some or all of the new immigrants?			
4. Native-Born Americans		5. New Immigrants	

© Houghton Mifflin Harcourt Publishing Company

Immigration and Urbanization

Immigration and Urbanization

Key Terms and People

urbanization The growth of cities

Americanization movement Program to assimilate people of wide-ranging cultures into American culture

tenement Multifamily urban dwelling

social stratification Organization of people into social classes by wealth

mass transit Transportation system designed to move large numbers of people along fixed routes

Social Gospel movement Movement that urged people to help the poor

settlement house Community center that addressed problems in slum neighborhoods

Jane Addams Social reformer who helped the poor; cofounder of Hull House

social mobility The ability of families or individuals to move into a higher social class

Before You Read

In the last lesson you read about the arrival of millions of immigrants to America's shores. In this lesson you will read how the arrival of so many immigrants caused cities' populations to swell—and their problems to increase.

As You Read

Use a chart to take notes on the problems of urbanization and the attempts made to solve the problems.

URBAN OPPORTUNITIES

Why **did people move to the cities?**

Many of the nation's new immigrants settled in the cities in the early 1900s. Cities were convenient and cheap places to live. Immigrants came there to find jobs in factories and businesses. They settled mainly in Northeast and Midwest cities. The result was rapid **urbanization,** or growth of cities, in those regions.

By 1910 immigrants made up more than half of the populations of 18 major American cities. Many immigrants settled in neighborhoods with others from the same country or even from the same village.

Newcomers to the United States learned about their new country through a social campaign known as the **Americanization movement.** Under this program, schools taught immigrants English and American history and government. Many immigrants, however, did not want to abandon their ethnic traditions. Over time, ethnic communities began to affect American culture. A new American culture began to develop in diverse American cities. This led to new movements in the arts.

Immigrants were not the only people who settled in the cities. On the nation's farms, new machines replaced workers. As a result, many workers in the rural areas lost their jobs. Unemployed farm workers soon moved to cities to find jobs.

Many of the southern farmers who lost their jobs were African Americans. Between 1890 and 1910 about 200,000 African Americans moved from the South to cities in the North. They hoped to escape economic hardship and racial violence. However, many found prejudice and low wages in the North.

1. Name two groups that settled in the cities.

_____

_____

URBAN PROBLEMS
What problems did city dwellers face?

City populations grew rapidly, which created problems. One problem was a housing shortage. New housing types let many people live in a small amount of space. One type was the row house, a single-family dwelling that shared side walls with other similar houses.

Another housing type was **tenements,** multifamily urban houses that were often overcrowded and unsanitary. This led some cities to pass laws to improve slum conditions.

In many cities, residents were not only divided along ethnic and racial lines but also along class lines. This **social stratification,** or organization of people into social classes by wealth, resulted in neighborhoods that could be identified as poor, working-class, or wealthy.

Cities also had transportation challenges. So they developed **mass transit.** These transportation systems moved large numbers of people along fixed routes. Streetcars and subways were used in some cities.

Supplying safe drinking water was also an issue. New York and Cleveland built public waterworks, but other city residents were still left without convenient water and had to get their water from street faucets. Over time, filtration and chlorination made water safer.

With no dependable garbage collection, people left garbage on the streets, so sanitation was a problem. Sewage flowed in the streets. By 1900 many cities solved these problems by building sewers and creating sanitation departments.

Crime led to full-time professional police departments in some cities. The same was true for fire departments since fire hazards were an issue. Wooden buildings were replaced with brick, stone, or concrete.

2. Name two problems that city residents faced.

_____

_____

REFORMERS MOBILIZE
How did reformers help the poor?

A number of social reformers worked to improve life in the cities. One early reform program was the **Social Gospel movement.** Leaders of this movement preached that people earned salvation

© Houghton Mifflin Harcourt Publishing Company

by helping the poor. Many reformers responded to the movement's call. They established **settlement houses.** These were community centers located in slum neighborhoods. Workers there provided help and friendship to immigrants and the poor.

Many of these houses were run by middle-class, college-educated women. The settlement houses also offered educational, cultural, and social services. They sent visiting nurses into homes and provided aid that was needed.

One of the more well-known social reformers of this time was **Jane Addams.** She helped establish Hull House in 1889.

This was a settlement house that helped the poor of Chicago. Reformers hoped that the services provided by settlement houses would increase the **social mobility** of immigrants so that they would benefit from living in the United States. Also, settlement houses made people aware of the difficulties facing the urban poor, and they worked for political solutions for the urban poor through lobbying state government.

3. Name two things a settlement house provided for the poor.

_____

_____

© Houghton Mifflin Harcourt Publishing Company

Name _____ Class_____ Date_____

Answer the questions in the chart about the rapid growth of American cities in the late 19th and early 20th centuries.

The People	Why was each group drawn to cities in the Northeast and Midwest?
1. Immigrants	
2. Farmers	
3. African Americans	

The Problems	What was done in response to each problem?
4. Overcrowding in cities	
5. Lack of safe and efficient transportation	
6. Not enough drinking water and water unsafe	
7. Lack of sanitation	
8. Fire hazards	
9. Crime	

© Houghton Mifflin Harcourt Publishing Company

Immigration and Urbanization

Politics in the Gilded Age

Key Terms and People

political machine A group that controlled a political party

graft Illegal use of political influence for personal gain

Boss Tweed Head of New York City's powerful Democratic political machine

patronage The giving of government jobs to people who had helped a candidate get elected

civil service Government administration

Rutherford B. Hayes 19th president of the United States

James A. Garfield 20th president of the United States

Chester A. Arthur 21st president of the United States

Pendleton Civil Service Act Act that implemented merit system in civil service hiring

Grover Cleveland 22nd and 24th president of the United States

Benjamin Harrison 23rd president of the United States

Before You Read

In the last lesson you read about problems that existed in America's growing cities. In this lesson you will read about the people and organizations that controlled the nation's major cities and how reformers tried to end corruption.

As You Read

Add details to a timeline featuring the people and events of the Gilded Age.

THE EMERGENCE OF POLITICAL MACHINES
How did political machines control the cities?

During the late 1800s a **political machine** ran many cities. This group controlled the activities of a city's political party and was headed by a boss. It offered services to businesses and voters in exchange for political or financial support.

The boss controlled city government and jobs in the police, fire, and sanitation departments. The boss controlled agencies that granted licenses to businesses and funded construction projects. Bosses won loyalty and influence because of the control they had and for solving problems. Many bosses were immigrants, too. They spoke to immigrants in their own language and helped them find jobs

© Houghton Mifflin Harcourt Publishing Company

Lesson 3, *continued*

and housing. In return, immigrants pledged their votes.

1. Name two ways in which political machines held power.

_____

_____

MUNICIPAL GRAFT AND SCANDAL
How were political bosses corrupt?

Political machines provided cities with vital services. But many bosses became corrupt and became rich through **graft,** or the illegal use of political influence for personal gain. To win elections, party members used fake names to cast enough votes to win.

Another illegal practice was the kickback. Workers on city construction projects would charge a higher price for their services and then "kick back" part of the fee to the bosses, who were also taking bribes from businesses in return for allowing illegal or unsafe activities.

William M. Tweed, known as **Boss Tweed,** was a powerful political boss. He became the head of Tammany Hall, New York City's most powerful Democratic political machine, and ran the Tweed Ring, a group of corrupt politicians.

Thomas Nast, a political cartoonist, made fun of Tweed in newspapers. Eventually, the public grew outraged by Tweed's corrupt practices. Authorities broke up the Tweed Ring in 1871. He was sentenced to prison.

2. Name two forms of corruption practiced by political bosses.

_____

_____

CIVIL SERVICE REPLACES PATRONAGE
How was civil service reformed?

For many decades, presidents had complained about the problem of **patronage.** This is the giving of government jobs to people of the same party who had helped a candidate get elected. As a result, many unqualified and corrupt workers were hired.

Reformers wanted to end patronage and begin a merit system. Jobs in **civil service,** or government administration, would go to the most qualified people, regardless of their political views.

President **Rutherford B. Hayes** attempted to reform civil service. He named independents to his cabinet and set up a commission to investigate customhouses, centers of patronage. Then he fired two top officials of the New York customhouse. When some members of the Republican Party objected, Hayes decided not to run for reelection in 1880.

The party quickly divided over the issue of patronage hiring. The Stalwarts opposed changes in the patronage system. The reformers supported changing the system. The party eventually settled on an independent candidate, **James A. Garfield,** who won the presidential election but turned out to have ties to the reformers. Shortly after being elected, he was assassinated by a Stalwart.

Garfield's vice-president, Chester A. Arthur, succeeded him. Despite being a Stalwart, Arthur turned reformer when he became president. He pushed through a civil service reform bill known as the **Pendleton Civil Service Act** of 1883. This act created a bipartisan civil service commission to give government jobs based on merit, not politics. It helped reform the civil service.

© Houghton Mifflin Harcourt Publishing Company

Meanwhile, in state government, some governors were attempting to make reforms as well. For example, New York's governor, Theodore Roosevelt, refused to fill civil service jobs through patronage. He ignored the state Republican machine's wishes relating to policy, which upset the Republican Party. The machine leaders sought to remove him by having Roosevelt nominated to replace the vice-president who had died in office. Roosevelt accepted the nomination, and New York's politics were back in the machine's control.

3. What was the purpose of the bipartisan civil service commission?

_____

_____

BUSINESS BUYS INFLUENCE
What happened to tariffs?

The Pendleton Civil Service Act had mixed results. More qualified workers did fill government positions. But because politicians had no jobs to offer, they had trouble seeking money from supporters. As a result, some politicians turned to wealthy leaders for financial support. This strengthened the ties between government and business.

Political reformers in the late 1800s also addressed the issue of tariffs. A tariff is a tax placed on goods coming into or going out of a country. Big business favored keeping or raising tariffs because they protected U.S. industry from foreign competition. The Democratic Party did not want high tariffs since they led to higher prices.

Tariffs were a key issue in presidential elections for years. In 1884 **Grover Cleveland,** a Democrat, won the presidency. He tried but failed to reduce tariffs because he had no congressional support. In 1890 Cleveland ran against Republican **Benjamin Harrison,** who was supported by big business. While Cleveland won more popular votes than Harrison, Harrison took a majority of electoral votes. He signed the McKinley Tariff Act into law, raising tariffs to their highest level ever. Then, in 1892 Cleveland defeated Harrison and became the only president to serve two nonconsecutive terms. He wanted to lower tariffs, but would not sign a bill that provided for a federal income tax. Nevertheless, Congress passed the Wilson-Gorman Tariff without Cleveland's signature, so tariffs were lowered.

In 1897 William McKinley became president. He raised tariffs again.

4. Which two presidents raised tariffs?

_____

_____

© Houghton Mifflin Harcourt Publishing Company

Lesson 3, *continued*

Fill in the chart below by writing answers to questions about the Gilded Age.

1876	Rutherford B. Hayes elected president →	1. What was Hayes's position on civil service reform? What did he do to promote it?
1880	James A. Garfield elected president →	2. In the debate over civil service reform, did Garfield seem to favor the Stalwarts or the reformers?
1881	Garfield assassinated; Chester A. Arthur assumes the presidency →	3. What position did Arthur take on civil service reform, and what did he do to support it?
1883	Pendleton Civil Service Act passed →	4. What did the Pendleton Civil Service Act do?
1884	Grover Cleveland elected president →	5. What was Cleveland's position on tariffs, and what did he do to promote this position?
1888	Benjamin Harrison elected president →	6. What was Harrison's position on tariffs, and what did he do to support that stand?
1892	Cleveland reelected president →	7. What happened to tariffs during Cleveland's second presidency?
1897	William McKinley elected president →	8. What happened to tariffs during McKinley's presidency?

© Houghton Mifflin Harcourt Publishing Company

Immigration and Urbanization

New Technologies

Key Terms and People

Louis Sullivan Early leader of architecture

Daniel Burnham Chicago architect

Frederick Law Olmsted Developer of Central Park

Orville and Wilbur Wright Brothers who flew the first airplane

George Eastman Inventor of the camera

Before You Read

In the last lesson you read about the people and organizations that controlled the nation's major cities and how reformers tried to end corruption. In this lesson you will read about how technology improved life in the cities and dramatically changed the world of communications.

As You Read

Use a chart to take notes on important changes in city design, communications, and transportation.

TECHNOLOGY AND CITY LIFE
How **did cities cope with their growing populations?**

By 1900 millions of Americans had settled in the nation's cities. To accommodate their growing populations, cities had to rely on technology. One example of this was the development of the skyscraper. Skyscrapers are tall buildings that allow people to live many floors above ground. So skyscrapers save space.

Two factors allowed architects to design taller buildings: the invention of elevators and the development of internal steel skeletons. An early skyscraper architect was **Louis Sullivan.** In 1890 he designed the ten-story Wainwright Building in St. Louis. In 1902 **Daniel Burnham** designed the

Flatiron Building, a skyscraper at one of New York's busiest intersections.

Skyscrapers became America's greatest contribution to architecture. They made use of limited and expensive space.

Changes in transportation helped cities spread outward. In 1888 Richmond, Virginia, became the first American city to use electric-powered streetcars. Soon, other cities installed electric streetcars. By the turn of the century, electric streetcars carried people from their homes in outlying neighborhoods to downtown stores, offices, and factories. People could now live in one part of a city and work in another.

To avoid overcrowding on streets, a few large cities moved their streetcars above street level. This created elevated, or "el," trains. Other cities built subways by moving rail lines underground.

Steel bridges joined sections of cities across rivers. The Brooklyn Bridge designed by John Augustus Roebling was one such bridge. It also provided recreational opportunities because it had an elevated walkway for people to walk over the bridge.

City planners also tried to restore serenity to the environment by creating parks and recreational areas. Landscape architect **Frederick Law Olmsted** led the movement for planned city parks. In 1857 he and another architect, Calvert Vaux, drew up plans for Central Park in New York. The finished park included boating and tennis facilities, a zoo, and bicycle paths. All of these were placed in a natural setting.

In Chicago, Daniel Burnham designed a plan that would change a swampy region near Lake Michigan into a recreational area. His plan resulted in elegant parks and sandy beaches along Chicago's Lake Michigan shores.

Large cities also looked for sources of food supplies. Breakthroughs in agriculture technology helped cities. George Washington Carver had revolutionized farming in the South with crop rotation and developing new uses for crops. Also, chemist Fritz Haber found a way to get nitrogen from the air, which led to chemical fertilizers. Now farmers could provide nutrients directly to their crops. Another new technology was refrigerated railroad cars. This made it possible for farmers to get their products to market without spoiling.

1. Name two technological advances that helped make cities more livable.

_____

_____

ADVANCES IN COMMUNICATION
How did technology transform communications?

Technology also improved the field of communications. American mills began to produce huge amounts of cheap paper from wood pulp. A new kind of high-speed printing press called the web-perfecting press was able to print on both sides of the paper, making magazines and newspapers more affordable.

Two brothers, **Orville and Wilbur Wright,** experimented with new engines. They built a glider and then used a four-cylinder internal combustion engine and a propeller to build an airplane. Their first successful flight occurred in 1903 at Kitty Hawk, North Carolina. It covered 120 feet and lasted 12 seconds. Within two years, the Wright brothers were making distant flights of 24 miles. By 1920 the United States had established the first transcontinental airmail service.

At one time, photography was only for professionals. They could not shoot a moving object and photos had to be developed immediately. Eventually, new techniques changed this.

In 1888 **George Eastman** invented his Kodak camera. With each camera, people got a roll of film. After taking the pictures, the camera would be sent back to Eastman's factory. There, the pictures were developed and the camera reloaded and sent back. This provided millions of Americans with an easy way to take pictures. The camera also changed journalism. Newspaper reporters could now photograph events as they occurred.

2. Name two inventions that helped change the world of communications.

_____

_____

© Houghton Mifflin Harcourt Publishing Company

Lesson 4, *continued*

Complete the chart about how technological changes at the turn of the 20th century affected American life. Leave the shaded boxes blank.

	Who was involved in its development?	What other inventions helped make this one possible?	How did this invention or development affect Americans' lives?
1. Skyscraper			
2. Electric transit			
3. Suspension bridge			
4. City planning			
5. Food supply			
6. Web-perfecting press			
7. Airmail			
8. Kodak camera			

© Houghton Mifflin Harcourt Publishing Company

Immigration and Urbanization

The Dawn of Mass Culture

Key Terms and People

Ashcan School A school of painting that featured urban life and working people with gritty realism

pragmatism School of philosophical thought developed in the 1870s

Mark Twain Pen name of the novelist and humorist Samuel Langhorne Clemens

Joseph Pulitzer Owner of the *New York World* newspaper

William Randolph Hearst Owner of the New York *Morning Journal* and the San Francisco *Examiner*

rural free delivery (RFD) System that brought packages directly to homes

Before You Read

In the last lesson you learned about new technologies that made a difference in people's lives. In this lesson you will read about how Americans developed new forms of entertainment and ways to spend their money.

As You Read

Use a chart to take notes on the development of leisure activities and mass culture.

AMERICAN LEISURE
How **did Americans spend their free time?**

The use of machines allowed workers at the turn of the century to do their jobs faster. This led to a shorter workweek. As a result, Americans had more leisure time.

Americans found new ways to use that time. Many city dwellers enjoyed trips to amusement parks. At Coney Island in New York, customers rode the roller coaster. The first Ferris wheel at the World's Columbian Exposition in Chicago in 1893 thrilled riders. People enjoyed new forms of entertainment.

Another recreational activity that became popular at the turn of the century was bicycling. Suffragist Susan B. Anthony noted that bicycling gave women freedom and independence. Bicycling entertained both men and women. Many Americans also played tennis.

Several kinds of snack foods also became popular. Americans turned to brand-name snacks such as a Hershey chocolate bar and drinks such as a Coca-Cola®.

Some Americans were interested in professional sports. They listened to boxing matches in barbershops and hotel lobbies. Baseball became popular. The National League was formed in

© Houghton Mifflin Harcourt Publishing Company

1876 and the American League in 1900. African American baseball players were not allowed in either league. They formed the Negro National League and the Negro American League.

1. What two activities were popular in the U.S. at the turn of the century?

_____

_____

THE SPREAD OF MASS CULTURE
How did newspapers attract readers?

As education expanded and more people learned to read, they became interested in cultural activities. By 1900 at least one art gallery could be found in every large city. American artists like Thomas Eakins of Philadelphia used realism to portray life as it was really lived. He was a leader of the **Ashcan School,** which showed urban life and working people with gritty realism and no frills. Many cities also had libraries.

With all the events that had occurred such as industrialization, immigration, and new technology, scholars turned to **pragmatism,** a school of philosophical thought. The value of a theory, idea, or innovation was related to its practical application. Thought was for solving problems. Eventually, these ideals would influence the government.

Different forms of entertainment offered Americans ways to spend their leisure time. Vaudeville was strictly American, and it offered something for everyone. It included song, dance, juggling, and slapstick comedy. The circus, which visited cities once a year, was also popular. P.T. Barnum and Anthony Bailey advertised their circus as the "Greatest Show on Earth." Motion pictures became widespread. They could be shown as often as 16

times a day, so they generated huge profits. Also, a new form of music called ragtime became popular. It blended African American spirituals and European music forms. Eventually, it would lead to jazz, rhythm and blues, and rock 'n' roll. Sheet music and phonograph records played a part in making the music popular.

Light fiction "dime novels" were popular as more people read books. These stories included adventure tales of the West and heroes. However, some readers wanted a more realistic portrayal of American life, so some writers wrote about characters that were less polished than upper-class men and women. **Mark Twain,** the pen name of the humorist and novelist Samuel Langhorne Clemens, wrote *The Adventures of Huckleberry Finn*. It became a classic of American literature. The efforts of American libraries and art galleries to raise public taste were not always successful. Many Americans had no interest in high culture. African Americans and others were denied access to most white-controlled cultural institutions.

Newspapers also entertained Americans. To attract more readers, many newspapers used sensational headlines. In 1889 a Pennsylvania newspaper introduced its story about the horrors of a flood in Johnstown, Pennsylvania with the headline "THE VALLEY OF DEATH."

Some publishers used other techniques. **Joseph Pulitzer,** the owner of the *New York World*, introduced a large Sunday edition. It included comics, sports coverage, and women's news. Pulitzer presented news in a sensational way to beat his main competitor, **William Randolph Hearst.** Hearst owned the New York *Morning Journal* and the

Lesson 5, *continued*

San Francisco *Examiner*. Hearst tried to outdo Pulitzer by publishing exaggerated stories. By 1898 both publishers were selling more than 1 million copies each day.

2. Name two ways in which publishers tried to sell more newspapers.

_____

_____

NEW WAYS TO SELL GOODS
How did Americans shop?

At the turn of the century, Americans also began to change the way they shopped. As cities grew, shopping centers emerged. These structures made many kinds of stores available in one area. Retail shopping areas grew in places where public transportation could easily provide shoppers.

These retail areas usually had department stores. Marshall Field of Chicago was the first department store in America. Field's store had specialized departments and a bargain basement.

Chain stores, groups of stores offering the same merchandise owned by the same person, also started in the late 1800s. F.W. Woolworth offered items at very low prices because he knew the consumer would buy it on the spur of the moment because it was cheap.

As shopping became more popular, so too did advertising. Companies filled magazines and newspapers with ads for their products. Advertisers also placed their products on barns, houses, and billboards.

In the late 1800s Montgomery Ward and Sears Roebuck introduced mail-order catalogs. These catalogs brought department store items to those who lived in small towns. Each company's catalog contained a description of its goods. By 1910 about 10 million Americans shopped by mail.

The United States Post Office increased mail-order business by starting a **rural free delivery (RFD)** system. This brought packages directly to every home.

3. Name two developments in the ways goods were sold.

_____

_____

© Houghton Mifflin Harcourt Publishing Company

Complete the chart with either an example of each item or one of the people who invented or popularized it. Then note one reason why you think the item became so popular around the turn of the 20th century.

	Example/Person	Reason
1. Amusement Parks		
2. Bicycling		
3. Brand-name Snacks		
4. Baseball		
5. Art Galleries		
6. Performing Arts		
7. Popular Fiction		
8. Newspapers		
9. Department Stores		
10. Mail-order Catalogs		

© Houghton Mifflin Harcourt Publishing Company

Progressivism

The Origins of Progressivism

Key Terms and People

progressive movement Social reform movement in the early-20th century

Florence Kelley Social reformer who worked to help women and children

prohibition Making the sale or use of alcohol illegal

muckraker Writer who exposes wrongdoing

scientific management Using scientific ideas to make work more efficient

Henry Ford Changed manufacturing with the introduction of the Model T automobile and the use of assembly lines

Robert M. La Follette Progressive Wisconsin governor and senator

initiative The procedure by which citizens can propose a law

referendum A way for people to approve changes in laws by a vote

recall A vote on whether to remove a public official from office

Seventeenth Amendment Amendment providing for senators to be elected directly

Before You Read

In the last lesson you read about popular culture at the turn of the century. In this lesson you will learn about the social reforms that made up the progressive movement.

As You Read

Use a chart to list the organizations and people who worked for social, political, moral, and economic reform and the successes they achieved.

FOUR GOALS OF PROGRESSIVISM
What did reformers want?

As the 1900s opened, reformers pushed for a number of changes. Together their efforts built the progressive movement. The **progressive movement** had four major goals: (1) to protect social welfare, (2) to promote moral improvement, (3) to create economic reform, and (4) to foster efficiency.

Reformers tried to promote social welfare by easing the problems of city life. The YMCA built libraries and exercise rooms. The Salvation Army fed poor people in the cities and cared for children in nurseries. Settlement houses helped families. One reformer, **Florence Kelley,** helped to win the passage of the Illinois Factory Act in 1893. The law prohibited child labor and limited women's working hours. The law became a model for other states.

Reformers promoted moral reform by working for **prohibition**—the banning of alcoholic drinks. Many of these reformers, called prohibitionists, were members of the Woman's Christian Temperance Union (WCTU). The WCTU saw much growth under the leadership of Frances Willard. The well-organized union became the largest women's group in the country.

Some temperance groups, such as the Anti-Saloon League, found themselves in conflict with immigrant groups. After all, immigrant customs often included the use of alcohol. Even so, the Anti-Saloon League had much political influence. The work of their members led to the banning of alcohol in many states. A large number of towns, city wards, and rural areas also voted to outlaw alcohol.

Reformers tried to make economic changes by pointing out the great inequality between the rich and the poor. They pushed for better treatment of workers. Some Americans questioned the capitalist economic system and supported socialism. Labor leader Eugene V. Debs helped found the American Socialist Party and spoke out about the power of business.

Journalists called **muckrakers** wrote stories about corruption and unfair practices in business. One such journalist was Ida M. Tarbell. Other muckraking journalists exposed dangerous working conditions, such as child labor and unsafe products.

To help make businesses more efficient and profitable, some reformers promoted the idea of **scientific management.** Scientific management was the brainchild of Frederick Winslow Taylor, who wanted to find ways to make industry more efficient. The idea was to apply scientific ideas to make each task simpler. One outcome was the assembly line.

Inventor and businessman **Henry Ford** introduced the assembly line, and this greatly changed American manufacturing. Ford used an assembly line to efficiently produce his Ford Model T automobile. Ford kept his car simple and identical so that it could be easily mass-produced. Such mass production made the cars cheaper to make and therefore more affordable to the general public.

The assembly line had drawbacks as well as benefits. The new system of manufacturing required people to work like machines. Not all workers could work at the same rate. At a fast pace, some workers became overtired and injured themselves on the job. Ford tried to keep workers happy by reducing the workday and paying workers five dollars a day. Workers seemed willing to accept the hardships of working on the assembly line for the attractive pay.

1. How did reformers try to make businesses more efficient and profitable?

_____

_____

CLEANING UP LOCAL GOVERNMENT
How did Progressives change city governments?

Progressives also reformed politics. City governments were sometimes corrupt, run by party bosses who gave jobs to their friends and bribed people to vote for them. One answer to this problem was a new system of city government called the commission system.

In the commission system, a group of experts runs the city. Each expert takes charge of a different city department.

© Houghton Mifflin Harcourt Publishing Company

By 1917 about 500 cities had commission forms of city government.

Another reform idea was the council-manager form of government. By 1925 nearly 250 cities had managers. These managers were appointed by councils elected by the people.

Some cities had progressive mayors. For example, progressive mayor Hazen Pingree served in Detroit and Tom Johnson led Cleveland. They improved cities without changing their system of government. They put in such reforms as fairer tax systems and lower public transportation fares.

2. How did the commission system improve city government?

    _____

    _____

REFORM AT THE STATE LEVEL
How did state laws change?

Reformers also worked at the state level. Many states had progressive governors. These states passed laws to regulate railroads, mines, telephone companies, and other large businesses.

Robert M. La Follette, as governor of Wisconsin, led the way in regulating big business. He worked hard to ensure that the voters rather than business leaders controlled government. His reforms of the railway industry taxed railroad property at the same rate as other business property. He set up a commission to regulate rates and forbade railroads to issue free passes to state officials.

Other governors also worked to limit the role of big business. These governors included Charles B. Aycock of North Carolina and James S. Hogg of Texas.

Progressives also helped improve working conditions and end child labor.

Factories hired children because children could do the same unskilled work as adults for less money. Often, wages were so low that every member of the family needed to work.

A group called the National Child Labor Committee investigated the harsh working conditions of children. Their efforts helped ensure passage of the Keating-Owen Act, which prohibited goods produced through child labor from being transported across state lines.

Progressive reformers did not get a federal law to ban child labor. They did, however, get state legislatures to prohibit it. States also set maximum hours for all workers.

Progressives also won some reforms from the Supreme Court. In the case *Muller* v. *Oregon,* the Court decided that a state could legally limit the working hours of women. Attorney Louis D. Brandeis successfully argued this case. In 1917 the Supreme Court upheld a ten-hour workday for men in its *Bunting* v. *Oregon* decision.

Electoral reforms at the state level gave voters more power. William U'Ren led his state of Oregon to become the first to adopt the secret ballot, giving voters privacy. Three other reforms of the times were important: (1) **initiative** gives voters themselves the right to propose a law, (2) voters could accept or reject the initiative by a direct vote on the initiative, called a **referendum,** and (3) voters got the right of **recall,** which meant they could force a government official to face another election.

Minnesota became the first state to use a mandatory statewide direct primary system. This meant that voters, instead of political machines, would choose candidates for public office through a special popular election. The

© Houghton Mifflin Harcourt Publishing Company

direct primary led to the passage of the **Seventeenth Amendment** to the Constitution. This amendment called for senators to be elected directly by the people instead of by state lawmakers.

3. What are three ways progressive reforms helped ordinary people?

_____

_____

Complete the chart about the goals, reformers, and successes of the reform movements.

Social Reforms	People and Groups Involved	Successes (laws, legal decisions, etc.)
1. Social welfare reform movement		
2. Moral reform movement		
3. Economic reform movement		
4. Movement for industrial efficiency		
5. Movement to protect workers		

Political Reforms	People and Groups Involved	Successes (laws, legal decisions, etc.)
6. Movement to reform local government		
7. State reform of big business		
8. Movement for election reform		

© Houghton Mifflin Harcourt Publishing Company

Progressivism

Education Reform

Key Terms and People

Booker T. Washington Prominent African American educator

Tuskegee Normal and Industrial Institute School headed by Booker T. Washington

W.E.B. Du Bois First African American to receive a doctorate from Harvard

Niagara Movement Insisted that blacks should seek a liberal arts education so that the African American community would have well-educated leaders.

Before You Read

In the last lesson you read about social reforms that made up the progressive movement. In this lesson you will read about the growth of public education in America.

As You Read

Use a chart to take notes on developments in education at the turn of the 20th century and their major results.

EXPANDING PUBLIC EDUCATION
***How* did education change in the late 1800s?**

During the late 1800s reformers tried to improve public education. They thought that it was a good way for young people to prepare for work and to become good citizens. They also believed that gaining an education helps people improve their economic and social status.

At that time, most children in the United States received little education. Many children did not even attend school. Those who did often left school after only four years.

Eventually, the situation began to improve. Between 1865 and 1895, states passed laws requiring children from 8 to 14 years old to attend school for at least three months out of every year. By 1900 almost two-thirds of American children between those ages attended

school. Schools taught reading, writing, and arithmetic.

Many people were unhappy with the emphasis on rote memorization and the varying quality of teachers in schools. Strict rules and physical punishments made many students miserable.

By the turn of the century, the number of schools had increased greatly. The number of kindergartens grew from 200 in 1880 to 3,000 in 1900. The number of high schools increased even more. By 1900 more than half a million students attended high school.

The high school curriculum also expanded. It included courses in science, civics, and social studies. Many people realized that the new industrial age needed people who had technical and managerial skills. As a result, high schools also included courses such as drafting and mechanics to prepare

© Houghton Mifflin Harcourt Publishing Company

male graduates for industrial jobs and business courses to prepare female graduates to work in offices.

The growth of public education mainly affected the nation's white communities. During the late 1880s, only 34 percent of African American children attended elementary school. Fewer than 1 percent attended high school.

Educator Mary McLeod Bethune sought to provide more educational opportunity for African Americans. She started a private school for African American girls in Daytona Beach. Later, this school became Bethune-Cookman College and was open to both male and female students.

Unlike African Americans, immigrants attended schools in large numbers. Some immigrant parents hoped that school would "Americanize" their children.

Many adult immigrants also went to school. They attended night classes to learn American culture and English. Some employers offered daytime programs to Americanize their workers.

1. Provide two examples of how public education changed in the late 1800s.

_____

_____

EXPANDING HIGHER EDUCATION
What changes did colleges make?

At the turn of the century, only about 2 percent of Americans attended college. During the years 1880 to 1920, the number of students enrolled in college quadrupled, however.

During this time, colleges added more kinds of courses. In response to the needs of expanding big business, the research university emerged offering courses in modern languages, physical sciences, and the new disciplines of psychology and sociology. Professional schools in law and medicine were started. Many private colleges and universities began requiring entrance exams, while some state universities required only a high school diploma for admission.

Thousands of freed African Americans began attending college in greater numbers after the Civil War. With the help of the Freedmen's Bureau and other groups, blacks founded Howard, Atlanta, and Fisk universities between 1865 and 1868. Still, blacks were excluded from many private institutions. Financially, it was difficult for private donors to support or educate enough black college graduates to meet the needs of their communities. In 1900 only about 4 percent of all African Americans were in attendance at colleges or professional schools.

Booker T. Washington founded the **Tuskegee Normal and Industrial Institute.** Washington believed that racism would end gradually over time when blacks acquired useful labor skills and were valuable to society. Washington taught those skills at his college, which is now known as Tuskegee University.

W.E.B. Du Bois was a black educator who disagreed with Washington. He believed that blacks should quickly enter American society. Du Bois had been the first African American to get a doctorate from Harvard. Du Bois founded the **Niagara Movement,** which insisted that blacks should seek a liberal arts education. In this way, the African American community would gain well-educated leaders.

2. Name two ways in which colleges changed during the late 1800s.

_____

_____

© Houghton Mifflin Harcourt Publishing Company

Describe the chief characteristics of each type of educational institution
and the developments that took place at the turn of the 20th century.

	Chief Characteristics and Important Developments
1. Elementary schools	
2. High schools	
3. Colleges and universities	
4. Education for immigrant adults	

© Houghton Mifflin Harcourt Publishing Company

Progressivism

Segregation and Discrimination

Key Terms and People

Ida B. Wells African American reformer who tried to end lynching through her reporting

poll tax Money one had to pay in order to vote

grandfather clause Clause that allowed poor, uneducated whites to vote

segregation The word used to describe racial separation

Jim Crow laws Laws that helped keep whites and blacks separate

Plessy v. *Ferguson* Court case that upheld the Jim Crow laws

debt peonage A system in which a person is forced to work to pay off debts

Before You Read

In the last lesson you read about improvements made to public education around the turn of the century. In this lesson you will read about how life for African Americans and other nonwhites remained one of hardship and discrimination.

As You Read

Use a chart to take notes on important events in race relations at the turn of the 20th century.

LEGAL DISCRIMINATION
How were African Americans kept from voting?

Reporter **Ida B. Wells** was a leader in the fight against discrimination. Wells crusaded against racial violence. After Reconstruction, many African Americans in the South could not exercise their right to vote. By 1900 all southern states had set up new voting restrictions meant to keep blacks from voting.

For example, some states required voters to be able to read. To determine this, officials gave each voter a literacy test. They often gave African Americans more difficult tests than they gave to

whites. The officials giving the test could pass or fail people as they wished.

Another voting requirement was the **poll tax.** This was a tax that had to be paid to enter a voting booth. African Americans and poor whites often did not have the money to pay the tax. So they were unable to vote.

Several southern states wanted to make sure that whites who could not read or pay a poll tax still could vote. So they added a **grandfather clause** to their constitutions. This clause stated that any person could vote if their father or grandfather was qualified to vote before January 1, 1867. This date was important because before that time,

© Houghton Mifflin Harcourt Publishing Company

Guided Reading Workbook

Lesson 3, *continued*

freed slaves did not have the right to vote. Therefore, the grandfather clause did not allow African Americans to vote. Some Americans challenged the literacy test and poll tax laws. But the Supreme Court allowed the laws to stand.

Separating people on the basis of race became known as **segregation.** Racial segregation developed throughout the South. The southern states passed **Jim Crow laws.** These laws separated whites and blacks in private and public places.

Eventually, a legal challenge to segregation reached the U.S. Supreme Court. However, in the case *Plessy* **v.** *Ferguson,* the Supreme Court ruled that separating the races in public places was legal. This case established the idea of "separate but equal."

1. Name two ways southern states restricted the voting rights of African Americans.

_____

_____

TURN-OF-THE-CENTURY RACE RELATIONS
How **did social customs restrict African Americans?**

In addition to laws, customs also restricted the rights of African Americans. African Americans had to show respect to whites. These customs often belittled and humiliated African Americans. For example, blacks had to yield the sidewalk to whites. Black men always had to remove their hats for whites.

African American reformers debated how to address racial discrimination. Booker T. Washington argued that blacks should not seek full equality at once but instead start by gaining

economic power. Other African Americans, like W.E.B. Du Bois and Ida B. Wells, demanded equality right away.

African Americans who did not follow the customs could face severe punishment. Often, African Americans accused of failing to perform the customs were lynched—or hanged without trial.

African Americans in the North also faced discrimination. They lived in segregated neighborhoods. They faced discrimination in the workplace.

2. Name two ways blacks had to show respect to whites.

_____

_____

DISCRIMINATION IN THE WEST
What **other groups faced discrimination in America?**

Mexican workers in the West and the Southwest faced discrimination, too. In the 1880s and 1890s, railroad companies hired many Mexicans to build new rail lines in the Southwest. Railroad managers hired Mexicans because they were used to the Southwest's hot, dry climate. Managers also felt they could pay Mexicans less than members of other ethnic groups.

Mexicans also played an important role in the Southwest's mining and farming industries. Mexicans provided much of the labor for western agricultural industries.

Landowners often forced Mexicans to work to repay debts. This system was called **debt peonage.** The Supreme Court ruled against this system in 1911, calling it a violation of the Thirteenth Amendment.

© Houghton Mifflin Harcourt Publishing Company

Guided Reading Workbook

Lesson 3, *continued*

The Chinese also faced discrimination in America. Whites feared losing their jobs to Chinese workers. Chinese workers lived in segregated neighborhoods. Their children attended segregated schools.

3. Name two groups that faced discrimination in the West.

_____

_____

Complete the chart by answering the questions about racial tensions at the turn of the 20th century.

	In what region or regions did it exist?	Who were its targets?	How did it affect the lives of these people?
1. Literacy test			
2. Poll tax			
3. Grandfather clause			
4. Jim Crow laws			
5. Racial etiquette			
6. Debt peonage			
7. Chinese Exclusion Act			

© Houghton Mifflin Harcourt Publishing Company

Progressivism

Lesson 4

Women in Public Life

Key Terms and People

NACW National Association of Colored Women; founded in 1896 to improve living and working conditions for African American women

suffrage The right to vote; a major goal of women reformers

Susan B. Anthony A leader of the woman suffrage movement who helped to define the movement's goals and beliefs and to lead its actions

Elizabeth Cady Stanton American reformer who cofounded the National Woman Suffrage Association (NWSA) with Susan B. Anthony

NAWSA National American Woman Suffrage Association; founded in 1890 to help women win the right to vote

Before You Read

In the last lesson you read about how life for African Americans and other nonwhites remained one of hardship and discrimination. In this lesson you will learn about the new, active roles women were taking in the workplace and in politics.

As You Read

Use a chart to take notes about working women in the late 1800s.

WOMEN IN THE WORK FORCE
What jobs did women do?

Before the Civil War, most married women worked at home. They cared for their families and did not have paid jobs. By the end of the 19th century, however, many women had to work outside the home in order to earn money.

Farm women continued to work as they always had. They did the cooking, cleaning, sewing, and child rearing. They helped with the crops and animals as well.

As better-paying opportunities in towns and cities became available, more women began working outside the

home. By 1900, one in five American women held jobs; 25 percent of them worked in manufacturing. About half of the women working in manufacturing were employed in the garment trades. They typically held the least skilled positions and were paid only half as much as men. Women also began filling new jobs in offices, stores, and classrooms. Women went to new business schools to learn to become bookkeepers and typists. These jobs required a high school education.

Women without a formal education took jobs as domestic workers, cleaning houses and taking care of children of other families. Almost 2 million African American workers—forced by economic necessity—worked on farms and in cities as domestic workers, laundresses, scrubwomen, and maids. Unmarried immigrant women did domestic labor, took in piecework, or opened their homes to boarders.

Women were not allowed to own property before the mid-1900s, so money they earned at jobs became the property of their husbands. This began to change in 1839 when the first state passed a law giving women the right to own property.

1. What were three jobs that women often held?

_____

_____

WOMEN LEAD REFORM
What reforms did women want?

Dangerous conditions, long hours, and low wages caused working women to fight for reforms. The Triangle Shirtwaist fire in New York City in 1911 killed 146 young workers, mostly Jewish and immigrant girls, and spurred the cause for reform.

Women who became active in public life attended college. New women's colleges such as Vassar, Smith, and Wellesley opened. By the late 19th century, marriage was no longer a woman's only choice. Many women joined the work force or attended college. These women often applied their skills to needed social reforms.

Women could not directly bring about changes in laws because they could not vote or hold public office. Because of this, they often concentrated their reform efforts in improving conditions at work and at home.

Uneducated laborers were among the first to seek workplace health and safety reforms. Early reform groups became stronger as educated women joined.

In 1896 African American women founded the National Association of Colored Women (**NACW**). This group helped improve educational opportunities for African Americans by managing nurseries, reading rooms, and kindergartens.

Women's crusade for **suffrage,** or the right to vote, began at the Seneca Falls Convention in 1848. The women's movement split over whether or not to support the Fourteenth and Fifteenth Amendments, which granted the vote to African American men but not to women of any race. **Susan B. Anthony** led the opposition. Anthony joined with reformer **Elizabeth Cady Stanton** to create the National American Woman Suffrage Association (**NAWSA**).

Women suffrage faced many obstacles. The liquor industry was afraid that if women gained the right to vote, they would cast their votes in favor of prohibition. The textile industry thought that they would vote to restrict child labor. Many men were happy with women's roles as they were and did not want change.

Women tried three approaches to win the vote: (1) they tried to convince state legislatures, (2) they went to court to clarify whether the provisions of the Fourteenth Amendment meant women should be allowed to vote, and (3) they pushed for a national constitutional amendment to grant women the vote.

Women had both successes and failures with these strategies. Wyoming, Utah, Colorado, and Idaho granted voting rights to women, but efforts in other states failed. The Supreme Court

Lesson 4, *continued*

ruled in 1875 that women were citizens, but denied that this meant they had the right to vote. The idea of a national constitutional amendment was voted down several times.

2. What are three ways in which women tried to win the vote?

_____

_____

Complete the chart about the roles of women.

1. What types of work were women in each group likely to do?			
Farm Women	Women in Cities	African American Women	Immigrant Women

2. How did educational opportunities for middle- and upper-class women change?

3. How did these new opportunities affect the lives of middle- and upper-class women?

4. What three strategies were adopted by the suffragists to win the vote?		
a.	b.	c.

5. What results did each strategy produce?		
a.	b.	c.

© Houghton Mifflin Harcourt Publishing Company

Teddy Roosevelt's Square Deal

Key Terms and People

Theodore Roosevelt United States president from 1901 to 1909

Square Deal President Theodore Roosevelt's program of progressive reforms

The Jungle Novel by Upton Sinclair describing meatpacking

Upton Sinclair Novelist who exposed social problems

Meat Inspection Act Law reforming meatpacking conditions, 1906

Pure Food and Drug Act Law to stop the sale of unclean food and drugs, 1906

conservation The planned management of natural resources

NAACP National Association for the Advancement of Colored People, founded in 1909 to work for racial equality

Before You Read

In the last lesson you read about women who worked for reforms in their communities and for the right to vote. In this lesson you will learn about President Theodore Roosevelt's success in promoting reforms at the national level.

As You Read

Use a chart to take notes on how the problems during Roosevelt's presidency were addressed.

A ROUGH-RIDING PRESIDENT
What **was Roosevelt like?**

   Theodore Roosevelt became president in 1901. He was bold, ambitious, and full of energy. He had been active in sports and politics. In the Spanish–American War, he led a fighting unit called the Rough Riders. His personality made him a popular president.

   Roosevelt used his popularity to get his programs passed. He wanted to see that the common people received what he called a **Square Deal.** This term referred to a program of progressive reforms sponsored by his administration.

1. How did Roosevelt's personality shape his presidency?

_____

_____

USING FEDERAL POWER
How **did Roosevelt handle big business?**

   President Roosevelt believed that modern America needed a powerful federal government. He used the power of the government to help solve the nation's problems.

   Roosevelt also used the power of his

© Houghton Mifflin Harcourt Publishing Company

government to deal with the problem of trusts. Trusts were large companies that had control over their markets. Trusts first drove smaller companies out by lowering their own prices. Then when the smaller companies were gone, the trusts could raise their prices. They no longer had any competition.

By 1900 trusts controlled about 80 percent of U.S. industries. Roosevelt supported big business, but he also wanted to stop trusts that harmed people. He had the government sue harmful trusts under the Sherman Antitrust Act of 1890. In all, Roosevelt filed 44 antitrust suits. He was called a trustbuster.

In 1902 about 140,000 coal miners in Pennsylvania went on strike. The mine owners refused to negotiate with them. President Roosevelt called both sides to the White House to talk. He threatened to have the government take over the mines. The two sides agreed to have an arbitration commission help settle their differences. The commission succeeded in reaching a compromise. From then on, the federal government would often step in to help settle a strike.

In 1887 the Interstate Commerce Commission (ICC) was established to regulate the railroad industry. It was not effective, however, because it had little power. Roosevelt pushed through laws that allowed the government to better regulate railroads. One such law was the Elkin Act of 1903, which made it against the law for railroad officials to offer rebates to shippers to use their railroad. Another was the Hepburn Act of 1906, which strictly limited the distribution of free railroad passes, a common form of bribery. Roosevelt's efforts resulted in fairer shipping

rates and strengthened the federal government's power to regulate the railroad industry.

2. How did Roosevelt use the power of the federal government to change business practices?

_____

_____

HEALTH AND THE ENVIRONMENT
What did President Roosevelt do for public health and the environment?

After reading *The Jungle* by **Upton Sinclair,** which described filthy conditions in the meatpacking industry, Roosevelt appointed a commission of experts to investigate the meatpacking industry. Their report backed up Sinclair's descriptions of filth in the industry. Roosevelt then pushed for passage of the **Meat Inspection Act.** This law, passed in 1906, called for strict cleanliness requirements for meatpackers. It created a program of federal meat inspection.

Also in 1906, Congress passed the **Pure Food and Drug Act,** which halted the sale of contaminated foods and medicines and called for truth in labeling. The government's Bureau of Chemistry was charged with enforcing the new law. This bureau later became the Food and Drug Administration.

Before Roosevelt became president, the federal government had paid little attention to the nation's natural resources. The U.S. Forest Bureau had been established in 1887, but the government seldom stepped in to prevent the loss of the ever-shrinking wilderness. John Muir, a naturalist and writer, persuaded Roosevelt to set aside

© Houghton Mifflin Harcourt Publishing Company

148 million acres of forest reserves. The president also reserved other land for waterpower sites, resource exploration, and wildlife sanctuaries. In addition, Roosevelt created several national parks and monuments. These included the Grand Canyon, Muir Woods, Crater Lakes, and Mesa Verde National Park.

Progressives had long believed in appointing experts in their field to study and make decisions about issues. With this in mind, Roosevelt appointed Gifford Pinchot as head of the U.S. Forest Service. Pinchot was a professional conservationist who was aware of the latest scientific and technical studies. Roosevelt and Pinchot believed in the **conservation** of land, meaning some land should be preserved as wilderness, while other areas would be developed for the common good.

Roosevelt and Pinchot were opposed by Muir, who believed in complete preservation of the wilderness. Indeed, Roosevelt signed the National Reclamation Act, which funded large-scale irrigation projects that transformed dry wilderness into land suitable for agriculture. This act became more commonly known as the Newlands Act. One such project under the Newlands Act was the creation of the Roosevelt Dam in Arizona. The Newlands Act established the precedent that the federal government would manage the precious water resources of the West.

3. What are two ways that Roosevelt helped to make people's lives safer and healthier?

_____

_____

ROOSEVELT AND CIVIL RIGHTS
What did Roosevelt do for African Americans?

The environment proved to be more of a focus of concern for Roosevelt than civil rights. Like most Progressives, the president failed to support civil rights for African Americans as a whole. He did work to assist a few individual African Americans, though.

Roosevelt stood up against southern whites to defend the civil rights of several African Americans. For example, he appointed an African American as head of the Charleston, South Carolina, customhouse even though whites in the city were against it. Also, he ordered that a post office be shut down when whites did not accept the black postmistress he appointed. Roosevelt also invited Booker T. Washington to dinner to show his respect for Washington's work. Washington was the African American leader who was most respected by powerful whites.

Washington urged that African Americans accept that whites would always discriminate against them. Not all African American leaders agreed with this idea. In 1909 black leaders, including W.E.B. Du Bois, founded the National Association for the Advancement of Colored People **(NAACP).** The organization pushed for civil rights and racial equality. The progressive movement, however, continued to focus on the needs of middle-class whites. The two presidents who followed Roosevelt also did little to attempt to ensure the goal of racial equality.

4. What action did the NAACP take?

_____

_____

Name _____ Class _____ Date _____

Complete the chart by answering questions about President Theodore Roosevelt. If Roosevelt took no steps to solve the problem or if no legislation was involved in solving the problem, write "none."

Problem	What steps did Roosevelt take to solve each problem?	Which legislation helped solve the problem?
1. 1902 coal strike		
2. Trusts		
3. Unregulated big business		
4. Dangerous foods and medicines		
5. Shrinking wilderness and natural resources		
6. Racial discrimination		

© Houghton Mifflin Harcourt Publishing Company

Progressivism

Progressivism Under Taft

Key Terms and People

William Howard Taft President from 1909 to 1913; successor to Theodore Roosevelt

Payne-Aldrich Tariff Bill meant to lower tariffs on imported goods

Gifford Pinchot Head of the U.S. Forest Service under Roosevelt, who believed that it was possible to make use of natural resources while conserving them

Bull Moose Party Nickname for the new Progressive Party, which was formed to support Roosevelt in the election of 1912

Woodrow Wilson Winner of the 1912 presidential election

Before You Read

In the last lesson you read about the reforms of Teddy Roosevelt's presidency. In this lesson you will learn about the reforms and political problems of the next president, William Howard Taft.

As You Read

Use a chart to identify the differences that caused divison among the Republicans, and the effect the split had on the 1912 election.

TAFT BECOMES PRESIDENT
Why did Taft have problems?

President Roosevelt promised not to run for another term. Instead, he wanted **William Howard Taft** to become president. Taft had been Roosevelt's secretary of war, and Roosevelt felt Taft would carry out his policies. Taft was elected in 1909 and continued some of the progressive programs. In fact, he busted 90 trusts during his four-year term. Taft was not as effective as Roosevelt had been, though, and faced many problems.

His first problem related to tariffs. Taft supported the tariff-lowering Payne bill, which was passed in the House. However, the Senate passed a weakened version of the bill called the

Payne-Aldrich Tariff. The revised bill did not lower tariffs much at all. Taft signed the bill anyway and defended it. The Progressives in Taft's own Party were annoyed.

Another problem for Taft arose over conservation. Conservationists like **Gifford Pinchot,** the head of the U.S. Forest Service, believed that wilderness areas could be managed for public enjoyment as well as private development. This meant, for instance, that someone could make a profit by logging land that belonged to the federal government. This was called a multi-use land program.

Taft appointed Richard A. Ballinger as secretary of the interior, angering conservationists. Ballinger did not want

© Houghton Mifflin Harcourt Publishing Company

Guided Reading Workbook

to keep so much federal land in reserve. He wanted to free up land for forestry and mining. He wanted to sell some land for private uses. When he did these things, Pinchot complained. Pinchot accused him of misusing the natural resources for commercial interests. As a result of Pinchot's criticism, Taft felt he had to fire Pinchot.

1. In what two areas did Taft have problems?

_____

_____

THE REPUBLICAN PARTY SPLITS
Why did the Republican Party split?

The Republican Party had two wings: (1) the Progressives, who wanted change, and (2) the Conservatives, who did not want reform. Taft was not able to hold the two wings of his party together.

The two groups disagreed over Taft's support of political boss Joseph Cannon. Cannon was Speaker of the House of Representatives, and he ran the House his own way. He appointed people to committee positions who weren't the next in line. As the head of the Committee on Rules, he had the power to control what bills Congress would take up. As a result, under Cannon, the House often did not even vote on progressive bills.

The Republican Party split over how to handle Cannon. The reform-minded Republicans wanted to remove Cannon as head of the Committee on Rules and were able to do so with the help of Democrats in the House.

Some citizens began to question Taft's policies. They blamed the Payne-Aldrich Tariff for a rising cost of living and believed that Taft did not support conservation.

The division between the two groups of Republicans gave the Democrats a chance to take over the House in the 1910 midterm elections. Democrats had control of the House for the first time in almost 20 years.

By 1912 Teddy Roosevelt had decided to run for a third term as president after all. Taft had an advantage because he was already in office. The Republican Party nominated Taft, but Roosevelt's supporters broke off and formed the Progressive Party. This third party was also called the **Bull Moose Party.** It ran on a platform of reform. The Democrats were in a stronger position now that the Republicans were split. They nominated the reform governor of New Jersey, **Woodrow Wilson.**

2. Who formed the Bull Moose Party?

_____

_____

DEMOCRATS WIN IN 1912
Who won the election of 1912?

The 1912 election offered Americans four main choices: Wilson, Taft, Roosevelt, and Socialist Eugene V. Debs.

Wilson campaigned on a progressive platform, called the New Freedom. He wanted stronger antitrust legislation, banking reform, and lower tariffs.

Both Roosevelt and Wilson wanted to give the government a stronger role in the economy. But they differed over ways that this would be accomplished. Roosevelt supported government supervision of big business but did not oppose all monopolies. Wilson supported small business and free-market competition, opposing all business monopolies or trusts. Debs went even further by calling for an end to capitalism.

© Houghton Mifflin Harcourt Publishing Company

Lesson 6, *continued*

Wilson won the 1912 election. He also brought in a Democratic majority in Congress. In all, about 75 percent of the vote went to the candidates who favored economic reform—Wilson, Roosevelt, and Debs. Because so many people supported reform, Wilson had more power to carry out his reforms once in office.

3. What did Wilson have in common with Roosevelt?

_____

_____

Fill in the chart by answering the questions about growing conflicts between reform and business interests.

THE REPUBLICAN PARTY SPLIT.		
	Progressives	**Conservatives**
1. Why did they support or oppose Taft?		
2. What party did they form or stay with?		

FOUR PARTIES RAN CANDIDATES IN THE 1912 GENERAL ELECTION.				
	Progressive Party	**Republican Party**	**Democratic Party**	**Socialist Party**
3. Who did they run for president?				
4. What was their candidate's position on big business?				

© Houghton Mifflin Harcourt Publishing Company

Guided Reading Workbook

Wilson's New Freedom

Key Terms and People

Clayton Antitrust Act Law that weakened monopolies and upheld the rights of unions and farm organizations

Federal Trade Commission (FTC) A federal agency set up in 1914 to investigate businesses to help enforce regulatory laws

Federal Reserve System National banking system begun in 1913

Carrie Chapman Catt President of NAWSA (National American Woman Suffrage Association) who led the campaign for women's suffrage during Wilson's administration

Nineteenth Amendment Amendment to the Constitution giving women the right to vote

Before You Read

In the last lesson you read about the problems Taft faced as president. In this lesson you will learn how Woodrow Wilson managed to get some parts of his progressive platform passed, but had to give up others.

As You Read

Use a chart to take notes on the key events during Wilson's first term.

WILSON WINS FINANCIAL REFORMS
What reforms did Wilson support?

Woodrow Wilson grew up in a religious family in the South. He started out as a lawyer, and then became a professor, university president, and finally state governor. As the governor of New Jersey, he worked for progressive causes. As president, he pushed for a reform program called the New Freedom.

Under Wilson, Congress passed two antitrust measures. The first was the **Clayton Antitrust Act** of 1914. The law

(1) made it more difficult for monopolies to form, (2) said that the people who ran a company could be held personally responsible if the company violated the law, and (3) ruled that labor unions and farm organizations were not to be considered trusts. This made strikes, peaceful picketing, and boycotts legal.

The second antitrust measure was the Federal Trade Act of 1914, which set up the **Federal Trade Commission (FTC).** This agency had the power to investigate businesses for the government and end unfair business

© Houghton Mifflin Harcourt Publishing Company

practices. The FTC became very active during Wilson's administration. It issued nearly 400 orders telling companies to stop breaking the law.

Wilson believed that high tariffs made big business more powerful. He supported the Underwood Tariff of 1913, which lowered tariffs for the first time since the Civil War.

With less money coming in from tariffs, however, the government needed another source of money. It turned to an income tax. This tax on people's earnings was created by the Sixteenth Amendment to the Constitution, which was ratified by the states in 1913. The tax gave to the federal government a percentage of all workers' income and business profits.

After reforming tariffs, Wilson turned his attention to the banking system. It was difficult for people far from banking centers to obtain credit. The new **Federal Reserve System** solved this problem by dividing the country into 12 decentralized districts, each with a federal reserve bank. This system controlled the money supply and made credit more easily available. Setting up the Federal Reserve was one of Wilson's most important reforms.

1. What were three areas that Wilson reformed?

_____

_____

WOMEN WIN SUFFRAGE
How did women get the vote?

The suffrage movement gained strength for three reasons. Local suffrage organizations increased their activism with door-to-door campaigns to win support. Also, women used new strategies to build enthusiasm for the movement. For example, they adopted the more bold tactics of British suffragists such as heckling government officials. In addition, **Carrie Chapman Catt** brought about the rebirth of the national suffrage movement as president of NAWSA.

It took World War I to bring women the vote. A great number of women became active in supporting the war effort by running committees, knitting socks for soldiers, and selling liberty bonds to raise funds for the war. They thought they deserved the right to vote for all their efforts. At last, in 1919 Congress passed the **Nineteenth Amendment.** This amendment giving women the vote was ratified by the states the next year.

2. How did World War I help women get the right to vote?

_____

_____

THE LIMITS OF PROGRESSIVISM
Did Wilson support civil rights?

Like Roosevelt and Taft, Wilson backed away from civil rights. During the 1912 campaign, he won the support of the NAACP by promising to treat blacks equally. He also promised to speak out against lynching, that is, mob killings of blacks. Yet once he was president, Wilson opposed federal laws against lynching. He felt that states, not the federal government, had the right to make such laws.

Another blow for those who wanted integration of blacks and whites was Wilson's appointment of his cabinet. Wilson chose cabinet members who extended segregation. Wilson's angry

© Houghton Mifflin Harcourt Publishing Company

Lesson 7, *continued*

meeting with an African American delegation brought African Americans' feeling of betrayal to a head.

World War I became a factor in dimming the reform spirit as legislators had less interest in reform.

3. Why did African Americans feel betrayed by President Wilson?

_____

_____

Complete the chart about President Wilson's approach to reform.

WHAT WERE THE AIMS OF EACH PIECE OF LEGISLATION OR CONSTITUTIONAL AMENDMENT?	
1. Federal Trade Act	
2. Clayton Antitrust Act	
3. Underwood Tariff	
4. Sixteenth Amendment	
5. Federal Reserve Act	
WILSON AND RIGHTS OF CITIZENS	
6. Which three new developments finally brought the success of the woman suffrage movement within reach?	
7. Which constitutional amendment recognized women's right to vote?	
8. How did Wilson retreat on civil rights?	

© Houghton Mifflin Harcourt Publishing Company

Imperialism and America

Key Terms and People

Queen Liliuokalani The Hawaiian queen who was forced out of power by a revolution started by American business interests

imperialism The practice of stronger countries extending economic, political, and military control over weaker countries

Alfred T. Mahan American imperialist and admiral who urged the United States to build up its navy and take colonies overseas

William Seward Secretary of state under presidents Lincoln and Johnson

Pearl Harbor Port in Hawaii where the United States built a naval base

Sanford B. Dole American businessman who headed the new government of Hawaii after the queen was overthrown

Before You Read

In the last lesson you read about the Woodrow Wilson administration. In this lesson you will learn how economic activity led to political and military involvement overseas.

As You Read

Use a diagram to take notes on the causes of U.S. imperialism.

AMERICAN EXPANSIONISM
Why did Americans support imperialism?

In 1893 **Queen Liliuokalani** of Hawaii gave up her throne. Hawaii was about to be taken over by the United States.

By the 1880s many American leaders thought the United States should establish colonies overseas. This idea was called **imperialism**—the policy in which stronger nations extend economic, political, or military control over weaker territories. European countries had competed for territory all over the world. Most Americans gradually accepted the idea of overseas expansion.

Three factors fueled American imperialism: desire for military strength, thirst for new markets, and a belief in the superiority of American culture.

Admiral **Alfred T. Mahan** of the U.S. Navy supported growing American naval power so the United States could compete with other nations. The United States built such modern battleships as the *Maine* and the *Oregon*. The new ships made the United States the world's largest naval power.

By the late 1800s technology had changed American farms and factories. They produced more than Americans could consume. So the United States needed foreign trade. American businesses needed markets for their products and raw materials for their factories.

© Houghton Mifflin Harcourt Publishing Company

The third factor of American imperialism was a belief that the people of the United States were better than the people of other countries. This racist belief came from people's pride in their Anglo-Saxon (Northern European) heritage. People sometimes felt they had a duty to spread their culture and Christian religion among other people.

1. What were three reasons Americans supported imperialism?

_____

_____

THE UNITED STATES ACQUIRES ALASKA; THE UNITED STATES TAKES HAWAII

How did the Hawaiian Islands become a U.S. territory?

William Seward was secretary of state for presidents Lincoln and Andrew Johnson. In 1867 he purchased Alaska from Russia for $7.2 million. Some opponents in Congress made fun of the deal, calling it "Seward's Icebox" or "Seward's Folly."

The Hawaiian Islands, in the Pacific Ocean, had been important to the United States since the 1790s. Merchants had stopped there on their way to China and India. In the 1820s American missionaries founded Christian schools and churches on the islands.

A number of Americans had established sugar plantations in Hawaii. In the mid-1800s these large farms accounted for about three-quarters of the wealth in the islands. Plantation owners brought thousands of laborers to Hawaii from Japan, Portugal, and China. This weakened the influence of the native Hawaiians. By 1900 the foreign laborers outnumbered the Hawaiians three to one.

In 1875 the United States agreed to import Hawaiian sugar duty-free. Over the next 15 years, Hawaiian sugar production increased nine times. Then the McKinley Tariff in 1890 caused a crisis for Hawaiian sugar growers. With the duty on their sugar, Hawaiian growers faced stiff competition from other growers.

The powerful Hawaiian sugar growers called for the United States to annex Hawaii. The U.S. military had already understood the value of Hawaii. In 1887 the United States forced Hawaii to let it build a naval base at **Pearl Harbor,** Hawaii's best port. Also in that year, white business leaders forced Hawaii's King Kalakaua to amend Hawaii's constitution, limiting voting rights to only wealthy landowners. But when Kalakaua died in 1891, his sister became queen. Queen Liliuokalani wanted a new constitution that would give voting power back to ordinary Hawaiians. American business interests did not want this to happen.

American business groups organized a revolt against the queen. The U.S. ambassador John L. Stevens helped them. The planters took control of the island. They established a temporary government headed by American businessman **Sanford B. Dole.**

Stevens urged the U.S. government to annex the Hawaiian Islands. President Grover Cleveland refused to take over the islands unless a majority of Hawaiians favored that. In 1897, however, William McKinley became president. He favored annexation. In 1898 Hawaii became a U.S. territory.

2. How did Hawaiians lose control of their islands?

_____

_____

Lesson 1, *continued*

As you read this lesson, fill out the chart below by summarizing reasons why the United States became an imperial power.

THE ROOTS OF AMERICAN IMPERIALISM		
1. Economic roots	2. Political and military roots	3. Racist roots

↓

4. What did Admiral Mahan urge the United States to do to protect its interests?

For each year on the timeline below, identify one important event in the history of U.S. involvement in Hawaii.

U.S. IMPERIALISM IN HAWAII	
1875	
1887	
1890	
1891	
1897	
1898	

© Houghton Mifflin Harcourt Publishing Company

Guided Reading Workbook

U.S. Imperialism

The Spanish–American War

Key Terms and People

José Martí Political activist who worked for Cuban independence

Valeriano Weyler General sent from Spain to Cuba to restore order in 1896

yellow journalism Reporting in newspapers and magazines that exaggerates the news in order to make it more exciting

USS *Maine* U.S. warship that exploded in a Cuban harbor in 1898

George Dewey U.S. naval commander who led the American attack on the Philippines

Rough Riders Fighting unit led by Theodore Roosevelt in Cuba

San Juan Hill Location of an important American land victory in Cuba

Treaty of Paris The treaty that ended the Spanish-American War

Before You Read

In the last lesson you learned how the United States became an imperialist power and took over the Hawaiian Islands. In this lesson you will learn how the United States became involved in Cuba and fought a war with Spain.

As You Read

Complete a cause and effect chart as you take notes on the Spanish-American War.

CUBANS REBEL AGAINST SPAIN
What happened when Cuba rebelled against Spain?

Between 1868 and 1878 Cubans fought their first war for independence from Spain. The rebels did not win, but they did force Spain to abolish slavery in 1886. After that, United States capitalists invested in sugarcane plantations in Cuba.

Sugar was the most important product of Cuba. The United States was the main market for the sugar. As long as the United States did not charge a tariff on Cuban sugar, the Cuban economy thrived. But the Cuban economy collapsed in 1894 when a tariff on sugar was imposed.

In 1895 Cubans began a second war for independence. The rebellion was led by **José Martí.** He was a Cuban poet and journalist who had been living in exile in New York. Martí organized a campaign of destroying property, especially American-owned sugar plantations, as a way of provoking the United States to action. The rebels wanted the United States to join their cause.

American opinion was mixed. Some wanted to support Spain in order to keep their investments safe. Others wanted to help the Cuban people win their freedom from Spain just as the United States had won its independence from England.

1. How did Cuba's two wars for independence affect American business interests?

   _____

   _____

WAR FEVER ESCALATES
Why did Americans become angry with Spain?

In 1896 Spain sent an army to Cuba to restore order. The army was led by General **Valeriano Weyler.** Weyler rounded up the entire rural population of central and western Cuba. He kept 300,000 people as prisoners in concentration camps. That way they could not help the rebels. Thousands died of hunger and disease.

This story was widely reported in the United States. Rival newspapers in New York made the terrible events sound even worse. They exaggerated the brutality of the story in order to attract readers. These sensational stories became known as **yellow journalism**— reporting that exaggerates the news in order to make it more exciting.

William McKinley became president in 1897. At that time, many Americans wanted the United States to help the rebels against Spain. McKinley tried to find a peaceful solution to the crisis. His efforts had several positive results. Spain sent General Weyler home, changed the concentration camp policy, and gave Cuba limited self-government.

Then two events made Americans very angry at Spain. The first was the publication of a letter that insulted the American president. The de Lôme letter

was written by a Spanish diplomat. It criticized McKinley for being weak. Although some Americans agreed that the president was weak, they did not want to hear this criticism from a Spanish official.

Only a few days after the letter was published, something worse happened. The battleship **USS *Maine*** was stationed in Cuba to protect American lives and property. On February 15, 1898, the ship exploded. The ship sank, and 260 officers and crew on board died. The cause of the explosion was not known. However, newspapers blamed Spain. Americans cried for war.

2. What two events led Americans to call for war against Spain?

   _____

   _____

WAR WITH SPAIN ERUPTS
Where and when did the fighting take place?

On April 20, 1898, the United States went to war with Spain. The first battle took place in the Philippines. The Philippines had been a Spanish colony for 300 years. They had rebelled many times. In 1896 they began another rebellion.

On May 1, 1898, the American naval commander **George Dewey** sailed into Manila Bay in the Philippines. His ships destroyed the Spanish fleet there. In the next two months, U.S. soldiers fought on the side of the Filipino rebels. The Spanish surrendered to the United States in August.

In Cuba, the American navy blocked off the harbor of Santiago de Cuba. Spanish ships could not leave. Then American troops landed on the island in June 1898.

© Houghton Mifflin Harcourt Publishing Company

Lesson 2, *continued*

One unit of volunteer soldiers was called the **Rough Riders.** Theodore Roosevelt was one of their leaders. They helped win the important battle of **San Juan Hill.** American newspapers made Roosevelt a hero.

When the Spanish ships tried to leave the harbor, their fleet was destroyed. This led the Spanish to surrender on July 25.

Spain quickly agreed to a peace treaty. The **Treaty of Paris** granted Cuba its independence. Spain gave Puerto Rico and the Pacific island of Guam to the United States. The United States paid Spain $20 million for the annexation of the Philippine Islands.

The Treaty of Paris touched off a great debate in the United States about imperialism. President McKinley was in favor of it. But some prominent Americans presented a variety of arguments against annexation. Booker T. Washington argued that the United States should settle race-related issues at home before taking on social problems elsewhere. Labor leader Samuel Gompers opposed the treaty because he believed Filipino workers would compete for American jobs. The Senate approved the treaty on February 6, 1899.

3. What three territories did the United States get from the war with Spain?

    _____

    _____

© Houghton Mifflin Harcourt Publishing Company

Lesson 2, *continued*

As you read about the Spanish-American War, write notes in the appropriate boxes to answer the questions about its causes and effects.

CAUSES: HOW DID EACH OF THE FOLLOWING HELP TO CAUSE THE OUTBREAK OF THE SPANISH-AMERICAN WAR?
1. American business owners
2. José Martí
3. Valeriano Weyler
4. Yellow journalism
5. De Lôme letter
6. USS *Maine*

EFFECTS: WHAT HAPPENED TO EACH OF THE FOLLOWING TERRITORIES AS A RESULT OF THE SPANISH-AMERICAN WAR?
7. Cuba
8. Puerto Rico
9. Guam
10. Philippine Islands

© Houghton Mifflin Harcourt Publishing Company

U.S. Imperialism

Acquiring New Lands

Key Terms and People

Foraker Act Law which ended military rule in Puerto Rico

Platt Amendment Provisions in the Cuban constitution that gave the United States broad rights in that country

protectorate A country that is partly controlled by another, stronger country

Emilio Aguinaldo Filipino rebel leader

John Hay U.S. secretary of state

Open Door notes Message sent by John Hay to other countries to protect U.S. trading rights in China

Boxer Rebellion Chinese rebellion against Western influence, 1900

Before You Read

In the last lesson you learned how the United States and Spain fought over Cuba and the Philippines. In this lesson you will read how the United States continued its imperialism.

As You Read

Use a chart to take notes on the key events relating to the relationships between the United States and Puerto Rico, Cuba, the Philippines, and China.

RULING PUERTO RICO
***How* did Puerto Ricans feel about U.S. control?**

Puerto Rico had become an American territory as a result of the Spanish-American War. American forces landed in Puerto Rico in July 1898. The commanding officer declared that the Americans were there to protect the Puerto Ricans. But other U.S. military officials insulted the Puerto Ricans. They spoke to them as children and set limits on their personal freedom. Many Puerto Ricans began to resent the military government.

Puerto Rico was strategically important to the United States, both for maintaining a U.S. presence in the Caribbean, and for protecting a future canal that American leaders wanted to build across the Isthmus of Panama. In 1900 Congress passed the **Foraker Act** that ended military rule in Puerto Rico and set up a civil government. The act gave the president of the United States the power to appoint Puerto Rico's governor and members of the upper house of its legislature. Puerto Ricans could elect only the members of the lower house.

The United States kept strict control over the Puerto Rican people and their

Lesson 3, *continued*

government. In 1917, however, Congress made Puerto Ricans U.S. citizens. It also gave them the right to elect both houses of their legislature.

1. Why did some Puerto Ricans resent U.S. control of their government?

_____

_____

CUBA AND THE UNITED STATES
How did the United States keep control over Cuba?

Cuba was officially independent after the war. The U.S. army, however, remained in Cuba for four years. It punished Cubans who did not like this American occupation.

In 1900 the new Cuban government wrote a constitution. The United States insisted they add the **Platt Amendment.** The amendment limited Cuba's rights in dealing with other countries. It gave the United States special privileges, including the right to intervene to preserve order.

Cuba became a U.S. **protectorate**— a country whose affairs are partially controlled by a stronger power. The United States insisted on these rights because of its economic interests in Cuba's sugar, tobacco, and mining industries, as well as it its railroads and public utilities.

2. What did the United States do to protect business interests in Cuba?

_____

_____

FILIPINOS REBEL
Why did the Filipinos rebel against the United States?

Filipinos had been fighting for independence for years. They were angry that the United States had annexed their islands. Rebel leader **Emilio Aguinaldo** believed that the United States had betrayed the Filipinos after helping them win independence. The rebels believed that the United States was doing the same thing Spain had done— imposing its authority and infringing on the freedom of the people.

In 1899 Aguinaldo started a rebellion, which lasted three years. After winning the Philippine-American War, the United States set up a government similar to the one it had set up in Cuba.

3. Why did Aguinaldo feel betrayed by the United States?

_____

_____

FOREIGN INFLUENCE IN CHINA
What were U.S. interests in China?

By 1899 many countries had economic interests in China. The United States wanted to be able to trade with China. China was seen as a vast potential market for American products.

The Secretary of State **John Hay** sent a series of policy statements to the leaders of other nations proposing that the nations share their trading rights with the United States. His policy statements were called the **Open Door notes.** They called for China's ports to remain open, and for China to remain independent. No country would have special trading rights. The other countries agreed.

Although China kept its freedom, Europeans dominated most of China's cities. In 1900 a secret society in China started a rebellion protesting the influence of Western countries. This group was known as the Boxers because members practiced martial arts.

© Houghton Mifflin Harcourt Publishing Company

Guided Reading Workbook

Lesson 3, *continued*

Troops from many countries, including the United States, fought against the Chinese rebels. After the **Boxer Rebellion** was defeated, the United States issued more Open Door notes to make sure that other countries did not try to make colonies in China.

4. Why did Secretary of State John Hay issue the Open Door notes?

_____

_____

THE IMPACT OF U.S. TERRITORIAL GAINS
How did Americans feel about U.S. imperialism?

President William McKinley was reelected in 1900. His opponent had been an anti-imperialist, William Jennings Bryan. The outcome of the election suggests that most Americans disagreed with Bryan. Imperialism was popular.

Before McKinley was reelected, an Anti-Imperialist League formed. The league included some prominent Americans: former president Grover Cleveland, industrial leader Andrew Carnegie, labor leader Samuel Gompers, social worker Jane Addams, and author Mark Twain. They all had different reasons for being against imperialism. For example, Gompers was concerned about the impact of imperialism on U.S. workers. Carnegie worried that U.S. imperialism would lead to endless wars with European countries. But all Anti-Imperialist League members agreed it was wrong for the United States to rule other people without their consent.

5. What did McKinley's reelection show about American attitudes toward imperialism?

_____

_____

© Houghton Mifflin Harcourt Publishing Company

Lesson 3, *continued*

As you read about America's relations with lands under its influence, write notes to answer the questions below. Some answers have already been filled in for you.

	Puerto Rico 1898–1916	Cuba 1898–1903	The Philippines 1898–1945	China 1900
1. What was its relationship to the U.S.?	very similar to that of a colony or protectorate		very similar to that of a colony or protectorate	
2. Why did the U.S. try to control its affairs?			to provide the U.S. with raw materials and new markets	
3. What laws and policies affected its relationship with the U.S.?				
4. What violent events affected its relationship with the U.S.?	Spanish-American War			

John Hay's "Open Door notes" paved the way for greater U.S. influence in Asia. Note three factors concerning the Open Door policy.

5.
6.
7.

© Houghton Mifflin Harcourt Publishing Company

Guided Reading Workbook

America as a World Power

Key Terms and People

Panama Canal A channel across Central America, between the Atlantic and Pacific Oceans, opened in 1914

Roosevelt Corollary Roosevelt's 1904 extension of the Monroe Doctrine, stating that the United States has the right to protect its economic interests in South and Central America by using military force

dollar diplomacy The policy of intervening in other countries to protect U.S. business interests

Francisco "Pancho" Villa Mexican revolutionary

Emiliano Zapata Mexican rebel

John J. Pershing U.S. general who led troops to capture Villa

Before You Read

In the last lesson you learned about the growth of American imperialism. In this lesson you will learn how Roosevelt and Wilson used American military and economic power.

As You Read

Use a chart to take notes on how Teddy Roosevelt and Woodrow Wilson used American power around the world.

TEDDY ROOSEVELT AND THE WORLD
How did Roosevelt use American power?

In 1901 President McKinley was assassinated, and Vice-President Theodore Roosevelt became president. Roosevelt continued the policies of American imperialism. He first used the influence of the United States to help settle the Russo-Japanese War.

The war began in 1904. Both Russia and Japan wanted to control Korea. Japan captured Korea and also invaded Manchuria, which was controlled by Russia.

Then Japan wanted to stop the fighting because they were running out of soldiers to fight and money to pay for the war. The Japanese secretly asked President Roosevelt to mediate the conflict. As a result, in 1905 representatives of Russia and Japan met. Roosevelt used his personal charm to help them negotiate a compromise. They signed a treaty, and Roosevelt received the 1906 Nobel Peace Prize for his efforts.

Roosevelt also used his influence to help build the **Panama Canal.** The idea of a canal connecting the Atlantic and Pacific Oceans had been discussed for some time. Such a canal would cut travel time for military and commercial ships. Ships would no longer have to go all the way around South America in order to get from one ocean to the other.

The narrow Isthmus of Panama was a logical place to cut a canal. Political problems stood in the way, however. Panama was a province of Colombia. When Colombia did not agree to the canal, the United States helped Panama to rebel against Colombia. Panama became independent. Then the United States got Panama's permission to build the canal.

Construction of the Panama Canal was one of the world's greatest engineering accomplishments. Work began in 1904 and took ten years. In 1913 there were 43,400 workers on the project. The work was hard and dangerous.

On August 15, 1914, the canal opened for business. It was a success from the start. More than 1,000 ships passed through during its first year. However, relations between the United States and Latin America had been damaged by the takeover of Panama.

President Roosevelt wanted the United States to be the major power in the Caribbean and Central America. He declared his policy in a message to Congress in 1904. His statement was called the **Roosevelt Corollary.** A corollary is a logical result of another statement, in this case the Monroe Doctrine of 1823. That doctrine had said the United States would not allow European influence in the Western Hemisphere. Roosevelt now said that the United States had the right to intervene in Latin American countries to protect U.S. business interests.

In 1911 President Taft used this policy in Nicaragua. A rebellion had left the country in debt. Taft arranged for U.S. bankers to loan Nicaragua money. In exchange, American business took control of the railroads and banks in the country. They also collected Nicaragua's custom duties.

Nicaraguans did not like this arrangement. They rebelled. The United States then sent troops to Nicaragua to preserve the peace. Those who did not like this kind of intervention called it **dollar diplomacy.**

1. What are two ways Roosevelt used U.S. power in other countries?

_____

_____

WOODROW WILSON'S MISSIONARY DIPLOMACY
Why did President Wilson send troops to Mexico?

President Woodrow Wilson took a step beyond Presidents Monroe and Roosevelt by adding a moral tone to Latin American policy. He said that the United States must act in certain circumstances.

This so-called "missionary diplomacy" meant that the United States could not officially recognize governments that were oppressive, undemocratic, or opposed to U.S. business interests. The new doctrine put pressure on countries to have democratic governments. A revolution in Mexico tested this policy.

In 1910 Mexican peasants and workers rebelled against their military dictator. Two new governments followed, the second headed by General Victoriano Huerta.

Wilson refused to support the Huerta government because it came to power through violence. However, the president looked for an opportunity to intervene.

© Houghton Mifflin Harcourt Publishing Company

Lesson 4, *continued*

That opportunity came through a minor incident. One of Huerta's officers arrested a small group of American sailors in Tampico, on Mexico's eastern shore. The Mexicans released them and apologized, but Wilson used the event as an excuse to order in American troops. As a result, 18 Americans and at least 200 Mexicans died in the fighting. The incident brought the United States and Mexico close to war. When the Huerta regime collapsed and a new leader, Venustiano Carranza, took power in Mexico, Wilson withdrew the troops and formally recognized the Carranza government.

Mexico remained in turmoil. Under the leadership of **Francisco "Pancho" Villa** and **Emiliano Zapata,** rebels revolted against Carranza. Some of Villa's followers killed Americans. The United States wanted to capture Villa.

Finally the Mexican government gave permission to send in troops. Wilson sent General **John J. Pershing** with 15,000 soldiers to capture Villa dead or alive. A year later, Villa was still free. Wilson then stationed 150,000 National Guardsmen along the border.

Mexicans were angered by the U.S. invasion. In 1916 U.S. troops fought with Carranza's army. In 1917 Wilson withdrew U.S. troops, in part because he was facing possible war in Europe. Later that year Mexico adopted a constitution that gave the government control of the nation's oil and mineral resources and placed strict regulations on foreign investors.

American intervention in Mexico showed how far the United States was willing to go to protect its economic interests.

In the early 20th century, the U.S. pursued several foreign policy goals. It expanded its access to foreign markets. It built a modern navy to protect its interests abroad. It used its international police power to influence Latin America.

2. What were two reasons Wilson sent troops to Mexico?

_____

_____

Lesson 4, *continued*

As you read this lesson, write notes summarizing the effects of
American military, diplomatic, and economic power around the world.

ROOSEVELT'S "BIG STICK" DIPLOMACY

American action taken		Consequences of that action
1. Treaty negotiated between Japan and Russia	→	
2. The United States helped Panama rebel against Columbia	→	
3. Panama Canal built	→	
4. Roosevelt Corollary adopted	→	

WILSON'S "MISSIONARY" DIPLOMACY

American action taken		Consequences of that action
5. Wilson used a minor incident with Mexico as an excuse to send in troops	→	
6. Wilson recognized the Carranza government	→	
7. Wilson refused Carranza's demand to withdraw U.S. troops sent into Mexico to capture Villa	→	

© Houghton Mifflin Harcourt Publishing Company

World War I

World War I Begins

Key Terms and People

nationalism A devotion to the interests and culture of one's nation

militarism Building up armed forces to prepare for war

Allies One side in World War I: Britain, France, and Russia, later joined by the United States

Central powers One side in World War I: Germany, Austria-Hungary, and the Ottoman Empire

balance of power Act of giving two different sides equal strength or power

Archduke Franz Ferdinand Young heir whose assassination triggered World War I

trench warfare Fighting between fortified ditches

"no man's land" The space between armies fighting each other

Lusitania British passenger ship attacked and sunk by Germans

Sussex **pledge** A promise by the Germans not to sink vessels without warning

Zimmermann note Message proposing an alliance between Germany and Mexico

Before You Read

In the last lesson you learned how presidents Roosevelt and Wilson used American power around the world. In this lesson you will read how war broke out in Europe while the United States tried to remain neutral.

As You Read

Use a chart to take notes on the causes of World War I.

CAUSES OF WORLD WAR I
***What* conditions led to war?**

Four main factors led to the outbreak of World War I in Europe. The first was **nationalism**—the belief that the interests of a single country are more important than cooperation among countries. This led to competition and hard feelings. It also made ethnic groups want to gain independence for their nations.

The second cause was imperialism. Countries tried to increase their power and influence around the world. This led to competition among them in the contest for colonies under their control. These colonies would provide them both with raw materials and markets for selling manufactured goods.

The third main cause was **militarism.** Militarism meant building up armed forces. For example, Germany tried to build up its navy to match the strength of Britain's. Both nations then competed to build the most battleships. Militarism

© Houghton Mifflin Harcourt Publishing Company

also meant using armed forces as tools for negotiating with other countries.

The fourth cause was the alliance system. Some countries in Europe had made treaties promising to defend each other. These mutual-defense treaties placed European countries in two main groups. The **Allies** were made up of France, Britain, and Russia. The **Central powers** were made up of Germany, Austria-Hungary, and the Ottoman Empire.

For a while, some European leaders thought the alliance created a **balance of power.** In other words, they believed the alliances gave the opposing sides equal strength. They hoped that this would keep a single nation from attacking another, which would lead to war. They would soon be proved wrong.

1. Name two causes of World War I.

_____

_____

WAR BREAKS OUT
What sparked the war?

In 1914 **Archduke Franz Ferdinand** was assassinated. He had been the heir to the throne of Austria-Hungary. His killer was a Serb who wanted to unite all Serbs (including those in Austria-Hungary) under one government. This touched off an action to punish the Serbs. Austria-Hungary declared war on Serbia.

The alliance system pulled one nation after another into the conflict. If a nation had sworn to protect another, it had to declare war on that nation's enemies. Germany and Austria-Hungary were facing France, Britain, and Russia. The conflict that became known as the Great War had begun.

Germany began by invading Belgium. It planned to overrun France and then to attack Russia. The British and French could not save Belgium. They did, however, manage to stop Germany's advance.

Europeans soon discovered that the war would not be quick, as they originally thought. This occurred in part because of the development of **trench warfare,** in which armies fight in ditches to gain small amounts of land. By the spring of 1915, two lines of deep trenches had developed in France. The trenches stretched from the Belgian coast to the Swiss Alps. Germans occupied one line. The Allies occupied the other line. Between the two lines lay **"no man's land."** The soldiers would climb out of their trenches and try to overrun enemy lines. They did this while facing machine-gun fire and poison gas. In the trenches, soldiers suffered both dysentery and trench foot, which sometimes led to amputation of toes or even entire feet.

This bloody trench warfare continued for more than three years. Neither side gained territory, but more than 1 million soldiers died.

2. Why did the assassination of Archduke Franz Ferdinand lead to fighting?

_____

_____

AMERICANS QUESTION NEUTRALITY
How did Americans feel about the war?

In the United States, public opinion about the war was strong but divided. Most Americans thought that the country should not join a fight thousands of miles away. Socialists saw the war as an imperialist struggle

© Houghton Mifflin Harcourt Publishing Company

Lesson 1, *continued*

between German and English businessmen. Pacifists believed that all wars were bad. They urged the United States to set an example for peace. Many other Americans simply did not want to send their sons to war.

Many naturalized U.S. citizens still had ties to the countries they came from. Many immigrants from Germany, for example, sympathized with Germany. Many naturalized citizens urged the United States to stay neutral and formed organizations to help the causes of their homelands.

Americans tended to sympathize with Britain and France. They shared a common language and heritage with Britain. They were horrified at Britain's claims of German brutality. And they had strong economic ties with the Allies.

American business found it hard to remain neutral. After all, trade with Britain and France had long been stronger than trade with Germany. During the war, the Allies began to order more and more military supplies from American businesses. Some businesses tried to remain neutral by shipping goods to Germany as well, but this proved risky. The British navy often stopped such shipments. Also, many Americans voiced concern about German brutalities and warned that a German victory would be a threat to democracy.

American banks loaned money to both sides but greatly favored Britain and the other Allies. Many Americans believed that United States prosperity depended on an Allied victory.

3. What were three things that influenced Americans' feelings about the war?

_____

_____

THE WAR HITS HOME
How did the war affect Americans?

The war affected American shipping. Britain set up a blockade along the German coast to keep goods from getting through. American ships would not challenge Britain's blockade. German U-boats attacked ships from all nations. A U-boat sank the British ship *Lusitania,* killing more than 1,000 people, including 128 Americans. Later, the Germans agreed in the *Sussex* pledge not to sink merchant ships without warning.

4. In what ways did the war affect American citizens?

_____

_____

THE UNITED STATES DECLARES WAR
Why did the United States join the war?

Three incidents brought the United States into the war. First, in January 1917 Germany announced it would sink all ships in British waters on sight whether they were hostile or neutral. Second, British agents intercepted the **Zimmermann note,** a telegram that proposed an alliance between Germany and Mexico against the United States. Third, a change in government led Russia to remove itself from the conflict. With Russia out, Americans considered the war a struggle of democracies against brutal monarchies. On April 6, 1917, at President Wilson's request, Congress declared war on Germany.

5. What are the three incidents that led the United States to declare war?

_____

_____

Lesson 1, *continued*

Answer the following questions about the international politics that led
to war in Europe.

How did the following help to ignite the war in Europe?
1. Nationalism
2. Imperialism
3. Militarism
4. Alliances
5. Assassination of Archduke Ferdinand

Why did the following groups of Americans tend to oppose U.S. participation in the war?
6. Naturalized citizens
7. Socialists
8. Pacifists
9. Parents

What did the following nations do to encourage U.S. participation in the war?		
10. Britain	11. Germany	12. Russia

© Houghton Mifflin Harcourt Publishing Company

World War I

The United States Joins the War

Key Terms and People

Selective Service Act Law requiring men to register for military service

convoy system Having merchant ships travel in groups protected by warships

American Expeditionary Force The name given to the American military force that fought in World War I

John J. Pershing The commander of the American Expeditionary Force

Eddie Rickenbacker Famous American fighter pilot

Alvin York American war hero

conscientious objector A person who believes fighting is wrong and therefore does not want to serve in the military

armistice Truce agreement

Before You Read

In the last lesson you learned how the United States was drawn into the war. In this lesson you will read how Americans prepared to fight and how they helped the Allies win.

As You Read

Complete a chart with details concerning how Americans responded to the war.

AMERICA MOBILIZES
How **did the U.S. prepare for war?**

The United States first needed to build up its armed forces. When war was declared, only about 200,000 men were in service. To solve this problem, Congress passed the **Selective Service Act.** It required men to register with the government so that some of them could be selected for military service. This process—called the draft—put about 3 million men in uniform.

The United States government appealed to minorities to help in the war effort. Many African Americans served in the military. They were placed in separate units. Many but not all African Americans were assigned to noncombat roles. Some who fought were among the first to receive the French honor of the Croix de Guerre. Native Americans, Asian Americans, and Hispanic Americans also contributed to the war effort. Many minorities hoped serving in the military would help them gain equal rights at home in the United States.

Women were not drafted. The army would not let them join. But the navy accepted women in noncombat positions. Woman served as nurses, secretaries, and telephone operators.

© Houghton Mifflin Harcourt Publishing Company

The United States also had to find ways to get men, food, and equipment overseas. The United States built new ships to do this. Shipyard workers were exempted from the draft. Prefabrication techniques were used to speed the production of ships.

1. How did the United States get ready for war?

_____

_____

THE FIGHT "OVER THERE"
How did the United States help the Allies?

The Allied forces were tired and eager for help in fighting the war. They welcomed the American troops and much-needed supplies.

To reduce the loss of ships to German submarine attacks, the United States convinced the British to use the **convoy system.** In this system, merchant ships traveled in a large group guarded by naval vessels. In addition, the United States helped create a barrier of mines across the North Sea to stop U-boats.

American soldiers helped turn the tide of battle in Europe. The Allies had experienced many casualties and were running out of men. Thousands of fresh American soldiers were full of energy and enthusiasm.

The **American Expeditionary Force** was led by General **John J. Pershing.** American infantrymen were called doughboys because of the white belts they wore and cleaned with pipe clay, or "dough."

New weapons played a decisive role in the war. The two most innovative weapons were the tank and the airplane. Air warfare developed rapidly during the war. Pilots went from shooting at each other with pistols to using mounted machine guns.

Eddie Rickenbacker was an American ace pilot. He fought in 134 air battles and shot down 26 enemy planes.

New weapons and tactics made World War I very destructive. Soldiers faced such dangers as machine-gun fire and poison gas.

2. How did the United States help the Allies?

_____

_____

AMERICAN TROOPS GO ON THE OFFENSIVE
How did American troops help end the war?

American soldiers arrived in Europe just in time to stop a German advance on Paris and other French cities. One soldier from Tennessee, **Alvin York,** became a war hero for his actions in battle. At the start, York had been a **conscientious objector** (a person who opposes war on moral grounds), but he then agreed to fight. When he returned to the United States, he became a celebrity for his brave actions in the war.

Germany, exhausted from the war, finally agreed to an **armistice** on November 11, 1918. The war took a bloody toll. Deaths numbered more than 22 million, about half of them civilians. About 20 million people had been injured, while 10 million more became refugees. The total economic costs of the war were about $338 million.

3. How did American troops help end the war?

_____

_____

Name _____ Class _____ Date _____

Lesson 2, *continued*

Answer the following questions about the American experience in World War I.

1. How did the United States raise an army?	2. How did women serve in World War I?
3. How did the United States build its naval force?	4. How did the U.S. Navy help win the war?

5. What new weapons of mechanized warfare threatened those in combat?

6. What did the war cost in terms of the number of . . .		7. What were the estimated economic costs?
civilian deaths?	injuries?	
military deaths?	refugees?	

World War I

The War at Home

Key Terms and People

War Industries Board Agency to improve efficiency in war-related industries

Bernard M. Baruch Leader of the War Industries Board

Committee on Public Information (CPI) A government agency established during World War I that used communication to influence people's thoughts and actions.

propaganda A kind of biased communication designed to influence people's thoughts and actions

George Creel Head of the Committee on Public Information

Espionage and Sedition Acts Laws that enacted harsh penalties against anyone opposing U.S. participation in World War I

Great Migration Movement of many African Americans to northern cities from the South in the early 1900s

---

Before You Read

In the last lesson you learned how the United States fought in World War I. In this lesson you will read about how the war changed American society at home.

As You Read

Use a chart to take notes on the changes the war brought about for African Americans, women, and immigrants.

GOVERNMENT OVERSEES THE WAR EFFORT
How did business and government work together?

Winning the war was not just a job for American soldiers alone. For example, the United States needed the help of industry. The economy had to change from making consumer goods to making weapons and war supplies. Congress gave President Wilson direct control over much of the economy. He had the power to fix prices and to regulate war-related industries.

Wilson created the **War Industries Board** (WIB) and named **Bernard M. Baruch** to run it. This agency helped boost industrial production by 20 percent. It did this by encouraging companies to use mass-production techniques to increase productivity. It also encouraged companies to standardize products as a way to eliminate waste. In addition, it set production quotas and allocated raw materials, or decided how they would be used. Not only that, it placed restrictions only at the wholesale level, which allowed retail prices to soar. This caused corporate profits to rise dramatically.

Other federal agencies also regulated the economy for the war effort. The Railroad Administration controlled the nation's railroads. The Fuel Administration watched over the use of coal, gasoline, and heating oil. Many Americans were willing to adopt "gasless Sundays" and "lightless nights" to conserve fuel. The Fuel Administration also introduced the idea of daylight-saving time. This innovation provided a way to make best use of the longer days of summer.

Wages in many industries went up. But workers often ended up actually losing money because of inflation. Corporate profits grew much more than average salaries. The difference in pay between labor and management was one cause of the growth of labor unions during this time. Other causes included increased working hours and the increasing speed of production.

Wilson established the National War Labor Board. This agency worked to settle disputes between management and labor. It also helped to improve working conditions.

Another new agency, the Food Administration, was established to help produce and conserve food supplies. This agency called on Americans to limit the amount of food they consumed. Herbert Hoover, the leader of the Food Administration, asked the American people to go without a different kind of food each day. For example, there was a "meatless" day, a "sweetless" day, and a "wheatless" day.

The Food Administration encouraged people to grow their own food. Soon many people were growing "victory gardens." Hoover also set a high government price on wheat and other food items people needed every day. This action led farmers to place 40 million additional acres of land into production. Such efforts made it possible to send more food to the Allies. In fact, American food shipments to the Allies tripled.

1. How did Wilson control the economy?

_____

_____

SELLING THE WAR
How did the government win over public opinion?

The government needed to raise money for the war. One way it did this was by increasing or adding several kinds of taxes. Taxes paid during the war included a progressive income tax and war-profits tax. Another way the government raised money was by selling war bonds. Thousands of volunteers sold the bonds. Famous people spoke at rallies to promote the sales. Newspapers and billboards carried advertisements free of charge.

To popularize the war, the government created the **Committee on Public Information (CPI).** It was the nation's first **propaganda** agency. The agency was headed by **George Creel.** He had been a muckraking journalist. He used artists and advertising people to create thousands of posters, paintings, and cartoons to promote the war. He distributed pamphlets in many languages. He also recruited about 75,000 men to act as "Four-Minute Men." Their job was to talk about the war effort. Topics included the draft,

Lesson 3, *continued*

rationing, bond drives, and victory gardens. The government did whatever it could to gain support for the war.

2. How did the U.S. government pay for the war?

_____

_____

ATTACKS ON CIVIL LIBERTIES INCREASE
How did the war affect civil liberties?

The war brought out anti-immigrant feelings. Immigrants from Germany were often targeted for attack. Americans with German-sounding names lost their jobs. Orchestras refused to play German music. Some towns with German names changed them. Some Americans even committed physical violence against German-Americans.

Congress passed the **Espionage and Sedition Acts** to punish people who did not support the war effort. People could not interfere with the draft or obstruct the sale of war bonds. They could not even speak against the war effort.

These laws violated the spirit of the First Amendment, which guarantees freedom of speech. The laws led to more than 2,000 prosecutions and about 1,000 convictions for antiwar activities. Newspapers and magazines that opposed the war or criticized any of the Allies lost their mailing privileges. People could also be fired for speaking against the war.

The chief targets of the Espionage and Sedition Acts were socialists and union leaders. Labor leader Eugene V. Debs was jailed for making a speech about the economic causes of the war. Anarchist Emma Goldman was imprisoned, fined, and later deported for speaking out against the draft. The Industrial Workers of the World urged

workers to strike. This was considered an antiwar activity, and leader "Big Bill" Haywood faced a jail sentence.

3. How did the Espionage and Sedition Acts contradict the First Amendment?

_____

_____

THE WAR ENCOURAGES SOCIAL CHANGE
How did the war affect women and African Americans?

The war brought many social changes for African Americans and women.

African American leaders were divided over the war. W.E.B. DuBois believed that helping the war effort would help the fight for equality. Others believed that blacks should not help a government that did not support equality for everyone.

The war sped up the **Great Migration.** This was the movement of thousands of African Americans from the rural South to cities of the North. They wanted to escape racial discrimination. They also wanted to find jobs in northern industries.

African Americans who migrated found more economic opportunities, particularly during wartime. Still, they faced some problems in the North, such as prejudice and overcrowding.

American women played new roles during the war. They did jobs that had previously been done only by men. They worked as railroad workers, cooks, dockworkers, and bricklayers. Women volunteered in the Red Cross and sold war bonds.

Women's activities made them more visible. They were not paid the same as men. Yet, soon after the war, Congress passed the Nineteenth Amendment,

© Houghton Mifflin Harcourt Publishing Company

giving them the right to vote.

Also, during the war a worldwide flu epidemic, probably spread by American soldiers, killed 500,000 Americans. The epidemic also caused major disruptions in the American economy.

4. How did women's roles change during the war?

_____

_____

Answer the following questions about how World War I changed American society.

What were the functions or results of the following wartime agencies and laws?		
1. War Industries Board	2. Railroad Administration	3. Fuel Administration
4. National War Labor Board	5. Food Administration	6. Committee on Public Information
7. Espionage and Sedition Acts		

What changes did the war bring about for the following groups of Americans?		
8. Immigrants	9. African Americans	10. Women

© Houghton Mifflin Harcourt Publishing Company

World War I

Wilson Fights for Peace

Key Terms and People

Fourteen Points Wilson's plan for world peace following World War I

Self-determination The right of people to choose their own political status

League of Nations An international peacekeeping organization proposed by Wilson and founded in 1920

Georges Clemenceau French premier

David Lloyd George British prime minister

Treaty of Versailles The 1919 treaty that ended World War I

reparations Payments made by defeated countries after a war

war-guilt clause Part of the Treaty of Versailles in which Germany took responsibility for the war

Henry Cabot Lodge Conservative senator who wanted to keep the United States out of the League of Nations

---

Before You Read

In the last lesson you learned how the war in Europe changed life at home. In this lesson you will read about the treaty that ended the war and about Wilson's proposal for a League of Nations.

As You Read

Use a timeline and chart to take notes on the provisions and weaknesses of the Treaty of Versailles and the opposition to it.

WILSON PRESENTS HIS PLAN
What were Wilson's peace plans?

President Wilson presented his plan for world peace to Congress in January 1918. The plan was called his **Fourteen Points.**

The first five points suggested ways that wars could be avoided. They stated that (1) countries should not make secret treaties with one another, (2) freedom of the seas should be maintained, (3) tariffs should be lowered or ended to promote free trade, (4) countries should reduce their arms,

and (5) the interests of the colonial people should be considered.

The next eight points suggested new national boundaries. Wilson believed in **self-determination:** different ethnic groups should be able to decide for themselves what nation they would belong to.

The 14th point called for a **League of Nations.** This international organization would address problems between countries before they led to war.

Wilson met with leaders of France and Great Britain, **Georges Clemenceau**

© Houghton Mifflin Harcourt Publishing Company

and **David Lloyd George,** to discuss the terms of peace. These leaders had won the war, and they wanted to punish Germany.

The Paris Peace Conference had been set up exactly with punishment in mind. In fact, the defeated Central powers were excluded from the conference. So too was Russia, which now had a Communist government.

Wilson was an idealist. He hoped the other leaders at the conference would share his dream of restoring peace to Europe without punishing Germany too much. However, he soon realized that the results of the meeting would not be in his favor. In the end, Wilson had to give up most of his fourteen points. The one he insisted on was the League of Nations.

1. What did Wilson's first five points address?

   _____

   _____

DEBATE OVER THE TREATY OF VERSAILLES
What did the treaty say?

On June 28, 1919, the leaders of the Allies and the Central powers met at the Palace of Versailles in France. They were to sign the **Treaty of Versailles.**

The treaty created new national boundaries by (1) establishing nine new nations, including Poland, Czechoslovakia, and Yugoslavia; (2) shifting the boundaries of other nations; and (3) carving out parts of the Ottoman Empire to create temporary colonies in the Middle East for Great Britain and France. The two Allies were to rule over the colonies until they were ready to rule themselves.

The treaty took away Germany's army. It required Germany to return the region of Alsace-Lorraine to France. It also forced Germany to pay **reparations,** or war damages, to the winners. These payments amounted to $33 billion. In addition, the treaty contained a **war-guilt clause.** Germany had to admit that it was responsible for causing the war.

The Treaty of Versailles had three basic weaknesses. The first was its harsh treatment of Germany. Germany was humiliated. Germany was not the only country that had also been militaristic, yet Germany alone was punished. And Germany would not be able to pay the huge reparations. Germany had lost all its colonies in the Pacific, so they could not make use of their resources. This eliminated one way to help pay Germany's steep reparation bill.

The second weakness was that the Soviet Union (formerly Russia) lost more territory than Germany did. Russia had been one of the Allies and had suffered more casualties than any other country. The Soviet Union was determined to get its territories back.

The third weakness concerned colonies. The treaty did not recognize the claims of colonies for self-determination. One example was Vietnam in Southeast Asia. The Vietnamese people wanted to gain political rights.

Wilson brought the treaty back to the United States for approval. He found several groups strongly opposed to it. Some thought the treaty too harsh. Others thought it favored imperialists. Some ethnic groups objected to the treaty because of the way it treated their homelands.

The main opposition to the treaty was over the League of Nations. The league was the only one of Wilson's fourteen points that was included in the treaty. Conservative senators, headed by **Henry Cabot Lodge,** opposed joining the

© Houghton Mifflin Harcourt Publishing Company

Guided Reading Workbook

Lesson 4, *continued*

league. They did not like the idea of working with other countries to take economic and military action against aggression. They wanted the treaty to include the constitutional right of Congress to declare war.

Wilson refused to compromise on the league. He believed that the league would allow nations a place to discuss disagreements and to reconcile them. He saw the league as a pathway to peace. Therefore, he would not accept amendments to the Treaty of Versailles that were proposed by Republican leaders.

The Republican majority of Senate had felt left out when Wilson had not included many Republicans as representatives of the American delegation in Versailles. Wilson's unwillingness to compromise about the League of Nations dismayed them even more.

As a result, the Senate failed twice to ratify the treaty. The United States never entered the League of Nations. It finally signed a separate treaty with Germany in 1921, when Wilson was no longer president.

2. Name the three weaknesses of the treaty.

_____

_____

THE LEGACY OF THE WAR
What was the legacy of the war?

The end of the war made Americans yearn for what Warren G. Harding called "normalcy." But the war had transformed the United States and the world. World War I had strengthened both U.S. military power and the power of government. It accelerated change for African Americans and women. However, the propaganda campaign left a legacy of mistrust and fear.

In Europe, the war left a legacy of massive destruction, loss of life, political instability, and violence. Communists ruled in Russia, and soon after the war, Fascist organizations seized power in Italy.

Americans hoped that the war had convinced the world to never fight again. But in Europe, the war settled nothing. In Germany, Adolf Hitler exploited Germans' discontent with the Treaty of Versailles and threatened to fight again. Hitler was true to his predictions; America did have to fight again years later in a second world war.

3. What were the long-term results of the war?

_____

_____

Answer the following questions related to the timeline below.

1918	Wilson delivers Fourteen Points speech to Congress	→	What were Wilson's points? 1. 2. 3. 4. 5. 6.–13. 14.
1919	Treaty of Versailles is signed	→	15. What terms of the treaty specifically affected Germany?
	Senate rejects Treaty of Versailles	→	16. Why did Henry Cabot Lodge object to the treaty?
1920	Senate again rejects Treaty of Versailles	→	17. How did Wilson help bring about the Senate's rejection of the treaty?
1921	U.S. signs separate treaty with Germany	→	18. What circumstance at this time would eventually lead many Germans to support Adolf Hitler?

© Houghton Mifflin Harcourt Publishing Company

The Business of America

Key Terms and People

Warren G. Harding 29th president of the United States

Charles Evans Hughes Secretary of state under Harding

Fordney-McCumber Tariff High tax on imports adopted in 1922

Ohio gang Harding's friends and advisors

Teapot Dome scandal Scandal surrounding Albert Fall

Albert B. Fall Secretary of the interior under Harding

Calvin Coolidge 30th president of the United States; succeeded to presidency on death of Harding; elected in 1924

urban sprawl The outward expansion of cities

consumerism The acquisition of goods in ever-greater amounts

installment plan An easy way to borrow money to buy goods

Before You Read

In the last lesson you read about Wilson's plan for peace. In this lesson you will read about the 1920s business boom and its effects.

As You Read

Complete a chart of events and trends of the era, and compare their strengths and weaknesses.

STRUGGLES FOR PEACE
How did Harding handle foreign affairs?

In 1921 **Warren G. Harding** and Secretary of State **Charles Evans Hughes** urged world powers to agree not to build warships for ten years and for major naval powers to scrap many of their existing warships. They agreed to disarm weapons.

Americans wanted to stay out of world affairs, but France and Britain owed World War I debts. Their economies were too weak to repay the loans. Congress passed the **Fordney-McCumber Tariff** in 1922, which protected American business from foreign competition. The tariff made it impossible for Britain and France to sell their goods in the United States. As a result, France and Britain pressured Germany to pay its war reparations. Germany's economy was too weak, so it could not pay. To avoid another war, banker Charles G. Dawes came up with the Dawes Plan, in which the United States loaned money to Germany to pay back Britain and France. Then Britain and France paid back the United States with its own money.

1. How did the Fordney-McCumber Tariff affect other countries?

_____

_____

HARDING'S DOMESTIC POLICIES AND PROBLEMS
How did scandal hurt Harding's administration?

Most of Harding's problems were caused by his cabinet appointments. Charles Evans Hughes, Herbert Hoover, and Andrew Mellon were excellent choices who did much for the country.

Others lacked ability and honesty. Some were part of the **Ohio gang,** the president's poker-playing buddies. One of the worst cases of corruption was the **Teapot Dome scandal.** It involved government-owned land, which held large reserves of oil. **Albert B. Fall** secretly leased the land to two oil companies and was later found guilty of bribery. Harding's presidency was tarnished.

Harding died suddenly in 1923, and Calvin Coolidge became president. He was then elected president in 1924.

2. What does the Teapot Dome scandal tell about President Harding?

_____

_____

AMERICAN INDUSTRIES FLOURISH
How did the success of the automobile industry affect America?

The new president, **Calvin Coolidge,** favored policies that promoted business and limited government interference.

Henry Ford and the Model T had a tremendous impact on the country. New roads were built and new businesses

came about. Automobiles ended the isolation of rural families. Cars made it possible for people to live farther from their jobs, which led to **urban sprawl,** as cities spread out in all directions. Cities in Ohio and Michigan grew as major centers of car manufacturing. States that produced oil, such as California and Texas, also prospered.

The automobile became a status symbol. Everyone wanted one. By the late 1920s, around 80 percent of all the cars in the world were in the United States.

The airline industry also grew. Planes carried the nation's mail, and passenger service began.

3. Name three ways the automobile changed American life.

_____

_____

AMERICA'S STANDARD OF LIVING SOARS
How did the American household change?

The 1920s were prosperous and people spent extra income. **Consumerism,** or acquiring goods, helped the economy. Electricity also changed the country. Homes had appliances of all kinds. They made work easier and led to more women working outside the home.

Advertising tried to appeal to people's wish to be young, beautiful, and wealthy by using psychology. Brand names became known nationwide.

4. How did advertising change American life?

_____

_____

Lesson 1, *continued*

A SUPERFICIAL PROSPERITY
What hidden problems did the economy have?

Most Americans had confidence in the 1920s prosperity. Most businesses seemed to make fortunes. The stock market reached new heights. But this prosperity hid problems.

First, business was not as healthy as it seemed. As workers produced more goods, businesses grew. Large businesses bought up, or merged with, smaller ones. But as businesses grew, managers made much more money than workers did. Also, mining companies, railroads, and farms were doing poorly.

Second, consumer debt rose.

Businesses needed to sell all the goods they were now producing. So they encouraged buying on the **installment plan,** a form of borrowing. Customers could make low payments over a period of time so they could afford to buy more. Banks provided money at low interest rates. Advertising also pushed the idea of buying on credit. Average Americans were spending more money than they actually had.

5. Describe two economic problems hidden by the 1920s business boom.

_____

_____

For each event or trend, identify strengths and weaknesses. Then in the bottom section of the chart, list three factors that were potential problems for the American economy.

Event/Trend	Stengths	Weaknesses
1. Harding cabinet		
2. automobile		
3. modern advertising		
4. installment plan		
Indicators of Future Economic Problems		
5.	6.	7.

The Roaring Twenties

Postwar Issues

Key Terms and People

xenophobia Unreasoned fear of things or people seen as foreign or strange

nativism Suspicion of foreign-born people

isolationism Pulling away from world affairs

communism An economic system that supports government control over property to create equality

anarchists People who oppose any form of government

Sacco and Vanzetti Immigrant anarchists accused of murder

quota system A system that established the maximum number of people who could enter the United States from each country

John L. Lewis President of the United Mine Workers

Before You Read

In the last lesson you read about the business boom that came about because of a rise in America's standard of living. In this lesson you will read about life in postwar America.

As You Read

Use a chart to take notes on postwar issues of communism and labor unrest.

POSTWAR TRENDS
How did World War I affect America?

World War I left much of America divided about the League of Nations. The war hurt the economy. Returning soldiers took jobs away from women and minorities, or faced unemployment themselves. **Xenophobia, nativism,** and **isolationism** swept America as people became suspicious of foreigners and wanted to pull away from world affairs.

1. What attitudes became prevalent in America after World War I?

_____

_____

FEAR OF COMMUNISM
Why did Americans fear communism?

Americans feared **communism,** an economic and political system that supports government control over property to create equality.

Communists came to power in Russia after a violent revolution that caused the Russian czar to step down. Vladimir I. Lenin and a group called Bolsheviks established a communist state. These Communists, or "Reds," waved their flag and called for a worldwide revolution to overthrow capitalism.

In the United States, about 70,000

© Houghton Mifflin Harcourt Publishing Company

people joined the Communist Party. A fear of communism, known as the "Red Scare," swept the nation.

Attorney General A. Mitchell Palmer and his agents hunted suspected communists, socialists, and **anarchists,** who opposed all forms of government. Palmer's agents ignored people's civil rights. They never found evidence of a plot to overthrow the government. But the Red Scare made people mistrust foreigners, such as Italian immigrants Nicola Sacco and Bartolomeo Vanzetti. Self-proclaimed anarchists **Sacco and Vanzetti** were arrested for robbery and murder. They denied the charges. The case against them was weak, but they were convicted. Many people protested the conviction. They said it was based on a fear of foreigners. The two were executed in 1927.

2. How did Americans show their fear of communism?

_____

_____

IMMIGRATION AND CITIZENSHIP ISSUES
How did Americans show their nativist feelings?

Some Americans used the Red Scare as an excuse to act against any people who were different. For example, the Ku Klux Klan used violence to keep certain groups "in their place." These included blacks, Jews, Roman Catholics, immigrants, and union leaders.

As a result of nativism, or anti-immigrant feelings, Congress passed the Emergency Quota Act of 1921. It established a **quota system,** which set a limit on how many immigrants from each country could enter the United States every year. In 1924 a new quota

limited immigration from eastern and southern Europe, mostly Jews and Roman Catholics.

The 1924 law also banned Japanese immigrants. It did not affect immigrants from the Western Hemisphere, such as those from Canada and Mexico.

3. What was the quota system?

_____

_____

A TIME OF LABOR UNREST
What were the three major strikes of 1919?

During World War I there were no strikes because they might have hurt the war effort. But in 1919, several strikes occurred. First, Boston police went on strike for a raise and to have a union. Massachusetts governor Calvin Coolidge used force to put down the strike. Then, a strike by steelworkers began at U.S. Steel Corporation. Workers wanted to join unions. In 1923 a report revealed harsh conditions in steel mills. Public opinion turned against steel companies, and workers were given an eight-hour day. But they still had no union. Next, **John L. Lewis,** the president of the United Mine Workers, had workers close the coalmines. President Wilson helped settle the dispute so that the miners got higher wages, but they did not get shorter hours.

During the 1920s union membership declined from 5 million to 3.5 million because immigrants were willing to work in poor conditions, language barriers made organizing people difficult, farmers who had migrated to cities were used to relying on themselves, and most unions excluded African Americans.

© Houghton Mifflin Harcourt Publishing Company

4. Why did union membership decline?

_____

_____

Answer questions about postwar conditions in America and the fear of communism.

FEAR OF COMMUNISM	
1. How did the Justice Department under A. Mitchell Palmer respond to this fear?	2. Why were Sacco and Vanzetti most likely convicted?
3. How did the Ku Klux Klan respond to this fear?	4. Why did Congress pass the Emergency Quota Act of 1921?
LABOR UNREST	
5. The strike by Boston police was unpopular with the public. Why might this have been so?	6. How did Massachusetts governor Calvin Coolidge handle the Boston police strike?
7. Why did public support turn against steel companies?	8. How did President Wilson respond to the steel strike?

© Houghton Mifflin Harcourt Publishing Company

Changing Ways of Life

Key Terms and People

Prohibition The era that banned the manufacture and sale of alcoholic beverages

speakeasy Hidden saloon or nightclub that sold liquor illegally

bootlegger Smuggler who brought in alcohol from Canada, Cuba, and the West Indies

fundamentalism Religious movement based on the belief that everything written in the Bible is literally true

Clarence Darrow Famous trial lawyer

Scopes trial Trial of John Scopes for teaching evolution

Before You Read

In the last lesson you learned about life in postwar America. In this lesson you will read about new lifestyles and values that emerged in the 1920s.

As You Read

Use a chart to show how the government attempted to deal with problems or conflicts related to Prohibition and with the teaching of evolution.

RURAL AND URBAN DIFFERENCES
What was Prohibition?

The 1920 census showed a change in America. For the first time, more Americans lived in large towns and cities than in small towns and on farms.

The values that most Americans had grown up with were small-town values. They included conservative moral and social standards, hard work, and close families.

By the 1920s urbanization, or the movement of Americans from rural areas to the cities, had increased. New York, Chicago, and Philadelphia had become huge cities. There were over 65 cities with more than 100,000 people.

Urban values began to dominate the nation. Life in big cities was different from in small towns. People with different backgrounds came into contact with one another. Also, thousands of workers, cars, buses, and streetcars moved through downtown areas.

City people were more open to new ideas in art, science, and politics. They went out at night. They were more tolerant of drinking and gambling. Life was fast paced. Sometimes it was impersonal and lonely. Many people who were new to city life found it hard to adjust.

One clash between small-town and city values led to an era known as **Prohibition.** Prohibition was the ban on alcoholic beverages as established by the Eighteenth Amendment. It took effect in 1920. Most support for Prohibition came from religious rural white Protestants.

Even though it was the law, the effort to stop drinking was doomed. There were not enough officers to enforce it. People made their own alcohol illegally.

In cities, even respectable middle-class people flocked to **speakeasies.** These were hidden saloons and nightclubs that served liquor illegally. People also bought liquor from **bootleggers,** or smugglers who brought it in from Canada, Cuba, and the West Indies.

Prohibition caused a general disrespect for the law. It also caused a great deal of money to flow out of lawful businesses and into organized crime. Gangsters took control of the illegal liquor business. The most famous gang was headed by Chicago's Al Capone. Chicago became known for bloody gang killings.

This rise in crime and violence led many people to demand the repeal of Prohibition. By the middle of the decade, only 19 percent of Americans supported it. Prohibition was repealed by the Twenty-first Amendment in 1933.

1. How did Prohibition affect the nation?

_____

_____

SCIENCE AND RELIGION CLASH
What was the Scopes Trial?

During the 1920s the nation saw the rise of Christian **fundamentalism.** This religious movement was based on the belief that everything written in the Bible was literally true. Fundamentalists rejected America's growing trust in science.

These beliefs led fundamentalists to reject Charles Darwin's theory of evolution. According to that theory, plant and animal species had developed over millions of years.

Fundamentalists believed that the Bible was correct in stating that the world and all its plants and animals were created by God in six days. They wanted laws prohibiting the teaching of evolution.

Fundamentalist preachers drew large crowds to religious revivals, especially in the South and West. They also gained political power. In 1925 Tennessee passed a law making it a crime to teach evolution.

Many people opposed this law. The American Civil Liberties Union (ACLU) promised to defend in court any teacher who would challenge the law.

John Scopes, a biology teacher from Dayton, Tennessee, challenged the law. He openly taught about evolution. He was arrested, and his case went to trial. The ACLU hired **Clarence Darrow,** the most famous trial lawyer in the nation, to defend Scopes. William Jennings Bryan was the prosecutor.

Scopes was guilty because he broke the law. However, the trial was really about evolution and religion in schools. Reporters came from all over the world to cover the **Scopes trial.**

The highlight of the trial was when William Jennings Bryan took the stand. Darrow questioned Bryan until Bryan said that while the earth was made in six days, they were "not six days of 24 hours." Bryan was admitting that the Bible could be interpreted in different ways.

© Houghton Mifflin Harcourt Publishing Company

Even so, Scopes was found guilty. His conviction was later overturned by the state Supreme Court. But the ban on teaching evolution remained a law in Tennessee.

2. How did fundamentalist beliefs lead to the Scopes trial?

_____

_____

Answer the questions about how the 1920s reflected conflicts and tensions in American culture related to Prohibition and the teaching of evolution

PROHIBITION	
1. a. Who tended to be supporters of Prohibition at this time?	b. Why do you think they supported it?
2. a. Who tended to be opponents of Prohibition at this time?	b. Why do you think they opposed it?
3. Why was Prohibition repealed?	
THE SCOPES TRIAL	
4. a. Who were Darrow's main supporters?	b. Why did they support him?
5. a. Who were Bryan's main supporters?	b. Why did they support him?
6. What was the outcome of the case?	

© Houghton Mifflin Harcourt Publishing Company

The Roaring Twenties

The Twenties Woman

Key Terms and People

flapper Young woman who embraced the new fashions and values of the 1920s

double standard Set of principles granting one group more freedom than another group

Before You Read

In the last lesson you read about Prohibition and the Scopes trial. In this lesson you will learn how women's lives changed during the 1920s.

As You Read

Use a chart to take notes on the changes women experienced in the 1920s.

YOUNG WOMEN CHANGE THE RULES
What was a flapper?

The twenties brought about a new world for young Americans. This was due in part to World War I, the growth of cities, and changing attitudes. Many young women began to take part in the rebellious, pleasure-loving life of the twenties. They rejected 19th century values in favor of independence. They wanted the same freedom as men.

The new symbol of women was the **flapper.** She was a liberated young woman with independent, urban attitudes. She was assertive. She liked the sophisticated new fashions of the day.

Instead of old style dark ankle-length dresses she now wore bright loose-fitting short skirts and dresses. Skin-toned stockings replaced corsets and petticoats. She wore pumps and strings of beads. She cut her long hair short and maybe even dyed it black. She often smoked cigarettes and drank alcohol in public. She danced new, exciting dances such as the tango, fox trot, camel walk, shimmy, and Charleston.

Other attitudes changed, too. Many young men and women began to see marriage as more of an equal partnership. However, housework and raising children remained a woman's job.

At the same time, churches and schools protested the new values. The majority of women were not flappers. Many people felt torn between the old values and the new ones.

One result of this clash between old values and the image of the flapper was the **double standard.** This was a set of principles or values generally accepted by society. One American double standard allowed men to have greater sexual freedom than women. Women were expected to observe stricter standards of behavior than men did.

© Houghton Mifflin Harcourt Publishing Company

Guided Reading Workbook

1. How did the flapper represent the spirit of the twenties?

_____

_____

WOMEN SHED OLD ROLES AT HOME AND AT WORK
How did women's roles change?

Many women had gone to work outside the home during World War I. This trend continued in the twenties. But their opportunities had changed after the war. Men returned from the war and took back traditional "men's jobs." Women moved back into the "women's professions" of being a teacher, nurse, or librarian.

Big business provided another role for women: clerical work. Millions of women became secretaries, typists, file clerks, and stenographers. Many others became salesclerks in stores. Many women also worked on assembly lines in factories. By 1930, 10 million women had paid jobs outside the home. This was almost one-fourth of the American work force.

Women did not find equality in the workplace. Few women rose to jobs in management. Women earned less than men. Men regarded women as temporary workers whose real job was at home keeping house and raising children. In the twenties, patterns of discrimination against women in the business world continued.

Family life changed, too. Families had fewer children. Electrical appliances made housework easier. Many items that had been made at home such as ready-made clothes, sliced bread, and canned foods could now be bought in stores.

Public agencies took over some family responsibilities, too. They provided services for the elderly and the sick. While most women remained homemakers, they had more free time. However, some women had to work and also run their homes. It was hard for them to combine these roles.

In the 1920s, marriages were more often based on romantic love than arranged by families. Children were no longer part of the work force. They spent their days in school and other activities with people of their own age. Peer pressure began to be an important influence on teens' behavior. Some adolescents went against their parents' wishes and rebelled. This reflected the conflict between traditional attitudes and modern ways of thinking.

2. Describe two changes in women's roles in the workplace.

_____

_____

© Houghton Mifflin Harcourt Publishing Company

Lesson 4, *continued*

Complete the chart about women's changing roles in the 1920s.

SOCIAL LIFE IN THE 1920S
1. What are two ways women's fashions changed?
2. What are two ways women's social behavior changed?
3. What two words describe the attitude reflected by these changes?
WORK AND HOME LIFE IN THE 1920S
4. What is one way women's work opportunities improved?
5. What are two ways women's home and family life improved?
6. What are three negative effects that accompanied women's changing roles in the 1920s?

© Houghton Mifflin Harcourt Publishing Company

The Roaring Twenties

Education and Popular Culture

Key Terms and People

Charles A. Lindbergh First person to fly nonstop solo across the Atlantic

George Gershwin Composer who merged popular concert music with American jazz

Irving Berlin Composer who wrote 1,500 songs, including "White Christmas"

Georgia O'Keeffe Artist who created colored canvases of New Mexico

modernism Artistic movement that rejected traditional art as outdated

Sinclair Lewis Author who was the first American to win a Nobel Prize in Literature

F. Scott Fitzgerald Author who revealed the negative side of the 1920s

Edna St. Vincent Millay Poet whose poems celebrated youth and freedom

Ernest Hemingway Author who introduced a tough, simple style of writing

Before You Read

In the last lesson you learned about women in the 1920s. In this lesson you will read about education and popular culture during the 1920s.

As You Read

Use a chart to take notes on the mass media and popular culture that defined the 1920s.

SCHOOLS AND THE MASS MEDIA SHAPE CULTURE
How did popular culture change in America?

America had become more prosperous. Business and industry required a more educated workforce. These factors caused an increase in the number of students going to high school. In 1914 only 1 million American students went to high school after elementary school. In 1926 the number was nearly 4 million.

Schools changed as they grew. Before the 1920s high schools were mostly for students who planned on attending college. In the twenties high schools had a variety of students. Schools offered vocational, or work-related, training for industrial jobs.

High schools also saw an increase in the number of children of immigrants. Many of them did not speak English. Even so, schools were successful in teaching large numbers of Americans to read.

As a result of increased literacy, more people read newspapers than before. Newspaper circulation rose. Big city papers and newspaper chains swallowed up small-town newspapers.

National magazines were also popular. Some of them delivered the news. By the end of the 1920s, ten magazines had a circulation of more than 2 million each.

The most powerful of the mass media was radio. Radio networks created something new in America: the shared national experience of hearing things as they happened. Listeners could hear speeches by the president or listen to the World Series.

1. What was an effect of increased literacy in the United States?

_____

_____

AMERICA CHASES NEW HEROES AND OLD DREAMS
Who was Charles Lindbergh?

In the 1920s Americans had more money and more free time than ever before. Fads, including crossword puzzles and games, swept the nation. People also flooded athletic stadiums to see sports stars.

Charles A. Lindbergh thrilled the nation by becoming the first person to fly nonstop solo across the Atlantic Ocean. Lindbergh took off from New York City in his plane, *The Spirit of St. Louis.* After 33 hours Lindbergh landed outside of Paris, France. On his return to the United States, Lindbergh became the idol of America. In an age of sensationalism and excess, Lindbergh stood for the honesty and bravery the nation seemed to have lost.

2. Why did Lindbergh become an American idol?

_____

_____

POPULAR CULTURE REFLECTS NEW ATTITUDES
Why did the music, art, and literature of the 1920s appeal to many Americans?

Even before the introduction of sound, movies became a national pastime. *The Jazz Singer,* the first movie with sound, was released in 1927. Walt Disney's *Steamboat Willie,* the first animated film with sound, was made the next year. By 1930 the "talkies" had caused movie attendance to double.

In the 1920s American artists broke away from European traditions. Eugene O'Neill wrote plays about the confusion of modern American life. Composer **George Gershwin** merged jazz with traditional elements creating music with a new American sound. **Irving Berlin,** another important composer, wrote 1,500 songs, many of which were heard in Broadway shows or in movies.

American painters recorded an America of dreams and contrasting realities. Edward Hopper painted the loneliness of American life. **Georgia O'Keeffe** showed the grandeur of New Mexico. Their works represented **modernism,** an artistic movement that rejected traditional art as outdated and no longer meaningful.

Many gifted American writers criticized American society. **Sinclair Lewis** was the first American to win a Nobel Prize in Literature. His novel *Babbitt* made fun of middle-class America.

Novelist **F. Scott Fitzgerald** coined the term "Jazz Age" to describe the twenties. His books, such as *This Side of Paradise* and *The Great Gatsby,* showed the negative side of the age. But the poems of **Edna St. Vincent Millay** celebrated youth and freedom from traditional restrictions.

© Houghton Mifflin Harcourt Publishing Company

Lesson 5, *continued*

Some Americans disliked American culture so much they went to live abroad. Many gathered in Paris. The writer Gertrude Stein called them the Lost Generation. They included Fitzgerald and **Ernest Hemingway.** Hemingway introduced a tough, simple style of writing that changed American literature.

3. How did American artists reflect new American ideas?

_____

_____

Fill in the chart describing the mass media and popular culture that defined the 1920s.

MASS MEDIA/POPULAR CULTURE	
1. Magazines	
2. Radio	
3. Charles Lindbergh	
4. Movies	
5. Composers	
6. Artists	
7. Writers	

© Houghton Mifflin Harcourt Publishing Company

Guided Reading Workbook

The Harlem Renaissance

Key Terms and People

National Association for the Advancement of Colored People (NAACP) Urged African Americans to protest racial violence

James Weldon Johnson Poet and civil rights leader

Marcus Garvey Black nationalist leader

Harlem Renaissance A literary and artistic movement of African American culture

Claude McKay Poet and novelist who urged African Americans to resist prejudice

Langston Hughes Best-known Harlem Renaissance poet; described lives of working-class African Americans

Zora Neale Hurston Author

Paul Robeson Dramatic actor who struggled with racism

Louis Armstrong Jazz trumpet player famous for his sense of rhythm and improvisation

Duke Ellington Jazz pianist and composer

Bessie Smith Female blues singer and outstanding vocalist of the decade

---

Before You Read

In the last lesson you read about education and popular culture in the 1920s. In this lesson you will learn about the Harlem Renaissance.

As You Read

Complete a chart on the achievements of the Harlem Renaissance.

AFRICAN AMERICAN VOICES IN THE 1920S
***How* did African Americans approach civil rights in the 1920s?**

Between 1910 and 1920, hundreds of thousands of African Americans had moved from the South to the big cities of the North. This was called the Great Migration. It was a response to racial violence and economic discrimination against blacks in the South. By 1929, 40 percent of African Americans lived in cities. As a result, racial tensions increased in Northern cities. There were race riots.

The National Association for the Advancement of Colored People (NAACP) worked to end violence against African Americans. W.E.B. Du Bois led a peaceful protest against racial violence.

The NAACP also fought to get laws

against lynching passed by Congress. **James Weldon Johnson,** a poet and lawyer, led that fight. While no law against lynching was passed in the twenties, the number of lynchings gradually dropped.

Marcus Garvey voiced a message of black pride that appealed to many African Americans. Garvey thought that African Americans should build a separate society. He formed a black nationalist group called the Universal Negro Improvement Association (UNIA).

Garvey promoted black-owned businesses. He also urged African Americans to return to Africa to set up an independent nation.

1. How did the NAACP and Marcus Garvey's followers respond to racial discrimination?

_____

_____

THE HARLEM RENAISSANCE FLOWERS IN NEW YORK
What **was the Harlem Renaissance?**

In the 1920s many African Americans moved to Harlem, a section of New York City. So did blacks from the West Indies, Cuba, Puerto Rico, and Haiti. Harlem became the world's largest black urban community as well as the birthplace of the **Harlem Renaissance.** This literary and artistic movement celebrated African-American culture.

The Harlem Renaissance was mainly a literary movement. It was led by well-educated middle-class blacks. They took pride in their African heritage and their folklore. They wrote about the problems of being black in a white culture. An important collection of works by Harlem Renaissance writers, *The New*

Negro, was published by Alain Locke in 1925.

The Harlem Renaissance produced many outstanding poets. **Claude McKay** wrote about the pain of prejudice. He urged African Americans to resist prejudice and discrimination.

One of the most famous Harlem Renaissance poets was **Langston Hughes.** He wrote about the daily lives of working-class blacks and the difficulties they faced. He gained international fame for his work.

Zora Neale Hurston collected the folklore of poor, uneducated Southern blacks and wrote about them. She celebrated the common person's art form. Hurston wrote novels, short stories, books of folklore, and poems.

Music and drama were important parts of the Harlem Renaissance, too. **Paul Robeson** became a major dramatic actor. He starred in Shakespeare's *Othello.* He experienced racism in the United States and lived for a time in England and the Soviet Union.

Jazz blended instrumental ragtime and vocal blues and was created in the early 20th century in New Orleans. Musicians from New Orleans traveled north, and they brought jazz with them. One of the most important and influential jazz musicians was trumpet player **Louis Armstrong.** He was known for his sense of rhythm and improvisation skills, and became a significant figure in jazz history.

Many whites came to Harlem to hear jazz. Edward Kennedy **"Duke" Ellington** led an orchestra at New York's Cotton Club. He was a jazz pianist and one of the nation's greatest composers.

Some considered **Bessie Smith** the outstanding blues singer of the decade. She was also the highest-paid black artist in the world in 1927.

The Harlem Renaissance inspired African Americans to take pride in their work. It represented part of the great social and cultural changes in America.

2. Describe the contributions of one artist of the Harlem Renaissance.

_____

_____

Describe briefly what each of the following artists was known for.

AFRICAN AMERICAN WRITERS AND PERFORMERS	
1. Claude McKay	
2. Langston Hughes	
3. Zora Neale Hurston	
4. Paul Robeson	
5. Louis Armstrong	
6. Duke Ellington	
7. Bessie Smith	

© Houghton Mifflin Harcourt Publishing Company

The Great Depression

The Nation's Sick Economy

Key Terms and People

deflation A decrease in the general price level of goods and services

price support Law that keeps prices above a set level

credit Short-term loans to buy goods with promises to pay later

Alfred E. Smith Democratic presidential candidate in 1928

Dow Jones Industrial Average Index of stock prices of select companies

speculation Investments in high-risk ventures

buying on margin Buying stock by paying only a portion of the full cost up-front with promises to pay the rest later

Black Tuesday October 29, 1929, the day the stock market crashed

Great Depression Period of bad economic times in the United States that lasted from 1929 through the 1930s

Hawley-Smoot Tariff Act Law that raised taxes on imports and worsened the Depression

Before You Read

In the last lesson you learned about the Harlem Renaissance in the 1920s. In this lesson you will read about the economic problems that led to the Great Depression.

As You Read

Complete a chart to identify the causes of the 1929 stock market crash.

ECONOMIC TROUBLES ON THE HORIZON
Why **was the nation's economy sick in the late 1920s?**

During the 1920s the economy boomed. But there were economic problems under the surface. Tariffs helped some businesses but harmed international trade. United States government revenues dropped because of tax breaks for the wealthy. Most Americans were not earning much.

Many businesses suffered because of this. New technology caused problems for some industries. For example, railroads faced strong competition because of the introduction of cars, buses, and trucks. Industries, such as clothing, steel-making, and mining, were hardly making a profit.

Industries such as mining and lumbering had expanded because of high demand for their products during World War I. After the war, that

Lesson 1, *continued*

demand decreased. Coal mining also suffered because of the introduction of new energy sources.

Many industries had been successful in the early 1920s. But by the late 1920s they were losing money. These industries included auto manufacturing, construction, and consumer goods.

A decline in housing starts was an important sign of economic problems. Fewer houses being built also meant that profits in related industries fell. For example, fewer new houses meant that less new furniture was needed.

The biggest problems were in farming. After the war, the demand for food dropped dramatically. Farmers suffered as **deflation,** or a decrease in the general price level of goods and services, took place. Their incomes went down. Many could not make the mortgage payments on their farms. As a result, many farmers lost their land.

Congress tried to help farmers by passing **price supports.** With price supports, the government would not allow food prices to fall below a certain level. But Calvin Coolidge vetoed the bill. Farmers' incomes continued to drop.

A decline in farmers' incomes was not the only problem with the economy. Americans were buying less. Many found that prices were rising faster than their salaries. Many people bought goods on **credit**—an arrangement in which consumers agreed to make monthly payments with interest. But too many Americans were accumulating debt they could not afford to pay off.

In the late 1920s much of America seemed prosperous, but there was an uneven distribution of income. A small number of rich people were getting richer. But a large number of people were not doing well and falling further

behind. In fact, most families earned less than the minimum needed to maintain a decent standard of living. That meant that most Americans did not have enough money to purchase all the many products flooding the market.

1. What problems did farmers face in the 1920s?

_____

_____

HOOVER TAKES THE NATION
How healthy was the stock market?

Few people recognized the problems with the economy in 1928. The Republican Herbert Hoover easily defeated the Democratic challenger, **Alfred E. Smith.** People believed Hoover when he said the American economy was healthy. The **Dow Jones Industrial Average,** a measure of 30 popular stocks, was way up. People rushed to buy stocks. Many people were engaging in **speculation,** buying risky stocks in hopes of a quick profit. To do so, they were **buying on margin**—paying just a small down payment and borrowing the rest. The problem of buying on margin was that there was no way to pay off the loan if the stock price declined sharply. After all, many Americans had bought stock using borrowed money.

2. What was dangerous about how Americans bought stock?

_____

_____

THE STOCK MARKET CRASHES
What was Black Tuesday?

Stock prices did begin to fall in September 1929. On Tuesday, October 29, 1929, called **Black Tuesday,**

© Houghton Mifflin Harcourt Publishing Company

Guided Reading Workbook

prices fell so sharply that people said the market had "crashed." People frantically tried to sell their shares, causing prices to go down further. There were no buyers. Many people lost all their savings. By mid-November, $30 billion—about the amount America had spent in World War I—had been lost.

3. What happened on Black Tuesday?

_____

_____

FINANCIAL COLLAPSE
How did the stock market crash affect businesses?

The stock market crash signaled the beginning of the **Great Depression.** This period of bad economic times when many people were out of work lasted from 1929 through the 1930s. Although the crash did not cause the Depression, it did make it worse. After the crash, many people panicked and took their money out of banks. Many banks were forced to close. When the banks failed, other depositors lost the savings they had in the banks.

Businesses also began to close. Millions of Americans lost their jobs. Workers who kept their jobs experienced pay cuts or reduced hours.

The Depression spread around the world. Germany was still paying war reparations. Other European countries were struggling with debts from the war. With Americans unable to buy their goods now, European economies suffered even more.

The situation became worse when Congress passed the **Hawley-Smoot Tariff Act.** Congress hoped that higher tariffs would push Americans to buy goods made in the United States. The result would be to help American industry. Instead, when the United States charged more to bring goods in, imports from Europe declined. Then Europeans had even less money to spend on U.S. goods, and American industry suffered.

The Great Depression had several causes:
• tariffs and war debt policies that cut down the foreign market for American goods
• a crisis in the farm sector
• the availability of easy credit
• an unequal distribution of income

These factors led to a falling demand for consumer goods. The federal government hurt the economy with its policy of low interest rates, causing businesses and consumers to borrow easily and build up too much debt.

4. Why did many banks fail after the stock market crashed?

_____

_____

Complete the chart to describe the serious problems in each area of the economy that helped cause the Great Depression.

1. Industry
2. Agriculture
3. Consumer spending
4. Distribution of wealth
5. Stock market

© Houghton Mifflin Harcourt Publishing Company

The Great Depression

Hardship and Suffering

Key Terms and People

shantytown A neighborhood where people live in shacks

soup kitchen Place where free food is served to the needy

bread line A line of people waiting for free food

Dust Bowl Area of the Great Plains made worthless for farming by drought and dust storms in the 1930s

direct relief Money or food given directly from the government to the needy

Before You Read

In the last lesson you learned about the start of the Great Depression. In this lesson you will read about the hardships caused by the Depression.

As You Read

Use a chart to summarize the effects of the Great Depression on farmers and city dwellers.

THE DEPRESSION DEVASTATES PEOPLE'S LIVES

***How* did the Depression affect people in cities and on farms?**

The Depression brought suffering and hardship to many Americans and ruined many lives. Millions of people lost their jobs. Some went hungry or became homeless. Those who could not meet their housing payments lost their homes.

Cities across the country were full of homeless people. Some slept in parks and wrapped themselves up in newspapers to keep warm. Others built **shantytowns,** where they lived in shacks they made from scrap material. Some ate in **soup kitchens,** where charities served meals to the needy. Those who could not afford to buy food stood in **bread lines** for free food.

African Americans and Latino

Americans who lived in the cities had a very hard time. They had a higher unemployment rate than whites. If they did have work, they were paid less than white workers.

There was even violence directed against African Americans and Latinos. Angry whites who had lost their jobs did not want to compete with these minority groups for the few jobs that were left. They sometimes attacked African Americans, lynching 24 in 1933. Some whites demanded that Latino Americans be sent back to the countries they came from. Thousands of people of Mexican heritage chose to move to Mexico to avoid prejudice. Others were deported by the United States government.

The Depression hurt people in rural areas, too. Food prices continued to go

© Houghton Mifflin Harcourt Publishing Company

down as the Depression deepened. Farmers earned less and less. Many farm families could not meet their mortgage payments. More and more of them lost their farms. From 1929 to 1932 about 400,000 farmers lost their land.

To make matters worse, a long drought hit the Great Plains. There was little rain from Texas to North Dakota. Much of this area had been grassland that farmers broke up with their plows in order to grow crops.

The soil was now exhausted from overfarming. The grass that had once held the soil in place was gone. When powerful winds swept across the Great Plains, the soil simply blew away. This dry area of blowing soil was called the **Dust Bowl.** Huge dust storms covered the plains and blew dust as far away as the East Coast.

The hardest-hit region included parts of Kansas, Oklahoma, Texas, New Mexico, and Colorado. Many Oklahoma farmers packed up their belongings and started for California to look for work. They became migrant workers, moving from place to place to pick crops. Because so many of them came from Oklahoma, migrant workers were often called Okies.

1. How did people in the cities and in rural areas suffer during the Great Depression?

   _____

   _____

EFFECTS ON THE AMERICAN FAMILY
How did the Depression affect families?

The Depression put a heavy strain on family life. Many families pulled together during the hard times. They shared what they earned. Instead of going out for entertainment, parents and children often stayed home. They played board games or listened to the radio.

Some families broke apart under the strain of poverty and unemployment, however. Many men felt ashamed because they had lost their jobs. Some of them simply left their families and wandered the country looking for work.

Women did all they could to help support their families. Many women who had not had to work before tried to find work. But they were usually paid less than men. Many people complained that employers should not hire women. They thought that men should have the jobs instead. These people argued that men were the ones who supported families, so it was more important for them to have jobs.

Children suffered terribly from poverty and the break-up of families. Many children had poor diets and no health care. Their parents could not afford to buy healthy food or to pay doctor bills. Many children suffered from malnutrition and diet-related illnesses like rickets. Many children ran away from home, hopping rides aboard freight trains. It was exciting, but also dangerous. Many were robbed or killed by criminals or beaten by railroad guards.

During the early years of the Great Depression, the federal government did not give **direct relief**—cash or food given directly to poor people. Charities and some city governments struggled to help. But they could not provide enough relief to keep people out of poverty.

Because so many people were out of work, cities and states collected less tax money. They had to cut their budgets for programs like child welfare. Some cities could not afford to keep their schools open for a full term. Many school boards shortened the school year. Other schools simply closed. Children often went to work to try to help their families survive.

The Great Depression caused great suffering. Many people became demoralized, some losing the will to live. Rates of suicide and mental illness increased dramatically. Many decided that compromises were more important than long-term health. For example, some Americans did not go to the doctor in order to save money. Hardship also forced young people to give up

dreams of college. Some people began to think that financial well-being was the most important concern in life. They were willing to give up everything else to get it.

While the Great Depression caused much suffering, it sometimes brought out the best in individuals, families, and communities. Many people shared resources with their neighbors or gave food and clothing to the needy.

2. Describe two ways the Great Depression affected families.

_____

_____

Summarize the Great Depression's effects on various aspects of
American life.

1. Employment
2. Housing
3. Farming
4. Race relations
5. Family life
6. Physical health
7. Emotional health

© Houghton Mifflin Harcourt Publishing Company

The Great Depression

Hoover's Failed Policies

Key Terms and People

Herbert Hoover 31st president

Boulder Dam Dam on the Colorado River built during the Depression to create jobs

Federal Home Loan Bank Act Law passed in 1931 to reduce mortgage rates to save farmers from foreclosure

Reconstruction Finance Corporation Agency established in 1932 to provide emergency relief to large businesses, insurance companies, and banks

Bonus Army Unemployed World War I veterans who marched to Washington to demand their war bonuses

Before You Read

In the last lesson you read about how the Depression affected common people. In this lesson you will learn how President Hoover tried to stop the Depression.

As You Read

Use a chart to list facts about President Hoover's response to the Great Depression.

HOOVER TRIES TO REASSURE THE NATION
How could the nation recover?

Over time, economies go through cycles, which means there are times of economic growth and prosperity followed by slumps when the economy slows down. In the 1930s many experts believed that it was best not to interfere with these cycles. They argued that slumps would end on their own and good times would return.

At first, President **Herbert Hoover** believed that the Great Depression was just another slowdown that would end on its own. Hoover did think that the government should take action in this situation. But he also believed that it

should not take too much power or give direct aid to poor people. Instead, Hoover believed government should help different groups work together to improve the economy. For example, he thought government should help managers and workers find solutions to their problems. But he did not think government should decide on the solution.

Hoover also believed in "rugged individualism," which is the idea that people should succeed through their own efforts. He thought that people should take care of themselves and each other, and that the government should encourage private groups to help the needy. He supported the idea that charities, not government, should give food and shelter to people who were poor or out of work.

Hoover adopted a cautious approach to dealing with the Depression. He began by meeting with businessmen, bankers, and labor leaders. He urged them to work together to help improve the economy. He asked employers not to fire workers or to lower their pay. He asked labor leaders not to demand higher pay or go on strike.

Hoover also devised a plan to help private charities increase the money they received to assist the poor. Nothing he did made a difference. The economy shrank and unemployment rose. Many companies closed their doors, and people continued to lose their jobs. Hungry Americans were forced to rely on soup kitchens for food. Some people lived in shantytowns or roamed from place to place as hoboes.

One project that helped was the **Boulder Dam,** a huge dam on the Colorado River. Still, economic difficulties increased, and the country turned against Hoover. In the 1930 elections, the Democrats gained more seats in Congress, winning control of the House of Representatives. The Republicans retained a majority in the Senate by just one seat. Citizens took other actions too. Farmers burned crops and dumped milk rather than sell it for less than it cost them to produce. People called the shantytowns "Hoovervilles." Despite criticism, Hoover stuck to his principles.

1. What did Hoover think government should do in bad economic times?

_____

_____

HOOVER TAKES ACTION; THE BONUS ARMY INCIDENT
What actions did Hoover take?

Hoover did not offer direct aid to the poor. However, he did take steps to use the government to improve the economy.

Hoover used the Boulder Dam project as a model of how the federal government could encourage cooperation between private groups. He tried to help farmers by backing the creation of the Federal Farm Board. One of its purposes was to help farmers find ways to raise prices of crops. He also tried to help banks by having them form the National Credit Corporation. This organization gave loans to banks that were in danger of failing.

By 1931 the economy had not improved. Congress passed the **Federal Home Loan Bank Act.** This law lowered mortgage rates. Congress hoped that low mortgage rates would help farmers change the terms of their mortgages. This would help protect their farms from foreclosure.

Hoover also created the **Reconstruction Finance Corporation** (RFC). The RFC provided money for projects to create jobs.

Hoover became less popular with the public. His popularity fell even more in 1932 when World War I veterans who had been promised bonuses to make up for their poor wartime pay came to the capital. Congress wanted to vote on a bill to give the veterans their bonuses immediately.

Thousands of out-of-work veterans and their families arrived in Washington. This so-called **Bonus Army** set up tents near the Capitol building. Hoover first sent the veterans food. But after the bonus was voted down in Congress, he told the veterans to leave. About 2,000

© Houghton Mifflin Harcourt Publishing Company

stayed. Hoover ordered the army to remove them. The sight of U.S. Army troops using tear gas on citizens outraged many people. It seemed unlikely that Hoover would be reelected.

2. What actions did Hoover take to try to improve the economy?

_____

_____

_____

Answer the questions below about President Hoover's response to the Great Depression.

Philosophy
1. What was Hoover's philosophy of government?
Response and Economic Results
2. What was Hoover's initial reaction to the stock market crash of 1929?
3. a. What was the nation's economic situation in 1930? b. How did voters in 1930 respond to this situation?
4. a. What did Hoover do about the economic situation? b. How did the economy respond to his efforts?
5. a. How did Hoover deal with the economic problem posed by the Bonus Army? b. How did his efforts affect his own political situation?

© Houghton Mifflin Harcourt Publishing Company

A New Deal Fights the Depression

Key Terms and People

Franklin Delano Roosevelt 32nd president

New Deal Franklin Roosevelt's programs to end the Depression

Glass-Steagall Act Law that created insurance for bank deposits

Federal Securities Act Law to regulate stock information

Agricultural Adjustment Act (AAA) Programs to help farmers

Civilian Conservation Corps (CCC) Program to employ young men in work projects

National Industrial Recovery Act (NIRA) Programs to help industry

deficit spending Spending more than the government receives in revenue

Huey Long Political leader from Louisiana who criticized the New Deal

Before You Read

In the last lesson you read about Herbert Hoover's reaction to the Great Depression. In this lesson you will learn about Franklin Delano Roosevelt's programs to fight the Depression.

As You Read

Use a chart to take notes on Roosevelt's New Deal programs, their purposes, and their long-term goals.

AMERICANS GET A NEW DEAL
***What* were the goals of the New Deal?**

In 1932 Americans elected Democrat **Franklin Delano Roosevelt,** known as FDR, president. He beat Hoover by a landslide. Democrats won majorities in Congress, too.

During Roosevelt's first Hundred Days, he and his advisers planned programs to end the Depression. They were part of the **New Deal,** which had three goals: relief for the needy, economic recovery, and financial reform. Congress passed many laws that expanded the government's role in

the nation's economy and citizens' lives.

Roosevelt declared a "bank holiday" by closing banks to stop more bank failures. Then Congress passed the Emergency Banking Relief Act, giving the Treasury Department the power to inspect and close banks. Sound ones reopened, while those in trouble stayed closed. Public confidence was restored. The **Glass-Steagall Act** set up the Federal Deposit Insurance Corporation (FDIC), which protects the money people put in banks. Congress also passed the **Federal Securities Act.** This

© Houghton Mifflin Harcourt Publishing Company

law required companies to give information on their stock offerings. Later, Congress created the Securities and Exchange Commission (SEC) to regulate the stock market.

FDR spoke directly to the American people in radio talks called "fireside chats." He explained the New Deal and asked for public support. These chats helped restore the nation's confidence.

1. Describe three goals of the New Deal.

_____

_____

HELPING THE AMERICAN PEOPLE
Who did the New Deal help?

Roosevelt helped farmers and other workers. The **Agricultural Adjustment Act (AAA)** paid farmers to raise fewer crops. As a result, the prices for farm products increased and farmers earned more money. The Tennessee Valley Authority (TVA) helped that region by creating jobs, building dams, and controlling floods.

The New Deal included programs that gave relief through work projects and cash payments. The **Civilian Conservation Corps (CCC)** put young men to work building roads, developing parks, and helping in conservation projects. The **National Industrial Recovery Act (NIRA)** set codes of fair practice for industries. It also set up the National Recovery Administration (NRA) to stop wage cuts, falling prices, and layoffs. The NIRA also created the Public Works Administration (PWA), which gave states money for construction jobs. The Civil Works Administration (CWA) provided additional jobs building schools and

roads and paid salaries for many teachers.

The Home Owners Loan Corporation (HOLC) provided government loans to homeowners who faced foreclosure because they could not make their loan payments. The Federal Emergency Relief Administration (FERA) provided direct relief to the needy.

2. How did the New Deal provide help to different groups of Americans?

_____

_____

THE NEW DEAL COMES UNDER ATTACK
Who criticized the New Deal?

The New Deal was financed through **deficit spending**—spending more money than the government gets in revenue. It helped, but it did not end the Depression, so people criticized it. Liberals said it did not do enough for the poor. Conservatives said the government had too much control.

The Supreme Court found the NIRA and the AAA unconstitutional. Roosevelt then proposed a bill so he could appoint more new Supreme Court justices. Critics said that he wanted to "pack" the Court with justices who supported him. People protested this proposal. However, justices resigned from the Court, so Roosevelt was able to appoint seven new justices. Court decisions began to favor the New Deal.

Three critics of Roosevelt appealed to poor Americans. Father Charles Coughlin used radio sermons to share his views against the New Deal. His anti-Jewish views eventually cost him support.

© Houghton Mifflin Harcourt Publishing Company

Dr. Francis Townsend proposed a pension plan to give monthly payments to the elderly. Elderly voters liked this plan.

A third critic was Louisiana senator **Huey Long.** Once a supporter of the New Deal, he now wanted to become president. He proposed a program called Share-Our-Wealth. In 1935 he was assassinated.

3. Name two critics of the New Deal and what changes they proposed.

_____

_____

Complete the chart about the New Deal programs listed below.

Federal Program	What was its immediate purpose?	What was its long-term goal?
Business Assistance and Reform		
1. Emergency Banking Relief Act (EBRA)		
2. Glass-Steagall Banking Act of 1933		
3. Federal Securities Act		
4. National Industrial Recovery Act (NIRA)		
Farm Relief/Rural Development		
5. Agricultural Adjustment Act (AAA)		
6. Tennessee Valley Authority (TVA)		
Employment Projects		
7. Civilian Conservation Corps (CCC)		
8. Federal Emergency Relief Administration (FERA)		
9. Public Works Administration (PWA)		
10. Civil Works Administration (CWA)		
Housing		
11. Home Owners Loan Corporation (HOLC)		

© Houghton Mifflin Harcourt Publishing Company

The New Deal

The Second New Deal

Key Terms and People

Eleanor Roosevelt First Lady, social reformer, political adviser

Works Progress Administration (WPA) New Deal jobs program

National Youth Administration Program to provide aid and jobs to young people

Wagner Act Law to protect workers' rights

Social Security Act Program that provided aid to people with disabilities and pensions for retired workers

Before You Read

In the last lesson you read about the early days of the New Deal. In this lesson you will learn about the Second New Deal.

As You Read

Use a chart to take notes on how the programs of the Second New Deal helped groups such as farmers, the unemployed, youth, and retirees.

THE SECOND HUNDRED DAYS
What did voters think about the New Deal?

The economy improved in the first two years of Roosevelt's presidency. But it did not improve much. Still, the New Deal was popular and FDR launched a second wave of reforms, often called the Second New Deal. These programs were meant to provide more help to farmers and workers.

The First Lady, **Eleanor Roosevelt,** traveled around the country and told her husband about the suffering of the poor. She made sure that the New Deal included relief programs for women and minorities. She focused on social issues and worked for civil rights and workers' rights.

The 1936 election was an overwhelming victory for Roosevelt, the Democrats, and the New Deal. It also marked the first time most African Americans voted Democratic. It also was the first time that labor unions supported a single candidate—Roosevelt.

1. What did the election of 1936 tell about the New Deal?

   _____

   _____

HELPING FARMERS
How did the Second New Deal help farmers?

Farmers were still struggling. Many had environmental problems from dust storms. Many farms were mortgaged. Thousands lost their land to the banks. So farmers needed a law to replace the AAA, which the Supreme Court had struck down.

Congress passed the Soil Conservation and Domestic Allotment Act, which paid farmers to reduce production of soil-depleting crops and to use soil conservation methods. Later, the second AAA was passed without the tax that had made the first AAA unconstitutional.

The Resettlement Administration helped tenant farmers, sharecroppers, migrant workers, and other poor farmers. It offered loans to farmers to buy land. It became the Farm Security Administration (FSA), and loaned money to farmers and set up better housing for migrant workers.

2. What action did the Second New Deal take to help farmers?

_____

_____

ROOSEVELT EXTENDS RELIEF
What were the WPA and NYA?

The **Works Progress Administration (WPA)** created jobs quickly. It used millions of workers to build airports, roads, libraries, schools, and hospitals. Sewing groups made clothes for the needy.

Some people criticized the WPA as a make-work program that created useless jobs just to give people a paycheck. But the WPA helped unemployment and poverty and gave working people a sense of hope and dignity along with their paychecks.

The WPA also employed teachers, writers, artists, actors, and musicians. It

helped women, minorities, and the young.

The **National Youth Administration (NYA)** provided aid and part-time jobs to many high school and college students. This allowed them to get an education even in tough economic times.

3. How did the WPA and NYA help people?

_____

_____

IMPROVING LABOR AND OTHER REFORMS
How did the Second New Deal help workers?

The Second New Deal created important reforms for labor and the economic security for retired workers. Congress passed the National Labor Relations Act to replace the NIRA, which the Supreme Court struck down. This law is often called the **Wagner Act.**

The Wagner Act supported workers' rights to join unions and take part in collective bargaining. It also banned unfair labor practices. The Wagner Act set up the National Labor Relations Board (NLRB) to enforce these reforms.

The Fair Labor Standards Act of 1938 set maximum hours and a minimum wage for the first time. It set a workweek of 44 hours and rules for workers under the age of 16.

The **Social Security Act** was one of the most important achievements of the New Deal. It had three parts:
- Old-age insurance: supplemental retirement plan that provided funds from what workers and employers paid into the system.
- Unemployment compensation: payments to workers who lost their jobs; paid for by a tax on employers.

Name _____ Class_____ Date_____

Lesson 2, *continued*

- Aid to the disabled and families with children: for people who could not be expected to work; paid for by federal funds available to states.

The Second New Deal also extended electricity to rural areas through the Rural Electrification Administration (REA).

4. How did the Second New Deal try to protect workers?

_____

_____

Complete the chart about the second phase of New Deal policies

Group	What problems did each group face during the Depression?	What laws were passed and agencies established to deal with these problems?
1. Farmers, migrant workers, and others living in rural areas		
2. Students and other young people		
3. Teachers, writers, artists, and other professionals		
4. All workers, including the unemployed		
5. Retired workers		
6. The disabled, the needy elderly, and dependent mothers and children		

© Houghton Mifflin Harcourt Publishing Company

Guided Reading Workbook

New Deal, New Opportunities

Key Terms and People

Frances Perkins Secretary of labor

Mary McLeod Bethune Head of the Division of Negro Affairs in the NYA

John Collier Commissioner of Indian Affairs

New Deal coalition Voters from different groups who supported the Democratic
Party because of the New Deal

Congress of Industrial Organizations (CIO) Labor union

Before You Read

In the last lesson you read about the Second New Deal. In this
lesson you will learn about some of the effects of the New Deal.

As You Read

Use a chart to take notes on how the New Deal affected minorities
and other groups.

WOMEN MAKE THEIR MARK
How did the New Deal affect women?

Women made some important gains
during the New Deal, including being
appointed to important federal jobs.
Frances Perkins became the first female
cabinet member when she was named
secretary of labor. She helped create the
Social Security system. Roosevelt also
appointed two female diplomats and a
female federal judge. He hoped that
these appointments would make him
more popular among women voters.

Women in the workplace had to
deal with discrimination because many
male workers felt women took jobs away
from men. Many New Deal agencies did
not discriminate in hiring. So women
had more opportunities, although
some agencies and many businesses did
not hire as many women as men. The
Civilian Conservation Corps only

hired men. The National Recovery
Administration hired women but paid
them less than men. However, women
kept working, so criticism did not stop
the trend of women working outside the
home.

1. Describe two ways that the New
   Deal expanded and limited
   opportunities for women.

   _____

   _____

AFRICAN AMERICAN ACTIVISM
How did the New Deal affect African
Americans?

President Roosevelt appointed more
than 100 African Americans to major
government positions. **Mary McLeod
Bethune** was an educator who became
head of the Division of Negro Affairs

© Houghton Mifflin Harcourt Publishing Company

Guided Reading Workbook

of the National Youth Administration (NYA). She worked to ensure that the NYA hired African Americans and offered job training and other benefits to minority students. She also helped organize a "Black Cabinet." This was a group of influential African Americans that advised Roosevelt on racial issues.

However, President Roosevelt did not push for full civil rights for African Americans. He was afraid of losing the support of white Democratic southerners. He did not approve a federal anti-lynching law or end the poll tax. Also, some New Deal agencies discriminated against African Americans with lower wages.

2. What gains did African Americans make during the New Deal?

_____

_____

MEXICAN AMERICAN FORTUNES; NATIVE AMERICANS GAIN SUPPORT
What **gains did Mexican Americans and Native Americans make?**

Mexican Americans tended to support the New Deal. But they received few benefits from New Deal programs. Many were farm workers who were not covered by federal laws. Some New Deal agencies discriminated against them. Some were disqualified from programs because they had no permanent address. Others were deported to Mexico.

Native Americans got support from the New Deal. In 1924 they were given full citizenship. In 1933 Roosevelt made **John Collier** commissioner of Indian Affairs. He supported Native American rights. Collier helped pass the Indian Reorganization Act. This law stopped assimilation and gave Native Americans

autonomy. It also strengthened their land claims.

3. How did Mexican Americans and Native Americans fare under the New Deal?

_____

_____

REVIVING ORGANIZED LABOR
Who **supported the New Deal?**

Roosevelt had support from southern whites, urban groups, African Americans, and union workers. These voting groups formed a coalition that supported FDR, the **New Deal coalition.**

Labor laws gave union members improved working conditions and more bargaining power. So labor unions made gains in the 1930s. Membership grew from 3 million to more than 10 million.

Divisions emerged between labor unions. The American Federation of Labor (AFL) consisted of mostly craft unions, such as electricians and carpenters. Other unions wanted to represent workers in a whole industry, such as the automobile industry. This led to the **Congress of Industrial Organizations (CIO).**

Labor employed an effective bargaining tool, the sit-down strike, in the 1930s. This kind of strike had workers staying at their workplace but refusing to work. So factory owners were prevented from using strikebreakers to get the work done.

Some strikes led to violence. On Memorial Day in 1937, ten people were killed during a steel strike. Business opposed labor unions, so the National Labor Relations Board forced the steel company to negotiate with the union. This helped labor gain strength.

© Houghton Mifflin Harcourt Publishing Company

As part of the New Deal coalition, urban voters helped Roosevelt and the Democratic Party. Powerful city political organizations provided jobs in exchange for votes. Labor laws and work-relief programs helped many religious and ethnic groups. Roosevelt also appointed immigrants and people of urban backgrounds to government jobs.

4. What was the New Deal coalition?

_____

_____

Complete the chart about how the New Deal affected minorities and other groups.

1. Women		
Example(s) of appointees to important government positions:	Gains women made under the New Deal:	Problems of women not solved by the New Deal:
2. African Americans		
Example(s) of appointees:	Gains African Americans made under the New Deal:	Problems of African Americans not solved by the New Deal:
3. Labor unions		
Example(s) of union(s) organized during the New Deal:	Gains unions made under the New Deal:	Problems of unions not solved by the New Deal:
4. Other coalition groups		
	Reasons they supported the Democratic Party:	

© Houghton Mifflin Harcourt Publishing Company

The New Deal

Culture in the 1930s

Key Terms and People

Gone With the Wind One of the most popular films of all time

Orson Welles Actor, director, producer, and writer; creator of renowned radio broadcast based on *The War of the Worlds*

Richard Wright African American author of *Native Son*

Zora Neale Hurston African American author of *Their Eyes Were Watching God*

The Grapes of Wrath Novel by John Steinbeck

Before You Read

In the last lesson you learned about the New Deal coalition. In this lesson you will learn about American culture during the Depression.

As You Read

Use a chart to take notes on culture of the 1930s in the fields of radio, literature, movies, music, and the arts.

THE LURE OF MOTION PICTURES AND RADIO
What did Americans do for fun during the Depression?

The 1930s were a golden age for the radio and film industries in spite of the hard economic times. About two-thirds of Americans went to a movie once a week.

Hollywood studios made a wide variety of movies including comedies, musicals, love stories, and gangster films. Some films offered escape from the realities of the Depression. One of the most famous and popular films of all time was *Gone With the Wind* (1939).

Fred Astaire and Ginger Rogers were dancing partners who made many movies together. Other popular movies in the 1930s included The *Wizard of Oz*

and the Disney animated film *Snow White and the Seven Dwarfs*. Audiences flocked to see Marx Brothers' comedies. They also went to gangster movies, featuring characters struggling to succeed in a difficult environment that people living in the Depression could understand. Some films such as *Mr. Deeds Goes to Town* (1936) by director Frank Capra showed New Deal accomplishments positively. Capra's films also included honest, kind-hearted people who won out over greedy people.

Radio showed the democratic spirit of the times. There were radios in nearly 90 percent of American homes. Radio was the most direct means of reaching the American people.

Most American families spent several hours a day listening to dramas and

© Houghton Mifflin Harcourt Publishing Company

variety programs. Soap operas, named for the soap companies that sponsored them, played during the late morning or early afternoon to reach homemakers. Children's programs, such as *The Lone Ranger*, played in the late afternoon.

Orson Welles created one of the most famous radio broadcasts of all time. He was an actor, director, and writer. In 1938 audiences heard that Martians had invaded Earth. Some people panicked. However, they were hearing a radio drama based on the novel *The War of the Worlds*. The broadcast showed the power of radio at a time when many Americans got their news that way.

Radio made Bob Hope, Jack Benny, George Burns, and Gracie Allen stars long before they had success on television. And to reach the greatest number of people, President Roosevelt went on the radio during his famous "fireside chats."

1. What was the appeal of movies during the Depression?

_____

_____

THE ARTS IN DEPRESSION AMERICA

How did the New Deal help artists?

The art, music, and literature of the Depression were more serious and sober than radio and movies. However, much of the artistic work had an uplifting message and emphasized the strength of character and democratic values of Americans.

Many New Deal officials believed the arts were important for the nation. They created several programs to put artists to work. For example, the Federal

Arts Project was part of the WPA. It paid artists to create posters, murals, and other works of art for public places to promote positive images of American society. Artists included Edward Hopper, Jackson Pollock, and Grant Wood. Wood's *American Gothic*, a portrait of a serious-looking man and woman standing in front of their farmhouse, remains symbolic of life during the Depression.

The Federal Theater Project, also part of the WPA, supported American playwrights and hired actors to perform plays.

Woody Guthrie was a folksinger who used music to capture Depression hardships. Forced from his home by the Dust Bowl, Guthrie traveled west and wrote about the trials of the journey. Guthrie's "This Land is Your Land" is a classic American folk song, and he had a major influence on American folk music.

The Federal Writers' Project funded writers such as African American writer **Richard Wright.** He received aid while writing *Native Son*, a novel showing the problems racism caused for a young African American man. **Zora Neale Hurston** wrote *Their Eyes Were Watching God*, the story of an African American woman growing up in rural Florida.

One of the country's most famous authors, John Steinbeck, also got help from the FWP. His novel ***The Grapes of Wrath*** shows the problems faced by Oklahoma farmers forced from their homes during the Dust Bowl. They became migrant workers and ended up in California, where their hardships continued.

From an Irish working-class neighborhood in Chicago, to the poverty

© Houghton Mifflin Harcourt Publishing Company

of Missouri coalfields, to sharecroppers in Alabama, writers told of difficulties during the 1930s for different groups. The play *Our Town* by Thornton Wilder captured the warmth and beauty of small-town life.

2. Describe two New Deal programs that supported the arts.

_____

_____

_____

Complete the chart about how the films, radio dramas, art, music, and literature of the 1930s influenced American culture.

Films	Radio
1. What were the main types of films?	5. What were the main types of radio shows?
2. What were several purposes of 1930s films?	6. Why was radio important? How do you know this?
3. What is *Gone With the Wind*?	7. Why did people panic when they heard the radio broadcast of *The War of the Worlds*?
4. What was unique about Frank Capra's films?	8. Who were some people made famous by radio?

Art	Music	Literature
9. What did the government pay artists to do? Why?	11. Who was Woody Guthrie? What did he do?	13. What are examples of writers helped by the Federal Writers' Project?
10. Who were some American artists of the 1930s?	12. What was one of Guthrie's famous songs?	

© Houghton Mifflin Harcourt Publishing Company

Lesson 5

The Impact of the New Deal

Key Terms and People

Securities and Exchange Commission (SEC) Agency to regulate stock markets

Federal Deposit Insurance Corporation (FDIC) Insurance for savings

National Labor Relations Board (NLRB) Agency to regulate business

parity An equal or fair amount

Tennessee Valley Authority (TVA) Regional work project of lasting value

Before You Read

In the last lesson you learned about American culture during the Depression. In this lesson you will read about the legacy of the New Deal.

As You Read

Use a chart to take notes on the lasting effects of the New Deal.

THE END OF THE NEW DEAL; NEW DEAL PROGRAMS ENDURE
How do some New Deal programs continue to affect Americans today?

President Roosevelt did not launch another New Deal. Although New Deal programs helped millions of Americans, they did not end the Great Depression. Also, the president was not in favor of deficit spending, and the federal government was already in debt. Congress urged Roosevelt to cut back on New Deal programs. He did, which caused industrial production to drop and unemployment to rise. In addition to the rising debt, Roosevelt was worried about events in Europe, particularly the rise of Hitler. The government was soon preparing for war, which led the deficit to rise again. However, this spending is what brought the nation out of the Depression.

Although Roosevelt did not begin any new New Deal programs after 1938,

many programs have continued and have an impact even today.

New Deal programs set up federal agencies to regulate banking and finance. They exist today. The **Securities and Exchange Commission (SEC)** regulates the stock market and enforces laws relating to the sale of stocks and bonds. The **Federal Deposit Insurance Corporation (FDIC)** created by the Glass-Steagall Act insures savings against loss if a bank fails.

The New Deal also has had an effect on workers' rights. The Wagner Act and the Fair Labor Standards Act set standards for wages and hours, stopped child labor, and allowed workers to form unions and bargain collectively. Today the **National Labor Relations Board (NLRB)** still mediates labor disputes.

One of the most important and lasting benefits of the New Deal is the Social Security Act, establishing the system by

© Houghton Mifflin Harcourt Publishing Company

Guided Reading Workbook

Lesson 5, *continued*

which large numbers of Americans receive financial help. It provides old-age insurance and unemployment benefits. It also helps families with children and those who are disabled. For the first time, the government took responsibility for the welfare of its citizens.

The New Deal affected agriculture, too. The second Agricultural Adjustment Act made loans to farmers. The loans were based on the **parity** value, which is a price intended to keep farmers' incomes steady. Projects that spread electric power to rural areas also helped farmers.

New Deal programs helped the environment. Roosevelt wanted to promote policies that protected the nation's resources. The Civilian Conservation Corps planted trees and created hiking trails. The Soil Conservation Service taught farmers how to use soil properly through contour plowing, terracing, and crop rotation. The Taylor Grazing Act helped reduce grazing on public lands. Overgrazing caused erosion, which led to the 1930s dust storms. The **Tennessee Valley Authority (TVA)** built dams, which helped prevent floods and provided electricity. And New Deal programs also added to the national park system and set up areas to protect wildlife.

1. What are two continuing benefits of the New Deal?

   _____

   _____

THE LEGACY OF THE NEW DEAL
What did the New Deal change?

New Deal reforms continue to affect American society and politics. Its greatest effect relates to the expansion of the federal government's power. It

gave the federal government, and particularly the president, a greater role in shaping the economy. It did this by putting millions of dollars into the economy, creating federal jobs, regulating supply and demand, and participating in settling labor disputes.

The expansion of the federal government changed the way in which the federal government and state government interacted, too. The federal government wanted states involved in New Deal programs, so federal aid to states increased. This allowed state governments to increase spending and provide additional services.

Conservative critics thought that the size of federal and state government was too large and threatened the basic character of the country. They said that the size and power of the government got in the way of free enterprise. They felt that government should not be so involved in the economy.

Liberal critics said that the New Deal did not go far enough. They thought that it should have done more to change the economy. They believed that Roosevelt should have done more to end the differences in wealth between the rich and the poor. Supporters of the New Deal say that it was well balanced between saving capitalism and reforming it, and that it helped the country recover from economic troubles.

The New Deal gave people hope. It changed what citizens expect from government, too. It also fueled the long-term debate over the role and size of the federal government.

2. How did the New Deal affect the federal government?

   _____

   _____

© Houghton Mifflin Harcourt Publishing Company

Name _____ Class _____ Date _____

Complete the chart about the impact of New Deal reforms and their lasting effects on American society.

	New Deal Laws and Agencies	Lasting Effects of These Laws and Agencies on American Government and Life
1. Labor		
2. Agriculture and rural life		
3. Banking and finance		
4. Social welfare		
5. Environment		

© Houghton Mifflin Harcourt Publishing Company

War Breaks Out

Key Terms and People

Joseph Stalin Communist dictator of the Soviet Union

totalitarian Government that has complete control over its citizens and puts down all opposition

Benito Mussolini Fascist dictator of Italy

fascism Political system that stressed nationalism and the interests of the state

Adolf Hitler Nazi dictator of Germany

Nazism Fascist political philosophy of Germany based on extreme nationalism

Hideki Tojo Prime minister of Japan during World War II

Neville Chamberlain Prime minister of Great Britain before World War II

Winston Churchill Prime minister of Great Britain during World War II

appeasement Trying to pacify an aggressor in order to keep the peace

nonaggression pact Agreement between Germany and Russia not to attack each other

blitzkrieg Lightning war strategy used by Germany against Poland

Before You Read

In the last lesson you saw the effects of the New Deal reforms in the United States during the Great Depression. In this lesson you will learn about how totalitarianism grew in Europe and Asia and led to World War II.

As You Read

Use a chart to take notes about the rise of dictators and the major events in German expansion leading to and during World War II.

FAILURES OF THE TREATY OF VERSAILLES; THE SPREAD OF TOTALITARIANISM
How did dictators take power in Europe and Asia?

Instead of leading to a "just and lasting peace," the Treaty of Versailles caused resentment. Germany was angry about losing territory and being blamed for starting the war. Italy was unhappy,

too. The Italians had hoped to be rewarded with territory, but that had not occurred. Similarly dissatisfied, the Soviets resented the carving up of parts of Russia.

The peace settlement failed to make the world "safe for democracy" as President Wilson had hoped. New democratic governments, hurt by economic and social problems, turned to

Lesson 1, *continued*

authoritarian leaders. The new democracies collapsed, and dictators were able to seize power.

In the Soviet Union, **Joseph Stalin** came to power in 1924. He focused on creating a model Communist state. He did away with private farms and created collectives, or huge state-owned farms. The state also took over industry. Stalin made the Soviet Union into a leading industrial power.

Stalin got rid of anyone who criticized him or his policies. Many were killed. Millions of others died in famines caused by the restructuring of Soviet society. Stalin created a **totalitarian** government—a government with complete control. Individuals had no rights, and the government put down all opposition.

At the same time, **Benito Mussolini** was creating a totalitarian state in Italy. His political movement was called **fascism,** which placed power with a strong leader and a small group of party members. Fascism stressed nationalism. Mussolini, who called himself *Il Duce*, or the leader, extended control to every aspect of Italian life. Like Stalin, he crushed all opposition.

In Germany, **Adolf Hitler,** who referred to himself as *Der Führer* (the Leader), promised to unite all German-speaking people into a new German empire. Hitler's political philosophy was called **Nazism**, a form of fascism. He believed that Germans—especially blond, blue-eyed "Aryans"—were the master race and were meant to have power over all "inferior races," such as Jews and nonwhites. Hitler believed Germany needed to expand its territory, even if that meant fighting.

Because of war debts, Germany's economy was in bad shape. Many people were unemployed. The German people were desperate, and the Nazi Party seemed to offer solutions to their problems. By the 1932 elections, the Nazis were Germany's strongest political party. Hitler became chancellor in 1933 and did away with the Weimar Republic. He set up the *Third Reich*, or third German empire.

Meanwhile, in Asia, military leaders had taken over Japan. They believed that Japan needed a strong army, more land, and resources.

In Spain, General Francisco Franco led a rebellion against the Spanish republic. Revolts led to the Spanish Civil War. Many American volunteers went to Spain to fight against Franco and the spread of fascism. Western democracies stayed neutral, but Hitler and Mussolini supported Franco with troops and weapons. Franco won in 1939, becoming Spain's Fascist dictator. Europe had another totalitarian government.

1. What five major countries had totalitarian governments in the 1930s?

_____

_____

DICTATORS EXPAND THEIR TERRITORY
Why did France, Britain, and Germany sign the Munich Pact?

In 1931 Japan's military government attacked Manchuria, a Chinese province. The League of Nations protested, but Japan left the league and kept Manchuria. This showed the failure of the league. Then, Japanese officials continued their expansion plans. **Hideki Tojo,** army chief of staff, invaded further into China. Eventually, Japan took control of French, Dutch, and British colonies in East Asia.

© Houghton Mifflin Harcourt Publishing Company

Lesson 1, continued

Europe's dictators noticed that the League of Nations had failed to stop Japan's aggressive actions. So in 1933, Hitler left the league and started building Germany's military, violating the Treaty of Versailles. Meanwhile in Italy, Mussolini began building a new Roman Empire. He sent troops to take over Ethiopia. Once again, the League of Nations failed to stop the aggression.

In March 1938 German troops marched into Austria. They met no opposition. Germany announced an Anschluss, or "union," with Austria.

Czechoslovakia was next for Hitler. He set his sights on the Sudetenland, the western border region where 3 million German-speaking people lived. He massed troops on the Czech border.

France and Britain promised to defend Czechoslovakia, but they were eager to avoid war. When their leaders met with Hitler in Munich, Germany, Hitler promised that the Sudetenland would be his "last territorial demand." So France, Britain, and Germany signed the Munich Pact in September 1938, giving Germany the Sudetenland.

Neville Chamberlain was the British prime minister who signed the Munich Pact. He called it "peace with honor." Another British leader, **Winston Churchill,** disagreed. He called the pact dishonorable **appeasement.** That means giving up your principles in order to pacify an aggressor. Churchill predicted that appeasement would eventually lead to war.

2. Why was Churchill against the Munich Pact?

_____

_____

THE GERMAN OFFENSIVE
How did Hitler's attacks on France and Britain turn out?

Hitler did not keep the promise he made at Munich. In March 1939 he conquered the rest of Czechoslovakia and set his sights on Poland by claiming that Germans living in Poland were being mistreated. Many people thought Hitler would never attack Poland. They thought he would be afraid that the Soviet Union, on Poland's eastern border, would then fight Germany. But Germany and the Soviet Union signed a **nonaggression pact,** an agreement not to fight each other. In a secret part of this treaty, Hitler and Stalin also agreed to divide Poland between them.

On September 1, 1939, Hitler launched World War II by attacking Poland. The Germans used a new strategy called a *blitzkrieg,* or lightning war. They used tanks and planes to take the enemy by surprise and crush them quickly. Poland fell to the Germans in a month. Britain and France declared war on Germany.

Meanwhile, the Soviets attacked Poland from the east and grabbed some of its territory. Then Stalin seized the Baltic States and Finland.

In April 1940 Hitler launched surprise attacks on Denmark and Norway. Then in May, he quickly took the Netherlands, Belgium, and Luxembourg.

Germany next headed to France, hoping to take its capital, Paris. With Italy's help from the south, France fell to Germany quickly.

Then Germany decided to invade Britain. It launched an air war, dropping bombs over Britain. The British air force, RAF, successfully defended Britain against these attacks, which were called the Battle of Britain. They used a

© Houghton Mifflin Harcourt Publishing Company

new technology called radar and shot down hundreds of German planes. Hitler's plan to take over Britain failed, but the Germans continued to bomb British cities.

3. What was *blitzkrieg?*

_____

_____

Answer the questions about the rise of dictators in Europe and Asia during the 1930s and the major events in German expansion leading up to and during World War II.

1.	What were Joseph Stalin's goals for the Soviet Union, and what actions did he take to achieve them?
2.	What dictator created Italy's totalitarian state, and how did he do this?
3.	What were the main ideas behind Hitler's political philosophy?
4.	How were military actions in Japan and Spain similar to those of Stalin, Mussolini, and Hitler?
5.	How did Hitler begin to expand Germany's territory?
6.	Why did Neville Chamberlain sign the Munich Pact? Why did Winston Churchill oppose it?
7.	What happened to Poland as a result of the invasion, and how did Britain and France respond to it?
8.	What type of battle was the Battle of Britain, and why was England's victory so important?

© Houghton Mifflin Harcourt Publishing Company

The Holocaust

Key Terms and People
Holocaust Systematic murder of more than 11 million Jews and other people in Europe by the Nazis
Kristallnacht Name given the night of November 9, 1938, when Nazis in Germany attacked Jews and their homes, businesses, and synagogues
genocide Deliberate and systematic killing of an entire people
ghetto A segregated neighborhood
concentration camp A prison camp operated by the Nazis where Jews and others were starved while doing slave labor, or murdered

Before You Read

In the last lesson you saw how Hitler began World War II. In this lesson you will see how Hitler put his plan of Aryan domination into place by killing Jews and other groups he considered inferior.

As You Read

Use a timeline to take notes on the events that led to the Holocaust.

THE PERSECUTION BEGINS
How did the persecution of Jews begin in Germany?

Part of Hitler's plan for Germany was to make the country racially pure. In 1933 Hitler stopped all non-Aryans from working in the government. He began an organized persecution of non-Aryans, mainly Jews. This led to the **Holocaust**—the systematic murder of more than 11 million people across Europe. Over half of the murdered people were Jews.

Anti-Semitism, or hatred of Jews, had a long history in Germany and in other parts of Europe. Germans had used Jews as a scapegoat, someone to blame for their own failures and frustrations. Hitler blamed Jews for Germany's defeat

in World War I. Many Germans agreed. Hitler blamed Jews for Germany's economic problems. Many Germans supported him.

Persecution of Jews increased under Hitler. In 1935 the Nuremberg Laws took away Jews' civil rights and property. Jews were forced to wear yellow Stars of David on their clothing.

On November 9, 1938, organized, violent persecution began with ***Kristallnacht.*** (*Kristallnacht* is a German word meaning "crystal night," or night of broken glass.) Nazi Storm Troopers attacked Jewish homes, businesses, and synagogues. The streets were littered with broken glass. Then, the Nazis blamed Jews for the destruction. Many Jews were arrested; others were fined.

© Houghton Mifflin Harcourt Publishing Company

Guided Reading Workbook

Lesson 2, *continued*

Jews started to flee Germany. Nazis wanted this, but other nations did not want to accept Jewish refugees. France already had 40,000 Jewish refugees, and the British did not want to accept more than 80,000 refugees because they feared greater anti-Semitism. Some refugees, such as Albert Einstein, were allowed into the United States. But the United States would not change its immigration quotas. This was partly due to anti-Semitism, and to Americans' fear of competition for the few jobs available during the Depression.

Once war started in Europe, some Americans feared that refugees were "enemy agents." The Coast Guard even turned away a ship carrying refugees who had emigration papers for the United States. More than half of those passengers were killed by the Nazis after the ship was forced to return to Europe.

1. How did the world react to Germany's persecution of the Jews and refugees?

_____

_____

HITLER'S "FINAL SOLUTION"
How **did the Nazis try to kill off the Jews and others?**

In 1939 there were only about a quarter of a million Jews left in Germany. But other countries that Hitler occupied had millions more Jews. Hitler's ultimate goal was to get rid of all of Europe's Jews. He began implementing the "final solution." This plan was **genocide,** the deliberate and systematic killing of an entire population.

The "final solution" was based on the Nazi belief that "Aryans" were a superior people, whose strength and racial purity must be preserved. So the

Nazis arrested people they identified as "enemies of the state." In addition to Jews, the Nazis rounded up political opponents—Liberals, Ccommunists, Socialists—and other groups including Gypsies, Freemasons, Jehovah's Witnesses, homosexuals, the disabled, and the terminally ill.

Some Jews were forced into **ghettos**—segregated Jewish areas where they were made to work in factories or left to starve. Despite brutal conditions, Jews resisted the Germans and set up schools.

Many Jews were sent to **concentration camps,** or labor camps. The hunger, illness, overwork, and torture usually ended in death.

2. Who were the targets of the "final solution"?

_____

_____

THE FINAL STAGE
How **did the Nazis kill so many people?**

The early concentration camps did not kill Jews fast enough for the Nazis. In 1941, six death camps were built in Poland. Prisoners were separated upon arrival at death camps by doctors. Those who were too old or too weak to work were led to gas chambers and killed. Other prisoners were shot, hanged, or subjected to horrible medical experiments by camp doctors.

By 1942 much of the world became aware of the Holocaust and the details of Hitler's "final solution." Reports about the concentration camps spread. The response to the Holocaust varied by nation and individual. Some ordinary people risked their own lives to hide Jews or to help them escape. But many countries, including the United States,

© Houghton Mifflin Harcourt Publishing Company

did little to help Europe's Jewish population. Many have criticized the United States for not doing enough.

Six million Jews died in death camps and Nazi massacres. Some Jews were saved, and some even survived the concentration camps.

3. Why were certain people separated from the others and led to the gas chambers?

_____

_____

Write answers to the questions related to events that are on the timeline.

1933 Hitler comes to power. Soon after, he orders non-Aryans to be removed from government jobs and begins to build concentration camps.

Thousands of Jews begin leaving Germany. →	1. Why didn't France and Britain accept as many German Jews as they might have?
1935 Nuremberg Laws are passed. →	2. What did the Nuremberg Laws do?
1938 *Kristallnacht* occurs. →	3. What happened during *Kristallnacht*?
1939 As war breaks out in Europe, U.S. Coast Guard prevents refugees from landing. →	4. Why didn't the United States accept as many German Jews as it might have?
Hitler implements "final solution."	
1941 Nazis build six death camps in Poland. →	5. What groups did the Nazis single out for extermination?
	6. How did the Nazis go about exterminating the approximately 11 million people who died in the Holocaust?

America Moves Toward War

Key Terms and People

Neutrality Acts Laws passed by Congress to ban the sale of arms or loans to nations at war

Axis powers Germany, Italy, and Japan

Selective Training and Service Act First peacetime military draft under which 16 million men between the ages of 21 and 35 were registered

Lend-Lease Act Law that allowed lending or leasing arms to any nation "whose defense was vital to the United States"

Atlantic Charter British and American statement of war goals

Allies Group of nations, including the United States, Britain, and the Soviet Union, who opposed the Axis powers

Before You Read

In the last lesson you learned about Hitler's effort to kill Jews and other groups he considered inferior. In this lesson you will see how the United States moved closer to entering the war against the Nazis.

As You Read

Use a timeline to take notes on the events that led to the entry of the United States into World War II.

ISOLATIONISM AMIDST CONFLICT
***Why* were the American people committed to staying neutral?**

Most Americans wanted the United States to stay out of foreign conflicts. Many people thought that the United States had made a mistake getting involved in World War I. During the 1930s antiwar feelings were strong and isolationism became more popular. Even when Japan invaded Manchuria, the United States did not get involved.

Congress passed the Neutrality Acts. These laws banned loans or arms sales to nations at war. Because of the Spanish Civil War, the **Neutrality Acts**

included countries involved in civil wars, too.

In 1937 President Roosevelt found a way around the Neutrality Acts. Since Japan had not declared war on China, Roosevelt felt free to send China military aid. In a speech, he talked of "quarantining the aggressors," but growing criticism from isolationists forced FDR to back down.

1. How did isolationism affect foreign policy?

_____

_____

MOVING AWAY FROM NEUTRALITY
Why did the United States change its policy of neutrality?

According to the Neutrality Acts, the United States could not enter the war in Europe. However, President Roosevelt asked for a change in the acts. He suggested a cash-and-carry provision. It would allow Britain and France to buy and transport American arms. Congress passed this new Neutrality Act in November 1939.

In 1940 Germany, Italy, and Japan signed a mutual defense treaty. They became the **Axis powers.** The treaty meant that if the United States went to war against any one of them, all three would fight. That would put America at war on two fronts: in Europe and in Asia. Nevertheless, Roosevelt gave the British "all aid short of war" to help them fight Hitler.

Roosevelt assured the nation that the United States would stay out of war. But he prepared for war. Congress increased spending for national defense. It passed the nation's first peacetime draft in September 1940, called the **Selective Training and Service Act.**

FDR broke the tradition of a two-term presidency and ran for reelection in 1940. His opponent, Wendell Willkie, shared Roosevelt's beliefs that the United States should help Britain but that it should not get involved in war. Voters chose the candidate they knew. FDR won a third term.

After the election, Roosevelt spoke to the American people. He said that it would not be possible to negotiate peace with Hitler. He said if Britain fell, there would be no one left to stop the Axis powers from taking over the world. Roosevelt suggested lending or leasing arms to any nation "whose defense was vital to the United States." Isolationists opposed his policy. But Congress passed the **Lend-Lease Act** in March 1941.

Meanwhile, Germany invaded its former ally, the Soviet Union. The United States gave lend-lease support to the Soviets as well as to Britain.

American industries began producing war supplies. They hired workers and unemployment began to shrink. The Great Depression was over.

2. What did President Roosevelt tell the American people after his reelection that hinted at the possibility of war?

_____

_____

FDR PLANS FOR WAR
How did the United States move toward war?

To prevent the delivery of goods to Britain and the Soviet Union, Hitler had his Nazi submarines, called U-boats, attack enemy supply ships. These U-boat attacks were successful in sinking tons of shipments of supplies. In June 1941 Roosevelt told the U.S. Navy to protect lend-lease ships and gave American warships permission to attack German U-boats in self-defense.

In August 1941 Roosevelt met secretly with British prime minister Winston Churchill. Roosevelt did not actually commit the United States to war. But he and Churchill did sign the **Atlantic Charter.** That was a statement of the goals for fighting World War II. These goals included collective security, disarmament, protecting people's rights to choose their own form of government, economic cooperation, and freedom of the seas.

Later, 26 nations signed a similar agreement. These nations, called the **Allies,** were united in fighting Germany,

© Houghton Mifflin Harcourt Publishing Company

Italy, and Japan.

On September 4, 1941, a German U-boat fired on an American destroyer. President Roosevelt ordered the U.S. Navy to fire on German ships on sight. U-boats responded by sinking an American merchant ship and several other American ships. In one attack, more than 100 American seamen were killed. The Senate finally allowed the arming of merchant ships. Full-scale war seemed inevitable.

3. What events moved the United States closer to war?

_____

_____

JAPAN ATTACKS THE UNITED STATES
What brought the United States into conflict with Japan?

In Japan, expansionists had long dreamed of creating a huge empire. Japan had already begun seizing Asian territory held as colonies by European nations. The United States also owned islands in the Pacific.

When Japan invaded Indochina in 1941, the United States cut off trade with Japan. Japan needed American oil to run its war machine. The prime minister of Japan, Hideki Tojo, started peace talks with the United States, but he also prepared for war.

The United States broke Japan's

secret communications code. The Americans knew Japan was preparing for a military strike. But they did not know exactly when or where the strike would be. After the United States cut off trade with Japan, the two countries met, but Japan refused to leave China. Then, the United States received a decoded message that told Japan's peacekeepers to refuse American proposals.

On December 7, 1941, Japan attacked the main U.S. naval base at Pearl Harbor in Hawaii. The Japanese damaged the U.S. Pacific Fleet in one blow. Planes and ships were destroyed. More than 2,400 people were killed.

Roosevelt did not want to fight a war on two fronts. He had expected to enter the war in Europe, not to fight in Asia, too. On December 8, 1941, Roosevelt addressed Congress asking for a declaration of war against Japan. He said: "Yesterday, December 7, 1941, a date which will live in infamy . . . [the Japanese launched] an unprovoked and dastardly attack." Congress quickly agreed to declare war. Germany and Italy then declared war on the United States.

4. What event caused the American declaration of war against Japan?

_____

_____

© Houghton Mifflin Harcourt Publishing Company

Answer the questions about how the United States entered
World War II.

1939	Congress passes Neutrality Act.	→	1. What did the 1939 Neutrality Act allow?
1940	Axis powers form alliance. U.S. passes the Selective Training and Service Act.	→	2. Who were the Axis powers? What did their alliance mean for the United States?
1941	Congress passes Lend-Lease Act.	→	3. What did the Lend-Lease Act do?
	Japan takes over French military bases in Indochina.	→	4. What did the United States do to protest Japan's action?
	Churchill and Roosevelt draft the Atlantic Charter.	→	5. What pledges were contained in the Atlantic Charter?
	German U-boats fire on American ships. U.S. Senate allows arming of merchant ships.	→	6. How did the United States react to German U-boat attacks?
	Japan launches a surprise attack on Pearl Harbor.	→	7. What did the attack do to the U.S. Pacific Fleet?
	As U.S. declares war on Japan, Germany and Italy declare war on U.S.	→	8. Why did Germany and Italy declare war on the United States?

© Houghton Mifflin Harcourt Publishing Company

World War II

The War Effort on the Home Front

Key Terms and People

George Marshall Army chief of staff during World War II

Women's Auxiliary Army Corps (WAAC) Women volunteers who served in noncombat positions

Office of Price Administration (OPA) Agency of the federal government that fought inflation

War Production Board (WPB) Government agency that decided which companies would make war materials and how to distribute raw materials

rationing Restricting the amount of food and other goods people may buy during wartime to assure adequate supplies for the military

Manhattan Project Secret research project that resulted in the atomic bomb

A. Philip Randolph Important African American labor leader

James Farmer Civil rights leader who founded the Congress of Racial Equality

Congress of Racial Equality (CORE) Interracial organization formed to fight discrimination

internment Confinement under guard, especially during wartime

Japanese American Citizens League (JACL) Civil rights group formed by Japanese Americans

Before You Read

In the last lesson you learned the reasons why the United States entered World War II. In this lesson you will learn how Americans joined in the war effort.

As You Read

Complete a chart featuring how different groups of Americans supported the war effort.

AMERICANS JOIN THE MILITARY
How did Americans react to Pearl Harbor?

The Japanese had expected Americans to react with fear to the attack on Pearl Harbor. Instead, Americans reacted with rage. "Remember Pearl Harbor" became a rallying cry. Five million men volunteered for military service.

But fighting a war on two fronts—in Europe and in the Pacific—required huge numbers of soldiers. Another 10 million men were drafted.

Because the new soldiers needed training and housing, hundreds of new military bases and training centers were built. The military built new bases in areas where there was a warm climate and plenty of open land.

The leader of the armed forces mobilization effort was Army chief of staff general **George Marshall.** His job was to make sure soldiers were properly trained and to help develop the nation's military strategy. Marshall suggested using women for noncombat military tasks. Congress created the **Women's Auxiliary Army Corps (WAAC)** in 1942. They worked in jobs such as nurses and pilots.

Men and women from minority groups also served in the war. Some African Americans had mixed feelings about defending a country where they were often segregated and denied the basic rights of citizenship. But some African Americans saw the war as a chance to fight discrimination. More than a million African Americans served, but in racially segregated units. These units were not allowed into combat until 1943. Many Mexican Americans, Asian Americans, and Native Americans also enlisted.

1. How did women and minorities join in the war effort?

_____

_____

THE FEDERAL GOVERNMENT MANAGES THE WAR EFFORT
How did the federal government get involved in the economy?

The United States was better prepared for World War II than it had been for World War I. It also worked to gain support from Americans by spreading propaganda through posters and films to influence thoughts and feelings in favor of the war effort.

Movies were popular, so the film industry helped in the war effort by producing patriotic films. Later, they made musicals and romances to help people forget for a few hours about the problems of the war.

The federal government was worried about economic issues. Congress wanted to prevent the high inflation that had occurred during World War I. Roosevelt and Congress set up the **Office of Price Administration (OPA).** It successfully fought inflation by freezing, or not increasing, prices on most goods. Congress also raised income taxes, which meant consumers had less to spend so there was less demand on scarce goods. These actions kept inflation low during the war. They also helped fund the war effort, along with war bonds bought by citizens.

The government also had to ensure that the armed forces and war industries had what they needed to win the war. The **War Production Board (WPB)** was created to decide which companies would make war materials and how to distribute raw materials.

The OPA also set up **rationing,** or setting up fixed allotments of goods essential for the military. Families were issued coupons to be used for buying scarce items, such as meat and gasoline. Most Americans cooperated with the rationing system. They also collected goods, such as tin cans and paper, that could be recycled. Some families started victory gardens to grow more food.

All of the products made in American factories and saved by citizens had to be shipped to the soldiers overseas. The U.S. merchant marine, a fleet of civilian merchant ships, transported goods to the war fronts.

In 1941 the government put together

© Houghton Mifflin Harcourt Publishing Company

the Office of Scientific Research and Development (OSRD). It involved scientists in the war effort. The group developed bombs and guided missiles and supported research and development of medications such as penicillin. Its most important role had to do with the development of the atomic bomb. The **Manhattan Project** became the code name for research work done that related to developing the atomic bomb.

2. What actions did the government take to control inflation, shrinking supplies, and the threat of destructive weapons?

_____

_____

A PRODUCTION MIRACLE
What changes took place in American life?

The nation's factories quickly switched to war production. Automobile factories made planes and tanks. Pencil-makers turned out bomb parts. Shipyards and defense plants expanded. They produced warships with amazing speed.

About 18 million workers kept these war industries going. Some 6 million new factory workers were women.

Before the war, most defense contractors had refused to hire African Americans. Now they hired more than 2 million minority workers including African Americans, Mexican Americans, Asian Americans, Native Americans, and others.

3. How did the war change life at home?

_____

_____

OPPORTUNITY, DISCRIMINATION, AND ADJUSTMENT
How did the war affect African Americans, Mexican Americans, and Native Americans?

The war created opportunities for women and minorities, but these groups still faced discrimination. **A. Philip Randolph,** the president of the Brotherhood of Sleeping Car Porters, was an important African American labor leader. He threatened to have African Americans march on Washington to demand an end to this discrimination. To avoid such a march, Roosevelt issued an executive order creating the Fair Employment Practices Committee. It required employers and labor unions to end discrimination.

On the home front, many African Americans left the South and moved to the Midwest. There they found skilled jobs that paid well. But they also found discrimination. In 1942 civil rights leader **James Farmer** formed an interracial organization to fight discrimination. It was called the **Congress of Racial Equality (CORE).**

African Americans also moved into crowded cities. Tension among the races grew. In 1943 it led to race riots. The worst one was in Detroit, where more than 30 people were killed. President Roosevelt sent federal troops to restore order. In response, many communities formed committees to improve race relations.

Mexican Americans experienced prejudice during the war years as well. In 1943 Mexican Americans were beaten by white servicemen and civilians in the "zoot-suit" riots.

Native Americans faced discrimination, too. Although many had volunteered for the military, many states prevented them from voting. Also, the

© Houghton Mifflin Harcourt Publishing Company

government reclaimed some reservations for use as military bases and weapons testing sites.

Americans in general had to make many adjustments during the war. People had to adjust to new family situations. Many fathers were in the armed forces, so women had to work and raise children.

4. How did World War II affect African Americans, Mexican Americans, and Native Americans?

_____

_____

INTERNMENT OF JAPANESE AMERICANS
What happened to Japanese Americans during the war?

After Pearl Harbor, government officials began to fear that people of German, Italian, and Japanese descent might help the enemy. Thousands of German and Italians were placed in prison camps. But the worst treatment was reserved for Japanese Americans.

Japanese Americans endured terrible treatment during the war. In Hawaii, the commanding general ordered the **internment,** or confinement, of about one percent of Hawaii's Japanese American residents.

On February 19, 1942, President Roosevelt ordered the internment of all Japanese Americans living in California and parts of other western states. More than 100,000 people were rounded up and shipped to internment camps.

No charges were ever filed against Japanese Americans. No evidence of subversion was ever found. In 1944, in the case of *Korematsu* v. *United States*, the Supreme Court said the government policy was justified by "military necessity." After the war, the **Japanese American Citizens League (JACL)** pushed the government to compensate, or pay back, those sent to the camps.

Finally, in 1990 cash payments were sent to all former internees. In a letter, President Bush said the nation recognized that "serious injustices were done to Japanese Americans."

5. What reason was given for the internment of Japanese Americans?

_____

_____

Explain how each group, act, or factor contributed to the war effort.

1. Women's Auxiliary Army Corps (WAAC)	2. Women
3. Minorities	4. Manufacturers
5. A. Philip Randolph	6. Office of Scientific Research and Development (OSRD)
7. Entertainment industry	8. Office of Price Administration (OPA)
9. War Production Board (WPB)	10. Rationing

© Houghton Mifflin Harcourt Publishing Company

World War II

The War for Europe and North Africa

Key Terms and People

Dwight D. Eisenhower American general who commanded Allied forces; 34th president of the United States

D-Day Allied invasion to liberate Europe

Omar Bradley American general who led American forces at Normandy

George Patton American general who helped liberate Paris

Battle of the Bulge German counteroffensive in December 1944

Before You Read

In the last lesson you learned how American involvement in World War II affected life at home. In this lesson you will see how the United States, Britain, and the Soviet Union defeated the Axis powers.

As You Read

Use a timeline to take notes on major events influencing the fighting in North Africa and Europe.

THE UNITED STATES AND BRITAIN JOIN FORCES

What **were the goals of the American and British alliance?**

A few weeks after Pearl Harbor, President Roosevelt met with British prime minister Winston Churchill to plan their war strategy. They decided that the first thing to do was to defeat Hitler's Germany. Roosevelt and Churchill began a lasting friendship and a strong alliance between their countries.

After war was declared, German U-boats increased attacks on American ships in the Atlantic to prevent food and war materials from reaching Great Britain and the Soviet Union. This action became known as the Battle of the Atlantic.

The Allies organized convoys for shared protection. Warships and airplanes escorted the convoys. At first, there were not enough vessels to form convoys. As U.S. industry began producing more ships and planes, however, the situation improved. Soon, there were more Allied cargo ships, or Liberty ships, being made than being sunk. They used sonar and radar to find and destroy many German submarines. By mid-1943 the Allies were winning the Battle of the Atlantic.

© Houghton Mifflin Harcourt Publishing Company

1. What was the Battle of the Atlantic, and how did the Allies win it?

_____

_____

THE EASTERN FRONT AND THE MEDITERRANEAN
What happened in the Soviet Union, North Africa, and Italy?

By the winter of 1943, the Allies were winning on land as well as on the sea.

The German invasion of the Soviet Union had begun in 1941. When it stalled in 1942, Hitler changed his tactics. He moved to capture Soviet oil fields and to take the industrial city of Stalingrad. The Germans bombed Stalingrad until almost the whole city was on fire.

Stalin refused to give up. During months of horrible hand-to-hand combat, the Germans took most of Stalingrad. Then as winter began, the Soviets counterattacked. They trapped a large German force in and around Stalingrad and cut off their supplies. The Germans froze and starved. In February 1943 the German soldiers surrendered. The Battle of Stalingrad was a turning point. From then on, Soviet forces moved steadily west toward Germany.

Meanwhile, in November 1942 the Allies invaded North Africa, which was controlled by the Axis powers. Control of the area was important to the Allies. They needed to protect Mediterranean shipping lanes because of the oil from the Suez Canal. American forces led by General **Dwight D. Eisenhower** defeated German troops under General Erwin Rommel. The Germans surrendered in May 1943.

Next, in July 1943 the Allies invaded Italy. They captured Sicily. The war-weary Italian king stripped Prime Minister Mussolini of power and had him arrested. But then Hitler seized Italy. It took many months of fighting for the Allies to drive the Germans out of Italy. In the Italian campaign, several units were made up of segregated groups of African Americans, Mexican Americans, and Japanese Americans. Many of these minority groups won honors for bravery.

2. How were the Allies victorious in the Soviet Union, North Africa, and Italy?

_____

_____

THE ALLIES GAIN GROUND IN EUROPE
Why did the Allies invade Normandy?

The Allies had been building a huge force for two years to invade the Normandy region of France. This invasion to liberate Europe was on June 6, 1944. It was **D-Day**—the day the Allies launched history's largest land-sea-air operation.

Allied forces landed on Normandy's beaches. They met German resistance, and many were killed. But they took the beaches. More Allied troops landed in France and began to advance. General **Omar Bradley** opened a huge hole in the German lines, which allowed General **George Patton** and his Third Army to liberate Paris in August. By September, the Allies had liberated other European nations and had entered Germany itself.

In the United States, Roosevelt won reelection to a fourth term as president.

To the Allies' surprise, Hitler began a counterattack in December. At first, the Germans cut deeply into Allied lines.

After a month of fighting, the Allies pushed the Germans back. The Germans had lost so many men and weapons in this **Battle of the Bulge** that they could only retreat.

3. How successful was the Allies' invasion of Europe?

_____

_____

Explain what made each event a critical moment or turning point in the war.

TURNING POINTS OF WORLD WAR II

December 1941	Roosevelt and Churchill meet	→ 1.
February 1943	End of Battle of Stalingrad	→ 2.
May 1943	End of North Africa campaign	→ 3.
Mid-1943	Victory in Battle of the Atlantic	→ 4.
Late 1943	Victory in Italy	→ 5.
June 1944	D-Day	→ 6.
August 1944	Liberation of Paris	→ 7.
September 1944	Liberation of other European nations and entry into Germany	→ 8.
January 1945	End of Battle of the Bulge	→ 9.

© Houghton Mifflin Harcourt Publishing Company

World War II

The War in the Pacific

Key Terms and People

Douglas MacArthur American commander in the Philippines

Bataan Death March Forced march of captured American and Filipino troops

Chester Nimitz Commander of American naval forces in the Pacific

Battle of Midway American victory that was the turning point in the Pacific War

Island hopping Allies' method of combining land, sea, and air forces to capture and secure islands

kamikaze Japanese suicide flight

Before You Read

In the last lesson you saw how the Allies made progress on the European front. In this lesson you will see how the Allies defeated Japan in the Pacific.

As You Read

Use a chart to take notes on military actions in the Pacific and their significance.

A SLOW START FOR THE ALLIES
Why **were the early attacks by the Japanese so successful?**

In the first six months after Pearl Harbor, the Japanese military had great success. They conquered huge areas of the Asian mainland and many islands in the Pacific. The Allies were shocked by Japan's success. They had underestimated the skill and training of Japanese soldiers.

In December 1941 the Japanese invaded the Philippines. At the time, the American army in the Philippines was under the command of General **Douglas MacArthur.** He led a small force of American and Filipino soldiers. They were no match for the 200,000 Japanese.

In March 1942 MacArthur retreated to the Bataan Peninsula. Once there, supplies were short and no help came from U.S. officials. The troops fought for four months, but many died from hunger, disease, and bombing attacks. With the loss of many men, President Roosevelt ordered MacArthur to leave. MacArthur left the Philippines but told people left behind, "I shall return."

After MacArthur's departure, the soldiers who were left were captured. Their suffering really began in what came to be called the **Bataan Death March.** Prisoners were forced to journey for five days and nights with little food or water. Those who could not continue were beaten or shot. Thousands died. Those who survived were put in Japanese prison camps. In these camps,

© Houghton Mifflin Harcourt Publishing Company

Guided Reading Workbook

with lack of food and medicine, hundreds more died.

1. What was the significance of the loss of the Philippines?

_____

_____

FORTUNES SHIFT IN THE PACIFIC
What was so important about the Battle of Midway?

After the defeat in the Philippines, the United States started to fight back against Japan. In the spring of 1942, Lt. Colonel James Doolittle led a bombing raid on Tokyo. Soon after, the U.S. Navy defeated the Japanese at the Battle of Coral Sea, which ended Japan's threat to invade Australia.

Then, in June 1942 the Japanese headed toward Midway, an island northwest of Hawaii. American forces broke the Japanese code and knew Midway was Japan's next target and the date of the planned attack. Admiral **Chester Nimitz,** commander of American naval forces in the Pacific, defended the island. He and his forces destroyed four aircraft carriers, a cruiser, and 250 planes. The **Battle of Midway** was a turning point in the Pacific War because it crippled the Japanese navy.

2. Why was the Battle of Midway important?

_____

_____

THE ALLIES GO ON THE OFFENSIVE
What were the important battles in the Pacific?

American forces turned their efforts toward winning control of the Solomon Islands beginning with Guadalcanal. Troops led by returning General MacArthur stormed Guadalcanal in August 1942. This marked Japan's first defeat on land.

However, with all the islands the Japanese still controlled, the United States knew it would be costly and take a long time to attack them all. So instead, they began **island hopping.** They avoided well-defended islands. Bases were built on captured islands from which future military actions could take place.

In addition, the United States began using Native Americans of the Navajo nation as code talkers. Using a coded version of their language, they transmitted messages that the Japanese could not figure out.

In October 1944, led by MacArthur once again, Americans landed on the island of Leyte in the Philippines. The Japanese launched **kamikaze** raids. In these suicide attacks, Japanese pilots crashed their bomb-laden planes into Allied ships. Despite the damage done by kamikazes, Japan lost so many ships in the Battle of Leyte Gulf that the Japanese navy was essentially knocked out of the war.

MacArthur and his troops next took the island of Iwo Jima, which was important to the United States because it became a base to launch bombers that might reach Japan. In addition, thousands of Japanese troops were in tunnels and caves here.

Okinawa was the major obstacle that stood between the Allies and Japan. When MacArthur and the U.S. marines invaded the island, the Japanese used more than 1,900 kamikaze attacks. On land, a fierce battle raged. Okinawa was Japan's last defensive outpost. The Americans finally won on June 22, 1945,

Name _____ Class_____ Date_____

but it cost 7,600 American lives. Japan lost 110,000 men including two generals. The Allies feared the human cost of invading Japan.

3. Why was the Battle of Leyte Gulf so important?

_____

_____

Explain what made each event a critical moment or turning point in the war.

THE WAR IN THE PACIFIC

Date and Place	Leader Involved	What happened?
1. April 1942, Bataan		
2. June 1942, Midway		
3. August 1942, Guadalcanal		
4. October 1944, Leyte Gulf		
5. March 1945, Iwo Jima		
6. June 1945, Okinawa		

© Houghton Mifflin Harcourt Publishing Company

World War II

The End of World War II

Key Terms and People

United Nations (UN) World peacekeeping organization created after World War II

V-E Day Victory in Europe Day, May 8, 1945

Harry S. Truman 33rd president of the United States

J. Robert Oppenheimer Scientist who led the Manhattan Project

Hiroshima City that was the site of the first atomic-bomb drop in Japan

Nagasaki Japanese city that was the site of the second atomic-bomb drop

Nuremberg Trials Tribunal that tried Nazi leaders for war crimes

GI Bill of Rights Law passed by Congress to help servicemen readjust to civilian life

Before You Read

In the last lesson you learned how the United States defeated the Japanese in the Pacific. In this lesson you will learn about preparations for the postwar world, the use of the atomic bomb, challenges countries faced, and benefits of the war for Americans.

As You Read

Use a chart to take notes on major World War II events at the end and after the war.

THE ALLIES LIBERATE EUROPE
How did the Allies try to shape the postwar world?

The Battle of the Bulge left Germany in a weakened state. Allied troops marched eastward into the center of Germany.

Meanwhile, the Soviets pushed westward across Poland toward Berlin, Germany. The Soviets were the first to liberate death camps and to describe the unbelievable horrors they saw there. Americans, who later liberated Nazi death camps in Germany, were just as horrified as the Soviets had been.

The Soviet army approached Germany from the east and Allied forces came from the west. The Germans were surrounded.

Meanwhile, in February 1945 Roosevelt, Churchill, and Stalin, the Big Three, met at the Yalta Conference. They were pleased over the defeat of Germany, which now seemed certain. Stalin wanted to keep Germany divided into occupation zones, areas controlled by Allied military forces, so Germany could no longer be a threat. Churchill disagreed and Roosevelt suggested concessions to Stalin. He wanted Stalin to help in the fight to defeat Japan. And he wanted Stalin to support the **United**

© Houghton Mifflin Harcourt Publishing Company

Nations (UN), a new world peacekeeping organization.

At Yalta, the Allies agreed to divide Germany into four zones: one zone for the Americans, the British, the Soviets, and the French. Stalin agreed to allow free elections in Poland and other Eastern European countries. He also agreed to join in the war against Japan.

The Yalta Conference made many decisions, but it signaled growing friction between the Soviet Union and the other Allies.

By April 25, 1945, the Soviets were in Berlin. Hitler responded to certain defeat by shooting himself.

A week later, General Eisenhower accepted the unconditional surrender of Nazi Germany. On May 8, 1945, the Allies proclaimed V-E Day—Victory in Europe Day.

President Roosevelt never saw V-E Day because he died on April 12, 1945. Vice-President Harry S. Truman became the nation's 33rd president.

1. How did the Yalta Conference shape the postwar world?

   _____

   _____

THE ATOMIC BOMB ENDS THE WAR
Why did the United States use the atomic bomb?

Although the Allies had won Iwo Jima and Okinawa, they knew invading Japan would be difficult because it still had a huge army. President Truman believed that the only way to avoid an invasion was to use the weapon developed by scientists working on the Manhattan Project, the atomic bomb. J. Robert Oppenheimer had led the research and development. On July 16,

1945, the first atomic bomb was tested. It was even more powerful than predicted. Many scientists felt it would be immoral to drop the bomb on Japan. Others said it would shorten the war and save lives. It would also give the United States an advantage over the Soviets after the war. Truman decided to use the bomb.

On August 6, 1945, an atomic bomb was dropped on Hiroshima, Japan. Almost every building collapsed into dust. But Japan did not surrender. A second bomb was dropped on Nagasaki, killing 200,000. Emperor Hirohito was horrified. Japan surrendered on September 2, 1945. The war was over.

2. Why did Truman decide to use the atomic bomb?

   _____

   _____

THE CHALLENGES OF VICTORY
How did losing the war affect the leaders of Germany and Japan?

Japan had surrendered, but the use of the atomic bomb had brought the world into the nuclear age. Over time, the Soviet Union and other nations tried to build their own atomic weapons. But the task at hand was what to do for the postwar world.

At the Yalta Conference and even before, leaders were planning for the United Nations. People hoped that the United Nations would help bring a time of peace. Instead, the UN became a place where the two superpowers, the United States and the Soviet Union, competed and tried to influence other nations.

Even before the war ended, there were tensions between the United States and the Soviet Union. Truman met with the

© Houghton Mifflin Harcourt Publishing Company

Lesson 7, *continued*

Allied leaders at the Potsdam Conference in July 1945. At Yalta, Stalin had promised to allow free elections in Eastern Europe. But now Soviet troops occupied Eastern Europe, and Stalin was not going to allow free elections.

In addition to democratic countries, Truman and Stalin disagreed about the reparations from Germany to help repay Soviet wartime losses. However, the leaders at Potsdam were able to compromise. They divided Germany into four occupation zones as was set up at the Yalta Conference. Each occupying country was able to take reparations from its own zone.

The **Nuremberg Trials** were held to try remaining Nazi leaders. For the first time, a nation's leaders were held legally responsible for their wartime acts. They were tried for crimes against humanity, crimes against the peace, and war crimes. The result of the trials was that 12 of the 24 defendants were sentenced to death and most of the others were sent to prison. Later trials saw 200 more found guilty of war crimes. These trials established the idea that individuals are responsible for their own actions even during a war. This principle became part of international law.

After its surrender, Japan was occupied by American forces headed by General MacArthur. This occupation lasted for six years. First, Japanese officials were put on trial for war crimes. Then, the United States helped Japan set up a free-market economic system and create a new democratic constitution.

3. How were defeated nations treated by the Allies?

_____

_____

CHANGES ON THE HOME FRONT
How did American society change as a result of the war?

Although Europe and Japan suffered tremendous devastation, World War II brought Americans opportunities. There were jobs and money to spend. Unemployment fell, and workers were able to save money.

Farmers also benefited. After the dust storms of the depression years, the 1940s saw good weather for growing crops. Improvements in farm technology also helped farmers make a profit.

The war had been good to women, too. More than 6 million women had started working. Many of these jobs were doing work traditionally done by men.

The war also brought about one of the largest mass migrations the country ever experienced. People who had lived for years in a place decided to look for jobs elsewhere. People left farms and small towns. They moved to the North and the West. African Americans were among these migrants. They were looking for new jobs and to escape discrimination.

In 1944 Congress passed the **GI Bill of Rights,** which was designed to help servicemen readjust to civilian life. This bill paid for veterans to get an education. Over half the returning soldiers took advantage of this opportunity. It also gave federal loan guarantees to veterans buying homes or farms or starting businesses. The GI Bill gave many people opportunities they otherwise would never have had.

4. How did the war benefit Americans?

_____

_____

© Houghton Mifflin Harcourt Publishing Company

Complete the chart about the end of World War II, postwar plans, the
challenges of victory, and life on the home front.

WORLD WAR II'S END AND BEYOND

1.	How did the Soviets and Americans react to the Nazi death camps?
2.	What plans did Roosevelt, Churchill, and Stalin make at the Yalta Conference?
3.	Why was V-E Day important?
4.	Why did some scientists believe that it was immoral to drop the atomic bomb on Japan?
5.	What major difference between the United States and the Soviet Union was demonstrated at the Potsdam Conference?
6.	What made the Nuremberg Trials so significant?
7.	What were positive results that came out of the U.S. occupation of Japan?
8.	Why did the war bring about one of the largest mass migrations in the United States?
9.	Why was the GI Bill of Rights a necessary law?

© Houghton Mifflin Harcourt Publishing Company

The Origins of the Cold War

Key Terms and People

Harry S. Truman 33rd president of the United States

satellite nation Country dominated by the Soviet Union

iron curtain The division of Europe between free and Communist countries

Cold War State of hostility between the Soviet Union and the United States but without military action

containment taking measures to prevent the spread of Communist rule to other countries

Central Intelligence Agency (CIA) Agency created to compile intelligence from the military and state department and to perform secret operations in foreign countries

Truman Doctrine U.S. policy of sending aid to any nation trying to prevent a Communist takeover

Marshall Plan Program under which the United States gave economic aid to rebuild postwar Western Europe

Berlin Airlift Resupply of West Berlin by U.S. and British planes during Soviet blockade of 1948

North Atlantic Treaty Organization (NATO) Defensive military alliance of the United States, Canada, and ten European nations

Before You Read

In the last lesson you saw the social and economic changes that would reshape postwar America. In this lesson you will see how the Allied coalition that won the war fell apart and how the United States and the Soviet Union came into conflict.

As You Read

Use a diagram to take notes on U.S. actions and Soviet actions that contributed to the beginning of the Cold War.

© Houghton Mifflin Harcourt Publishing Company

FORMER ALLIES CLASH
What caused Soviet-American problems?

The end of World War II saw many countries in Europe devastated economically and militarily. The United States and the Soviet Union were the world's leading nations. They were superpowers, and as such had the strength and influence to shape events. But they had different goals, and these differences made for tension between the two powers.

A major reason for their differences was that the United States followed democratic principles, while the Soviet Union was a totalitarian government. The Soviets were angry that the United States had not recognized their Communist government. Economically, the countries were at odds as well. Under Soviet communism, the state controlled all property and economic activity. In the United States, citizens and corporations controlled economic activity.

The United States was also angry that the Soviet leader, Stalin, had once been an ally of Hitler. Stalin was annoyed that the United States had taken so long to launch an attack against Hitler in Europe. Stalin also did not like that the United States had kept the development of the atomic bomb a secret. Also adding to the tensions was the fact that Stalin refused to allow democracy in Poland and other parts of Eastern Europe. President **Harry S. Truman** reminded Stalin of his promise at Yalta to allow free elections in Eastern Europe. But Stalin would not listen to Truman. He set up Communist governments in the European nations occupied by Soviet troops. They became **satellite nations,** countries that depended on and were dominated by the Soviet Union.

In 1946 Winston Churchill described "an **iron curtain**" coming down across Europe. It separated the nations in the "Soviet sphere" from the capitalist democracies of the West.

1. What were three issues that led to hard feelings between the Soviet Union and the United States?

_____

_____

NEW FOREIGN POLICIES
What did Stalin and Truman want for postwar Europe?

The conflicting aims of the United States and the Soviet Union led to the **Cold War.** This was a state of hostility between these superpowers, but one without military action. Each tried to spread its political and economic influence worldwide.

The United States began to follow a policy of **containment.** This was an effort to block Soviet influence by making alliances and supporting weaker nations. Containment began to guide Truman's foreign policy, which placed the United States in direct opposition to the Soviet Union. The United States provided diplomatic and financial help to countries so they could fight Soviet influence. Later, the United States used military intervention to keep communism out of countries.

To deal with the complex foreign relations of the Cold War, the United States created new intelligence gathering organizations. One agency was the **Central Intelligence Agency (CIA).** It would compile intelligence from the military and state department and perform secret operations in foreign countries.

© Houghton Mifflin Harcourt Publishing Company

Lesson 1, *continued*

2. What methods were used to implement the policy of containment?

_____

_____

EFFORTS TO REBUILD EUROPE
What were the Truman Doctrine and the Marshall Plan?

Truman's first test of containment was when Greece and Turkey needed economic and military aid in 1947. In the **Truman Doctrine,** the president argued that aid should be sent to any nation trying to stop Communists from taking over. Congress agreed. Aid was sent to Turkey and Greece.

Western Europe was also in terrible economic shape. A terrible winter in 1946–1947 increased hardship. Crops were damaged, water transportation was cut off, and there was a fuel shortage. Secretary of State George Marshall wanted to send aid to nations that cooperated with American economic goals. The **Marshall Plan** provided aid to 16 countries and was a great success in rebuilding Western Europe and halting the spread of communism.

3. How did the United States begin to send aid to nations fighting communism?

_____

_____

SUPERPOWERS STRUGGLE OVER GERMANY
How did the Soviets and the West disagree over Germany?

The United States and its allies disagreed with the Soviet Union over German reunification. Allied leaders had originally agreed to leave Germany divided into four zones occupied by the United States, Great Britain, and France in the west and the Soviet Union in the east. The west decided to combine their zones into one nation. Berlin, however, was surrounded by Soviet-occupied territory. The United States, Great Britain, and France, however, had no agreement with the Soviets that would allow them free access to Berlin.

Stalin cut off all transportation to West Berlin. No food or fuel could reach that part of the city.

The United States and Britain started the **Berlin Airlift.** For 327 days, planes brought food and supplies to West Berlin. Finally, the Soviets gave up the blockade.

The western part of Germany became a new nation, the Federal Republic of Germany, or West Germany. It included West Berlin. The Soviet Union then created the German Democratic Republic, called East Germany, and it included East Berlin.

The Berlin blockade made the West worry about Soviet aggression. The United States and Canada joined with ten European nations in a defensive military alliance called the **North Atlantic Treaty Organization (NATO).** Members agreed that an attack on one was an attack on all.

4. What led to the Berlin blockade?

_____

_____

Complete the cause-and-effect diagram with the specific U.S. actions made in response to Soviet actions. Use the following terms in filling out the diagram:

containment   **Truman Doctrine**   **Berlin airlift**   **NATO**

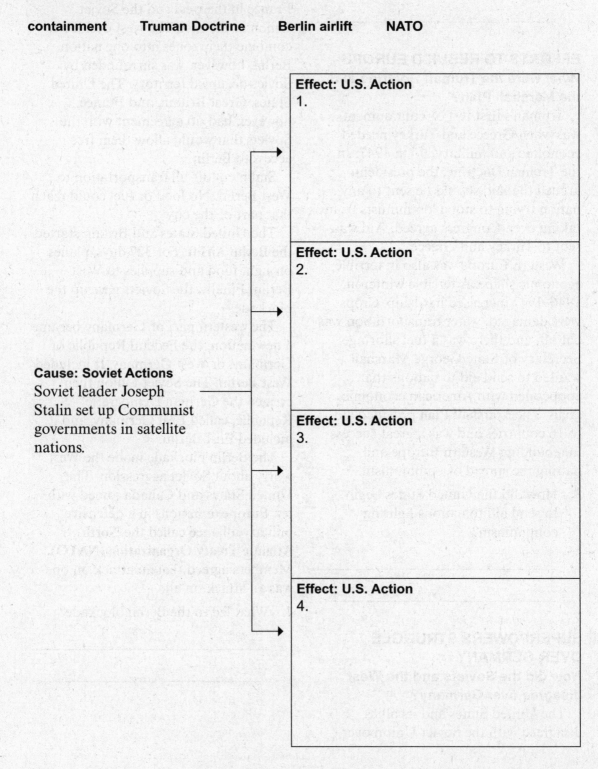

Effect: U.S. Action
1.

Effect: U.S. Action
2.

Cause: Soviet Actions
Soviet leader Joseph Stalin set up Communist governments in satellite nations.

Effect: U.S. Action
3.

Effect: U.S. Action
4.

© Houghton Mifflin Harcourt Publishing Company

The Cold War

The Cold War Heats Up

Key Terms and People

Chiang Kai-shek Leader of the Nationalist forces in China

Mao Zedong Leader of the Communist forces in China

Taiwan Island off the coast of China

38th parallel Imaginary line that divides Korea at 38 degrees north latitude

Korean War War begun when North Korea invaded South Korea in 1950

Before You Read

In the last lesson you read about postwar Europe. In this lesson you will read about the postwar situation in Asia and about the Korean War.

As You Read

Use a chart to take notes on events in China and Korea.

CHINA BECOMES A COMMUNIST COUNTRY
How did the Communists gain control of China?

For two decades, the Chinese Communists struggled against the Nationalist government led by **Chiang Kai-shek.** The United States supported Chiang and sent him aid because he opposed communism. But U.S. officials knew that Chiang's government was inefficient and corrupt. He overtaxed the Chinese people even during times of famine.

Mao Zedong led the Communist forces in the North. He won the support of many Chinese peasants. His forces encouraged peasants to learn to read and helped them improve food production. By 1945 much of northern China was Communist.

President Truman refused to send American troops to help the Nationalists

fight communism. But he did send $2 million worth of military equipment and supplies. Even so, in 1949 Chiang and his forces had to flee to **Taiwan,** an island off the coast of China. The Communists ruled all of mainland China and set up the People's Republic of China, which the United States refused to accept as China's true government.

Americans were stunned that China had become Communist. American conservatives said that the United States had "lost" China because there was not enough help for the Nationalists. Containment had not worked in Asia. Truman's supporters said that the Communist success was because Chiang could not win the support of the Chinese people. Conservatives claimed that the U.S. government was filled with Communist agents. American fear of communism began to burn out of control.

© Houghton Mifflin Harcourt Publishing Company

1. How did Communists gain control of China?

_____

_____

THE KOREAN WAR; THE UNITED STATES FIGHTS IN KOREA
What caused the Korean War?

Japan had ruled Korea since 1910. At the end of World War II, Japanese forces in the north surrendered to the Soviets. In the south, the Japanese surrendered to the Americans. Two nations then developed. They were separated by the **38th parallel,** an imaginary line that divides Korea at 38 degrees north latitude.

In 1948 South Korea became an independent nation. North Korea became a Communist nation.

In June 1950 North Korea started the **Korean War** by invading South Korea. Its efforts were supported by the Soviet Union. Truman was afraid another Asian nation was about to fall to communism. He ordered air and naval support for South Korea. Then, the United Nations agreed to help South Korea. Troops from 16 nations, most of them American, were sent to South Korea. They were led by General Douglas MacArthur.

North Korean troops moved steadily south. They conquered the capital of South Korea, Seoul. Then MacArthur launched a counterattack. His forces trapped about half the North Korean army, which surrendered. MacArthur's success in Korea made him a national hero.

United Nations and South Korean forces advanced toward the 38th parallel. If they crossed it, the war would become an offensive rather than a defensive one. In October 1950 the UN told MacArthur to cross the 38th parallel and reunite Korea.

The Chinese opposed UN forces moving into North Korea. China said it would not let the Americans near its border, and China joined the war on the side of North Korea. Chinese troops drove UN forces southward. In January 1951 the Communists recaptured Seoul.

For two years, fighting continued. MacArthur wanted to extend the war into China. He even suggested using nuclear weapons. Truman was against this strategy. The Soviets were allies of the Chinese. Truman felt bombing China would start World War III.

MacArthur continued to argue for his plan. He spoke to the press and to Republican leaders. Truman felt that he could no longer allow MacArthur's behavior. He fired MacArthur as commander. At first, the American public sided with MacArthur. Later, they came to agree with Truman's idea of a limited war.

Meanwhile, a cease-fire went into effect in June 1951. Both sides agreed on a demilitarized zone at the 38th parallel. An armistice was signed in July 1953. The agreement was a stalemate. Korea was still divided between Communist North Korea and non-Communist South Korea.

Many people felt that American lives and money had been lost for little gain. As a result, the American people rejected the party in power, the Democrats, in the 1952 election. Republican Dwight D. Eisenhower was elected president. Americans also became even more worried about Communist expansion abroad and Communist spies at home.

2. What was gained by the Korean War?

_____

_____

© Houghton Mifflin Harcourt Publishing Company

Lesson 2, *continued*

Complete the chart below by writing answers to the questions in the appropriate boxes.

	Civil War in China	Civil War in Korea
1. Which side did the United States support, and why?		
2. What did the United States do to affect the outcome of the war?		
3. What was the outcome of the war?		
4. How did the American public react to that outcome, and why?		

© Houghton Mifflin Harcourt Publishing Company

Lesson 3

The Cold War at Home

Key Terms and People

House Un-American Activities Committee (HUAC) Committee of the U.S. House of Representatives that investigated people thought to be Communists

Hollywood Ten People called before HUAC who did not cooperate

blacklist List of people in the Hollywood film industry who were refused jobs because they did not cooperate with HUAC

Alger Hiss Former State Department official

Ethel and Julius Rosenberg Activists in the American Communist Party who were executed as spies

Joseph McCarthy Republican senator who claimed Communists were taking over the federal government

McCarthyism Attacks on suspected Communists in the early 1950s

Before You Read

In the last lesson you read about the conflicts with Korea and China. In this lesson you will read about the effects of the Cold War at home.

As You Read

Use a chart to take notes on the ways that anti-Communist fear gripped the United States.

FEAR OF COMMUNIST INFLUENCE
How did Americans react to the threat of Communist influence?

Many Americans felt threatened by Communist governments in Europe and Asia. Some felt that Communists could threaten the government in the United States, too.

Republicans accused the Truman administration of being "soft on communism." So Truman set up a Loyalty Review Board that investigated over 3 million people. About 200 were fired. Many people felt that these investigations were unconstitutional because the accused were not allowed to

see the evidence against them or to face their accusers.

In 1947 Congress set up the **House Un-American Activities Committee (HUAC)** to look for Communists both inside and outside government. HUAC concentrated on the movie industry because of suspected Communist influences in Hollywood and the belief that propaganda was getting into films.

Many people were brought before HUAC. Some agreed that Communists had infiltrated the movie industry.

Ten people called before HUAC refused to testify. They said the hearings were unconstitutional. They were the

Lesson 3, *continued*

Hollywood Ten, and they were accused of disloyalty and of being Communists. They were sent to prison for their refusal.

In response to the HUAC hearings, Hollywood executives named some 500 people they thought were Communists, including the Hollywood Ten. Executives refused to hire people on this **blacklist.** Many people's careers were ruined.

In 1950, Congress passed the McCarran Internal Security Act. It outlawed the planning of any action that might lead to a totalitarian dictatorship in the United States.

1. What are three ways that Americans reacted to fear of communism?

_____

_____

SPY CASES STUN THE NATION
How did spies increase fear of communism?

Two spy cases added to the fear of communism sweeping the nation. One involved State Department official **Alger Hiss.** A former Soviet spy accused Hiss of being a Soviet spy and giving away government documents. He claimed that documents implicated Hiss. Hiss said the documents were forgeries. Too much time had passed for Hiss to be charged with espionage. But he was convicted of perjury, or for lying about the documents, and went to jail.

In 1949 the Soviet Union tested an atomic bomb. A German-born scientist admitted giving the Soviets secret information about the American bomb. He also implicated two Americans: **Ethel and Julius Rosenberg.**

The Rosenbergs were members of the American Communist Party. They denied the charges of spying. But they were convicted and sentenced to death. People appealed for clemency for the Rosenbergs. They said the evidence against them was weak. The Supreme Court refused to overturn the decision. The Rosenbergs were executed in 1953.

2. What two spy cases increased fear of communism in the United States?

_____

_____

MCCARTHY LAUNCHES HIS "WITCH HUNT"
Who was Senator McCarthy?

In the early 1950s Republican senator **Joseph McCarthy** claimed that Communists were taking over the government. He may have been motivated by the desire to be reelected, because he blamed the Democrats for allowing this to occur. McCarthy's accusations fed on the American public's fear and suspicion of communism.

McCarthy never produced any evidence to support his charges. These unsupported attacks on suspected Communists became known as **McCarthyism.** McCarthyism also came to mean the unfair tactic of accusing people of disloyalty without producing evidence.

Many Republicans encouraged McCarthy because they wanted to win the 1952 elections. But some said that McCarthy was violating people's constitutional rights.

In 1954 McCarthy made accusations against the U.S. Army. The Senate hearings were broadcast on national television. People watched McCarthy bully witnesses but produce no evidence. McCarthy lost public favor. The Senate criticized him for improper conduct.

© Houghton Mifflin Harcourt Publishing Company

Guided Reading Workbook

Lesson 3, *continued*

Communist witch hunts in the early 1950s met with much support. Many people were forced to take loyalty oaths to get jobs. States passed laws making it a crime to speak of overthrowing the government, which violated first amendment rights.

3. What are two meanings for the term *McCarthyism*?

_____

_____

Complete the chart below by writing answers to the questions in the appropriate boxes.

	a. What were they accused of?	b. How were they affected by the accusations?	c. Do the accusations seem to have been fair? Explain.
1. The Hollywood Ten			
2. Alger Hiss			
3. Ethel and Julius Rosenberg			

MCCARTHYISM		
4. What seems to have motivated it?	5. Why did it succeed at first?	6. Why did it fall out of favor?

© Houghton Mifflin Harcourt Publishing Company

Guided Reading Workbook

Two Nations Live on the Edge

Key Terms and People

H-bomb Hydrogen bomb

arms race An international contest between countries seeking a military advantage over each other

Dwight D. Eisenhower 34th president of the United States

massive retaliation Strategy that deterred the United States and Soviet Union from launching a nuclear attack

mutually assured destruction Policy that meant that any attack with nuclear force would result in the total destruction of both countries

John Foster Dulles Secretary of state

brinkmanship Willingness to go to the edge of all-out war

Warsaw Pact Military alliance of the Soviet Union and its satellite nations

Eisenhower Doctrine Policy of the United States that it would defend the Middle East against attack by any Communist country

Nikita Khrushchev Soviet leader

Francis Gary Powers Pilot of an American U-2 spy plane

U-2 incident Downing of a U.S. spy plane and the capture of its pilot by the Soviet Union in 1960

Before You Read

In the last lesson you saw how the fear of communism affected life in the United States. In this lesson you will see how Cold War tensions increased as both the United States and the Soviet Union tried to spread their influence around the world.

As You Read

Use a chart to take notes on the involvement of the United States in Cold War trouble spots around the world.

BRINKMANSHIP RULES
U.S. POLICY
What was the arms race?

The Soviet Union exploded its first atomic bomb in 1949. In an effort to maintain an advantage in weaponry, American leaders wanted to develop a more powerful weapon. In 1952 the United States exploded the first hydrogen bomb, or **H-bomb.** The Soviets tested their own H-bomb in 1953.

Leaders in the United States and Soviet Union feared that the other would gain an advantage. This lead to an **arms race,** a contest between countries seeking a military advantage.

Dwight D. Eisenhower was president. His foreign policy focused on leading in the arms race, which would allow for **massive retaliation** strategy. He wanted to discourage the Soviets from launching a nuclear offensive. He vowed to launch a counterstrike to any attack. With both countries having matching nuclear capabilities, any attack would result in total destruction of both superpowers. So neither country was willing to attack the other. This was the policy of **mutually assured destruction.**

Eisenhower's secretary of state, **John Foster Dulles,** was anti-Communist. He said that the United States must be prepared to use all of its nuclear weapons against any aggressor. This willingness to go to the edge of all-out war was called **brinkmanship.**

The United States and Soviet Union began making more nuclear weapons. Many Americans feared a nuclear attack.

The arms race affected the American economy, too. Many weapons were produced, which caused munitions companies to grow. Even President Eisenhower became concerned about increasing defense spending and the growth of these companies.

1. Why did the arms race begin?

_____

_____

THE COLD WAR SPREADS
AROUND THE WORLD
What events increased Cold War tensions?

With growing dependence on nuclear arms, President Eisenhower began to rely on the Central Intelligence Agency (CIA). The CIA used spies to get information abroad. It also carried out covert, or secret, operations to weaken or overthrow governments unfriendly to the United States.

One CIA action involved Iran. In 1951 Iran's prime minister nationalized Iran's oil fields. When Great Britain stopped buying Iranian oil, Iran's economy faltered. Afraid that the Iranians would ask the Soviets for help, the CIA convinced the shah, or monarch, of Iran to get rid of the prime minister. The shah turned over control of Iranian oil fields to the West.

In 1954 the CIA took action in Guatemala. Eisenhower believed Guatemala was friendly to the Communists because it had given acres of American-owned land to peasants. The CIA trained an army that overthrew Guatemala's government.

The U.S. government helped many nations fight communism. In Africa and Asia, the United States offered aid to new African and Asian governments to help convince the new countries to form democratic governments. Some of these new nations felt trapped between the United States and the Soviet Union, so they chose to stay unaligned with either country. Other countries were eager to align, however. Governments in Asia such as the Philippines, Thailand, and Pakistan joined with the United States, France, Britain, Australia, and New Zealand to fight Soviet domination.

Soviet dictator Joseph Stalin died in 1953. At first, tensions eased between the superpowers. People called it a thaw in the Cold War. But when West Germany joined NATO, the Soviet Union formed a military alliance with its satellite nations in 1955. This alliance was called the **Warsaw Pact,** and it was firmly under Soviet control. The Soviets used it to counter NATO threats and to crush internal rebellions.

In 1955 the United States and Great Britain agreed to help Egypt build a dam at Aswan on the Nile River. When Egypt's head of government tried to pit the Soviets against the United States, however, a crisis developed in the Middle East. Egypt seized control of the Suez Canal. The canal was located in Egypt but owned by Britain and France, who had built it. Egypt's leader, Gamal-Abdel Nasser, refused to let ships headed for Israel pass through. Britain, France, and Israel then invaded Egypt to take the canal back. Both the United States and the Soviets objected to the use of force to regain the canal. War was prevented when the UN stepped in to stop the fighting. The troops withdrew, and Egypt was able to keep control of the canal.

During the crisis, Eisenhower issued a warning known as the **Eisenhower Doctrine.** It said the United States would defend the Middle East against Communist attack.

In 1956 the people of Hungary rose in revolt against the Soviet Union and called for a democratic government. The new government promised free elections. When the Hungarians asked to leave the Warsaw Pact in 1956, Soviet tanks rolled into Hungary. They crushed the reform

movement. Many Hungarian reformers were killed, and others fled the country. The United States did nothing to help Hungary because the containment policy did not extend to driving the Soviet Union out of its satellites.

2. How did hostilities increase between the United States and the Soviet Union during the 1950s?

_____

_____

THE COLD WAR TAKES TO THE SKIES
What was the space race?

The Soviet leader, **Nikita Khrushchev,** came to power after Stalin's death. Unlike Stalin, he believed communism could triumph through peaceful means.

On October 4, 1957, the Soviets leaped into an early lead in a competition for prestige that became known as the space race. They shocked the world by launching *Sputnik.* It was the first artificial satellite to orbit the earth. American scientists worked hard to catch up. The first attempt to launch a U.S. satellite was a failure when the rocket toppled to the ground. Finally, on January 31, 1958, the United States successfully launched its first satellite.

Meanwhile, the United States had been flying spy missions over the Soviet Union. The CIA used U-2 aircraft that flew so high they could not be detected. However, by 1960 U.S. officials knew the Soviets were aware of them. On the United States' last flight, pilot **Francis Gary Powers** was shot down and sentenced to ten years in a Soviet prison. Later, he was released in exchange for a Soviet spy.

This event, called the **U-2 incident,** happened right before a meeting between

Lesson 4, *continued*

Eisenhower and Khrushchev. At first, Eisenhower denied the U-2 had been spying, but before the meeting, he had to admit it. At the meeting, Khrushchev criticized the United States and walked out. The U-2 incident hurt Eisenhower's ability to deal with the Soviets.

3. In what two ways was the Cold War fought in the skies?

_____

_____

For each event, write your answer to the question in the appropriate box.

Event	How did the United States react, and why?
1. The Soviet Union exploded its first atomic bomb in 1949.	
2. In 1951 the Iranian prime minister placed the oil industry in Iran under the Iranian government's control.	
3. The Guatemalan head of government gave American-owned land in Guatemala to peasants.	
4. In 1956 Britain, France, and Israel invaded Egypt and occupied the Suez Canal.	
5. Soviet tanks invaded Hungary and fired on protesters in 1956.	
6. In 1957 the Soviet Union launched *Sputnik.*	
7. In 1960 the Soviet Union brought down an American U-2 piloted by Francis Gary Powers.	

© Houghton Mifflin Harcourt Publishing Company

The Cold War

Mounting Tensions in the Sixties

Key Terms and People

John F. Kennedy 35th president of the United States

flexible response Policy of using nonnuclear weapons to fight a war

domino theory Theory that one country falling to Communist influence would quickly lead to other countries in the same area falling, too

Lyndon B. Johnson 36th president of the United States

Fidel Castro Ruler of Cuba

Berlin Wall Barrier built to keep East Germans from fleeing to West Berlin

hot line Direct phone line between the White House and the Kremlin

Limited Test Ban Treaty Treaty that barred nuclear testing in the atmosphere

Nuclear Non-Proliferation Treaty Treaty in which nuclear powers agreed not to sell or give nuclear weapons to any other country

Before You Read

In the last lesson you read about the increase of Cold War tensions. In this lesson you will read about how the Kennedy administration dealt with Soviet confrontations.

As You Read

Provide details for a timeline on events and crises that the Kennedy administration faced.

A NEW MILITARY POLICY; CRISES OVER CUBA
What **two crises involving Cuba did Kennedy face?**

Improvements in the space program were supported by President **John F. Kennedy.** He thought the Soviets were ahead of the United States in technological developments. He also believed that they had the loyalties of economically less-developed third-world countries in Asia, Africa, and Latin America.

Beginning in 1961 Kennedy focused

on foreign affairs. He supported a policy called **flexible response.** This policy called for the use of conventional weapons rather than nuclear weapons in the event of a war. Conventional weapons included jets, tanks, missiles, and guns. To build more conventional weapons, Kennedy increased defense spending. He hoped that this would reduce the risk of nuclear war.

The developing conflict in Vietnam threatened to lead to war. This conflict had been continuing for more than a decade. Vietnam was divided. A

Communist government was in power in the north, and a democratically elected government controlled the south. Kennedy wanted to stop any further spread of communism in Southeast Asia. His policy was based on the **domino theory,** the theory that says that one country falling to Communist influence will quickly lead to other countries in the same area falling as well. After Kennedy's death, **Lyndon B. Johnson** became president and continued Kennedy's policies. He, too, was determined to contain communism in Vietnam, and ended up sending U.S. soldiers there.

President Kennedy faced a Communist government close to the United States in Cuba. Cuba's leader was **Fidel Castro.** Castro had seized power in 1959. Soon after that, he declared himself a Communist. He then formed ties with the Soviet Union.

The United States was wary of Castro, but it did recognize Cuba's government. However, Castro seized three American and British oil refineries, and relations worsened. Castro also broke up commercial farms into communes to be worked by peasants. American sugar companies controlled this cropland, so the United States established trade barriers against Cuban sugar.

Castro used Soviet aid and political repression to put his reforms into place. Many Cubans went into exile and came to the United States.

American leaders were afraid of a Communist government so close to the United States. Kennedy approved a plan to remove Castro from power. The plan called for Cuban exiles to invade Cuba and overthrow Castro. The U.S. government would supply air support for the exiles.

The attack failed. Many exiles were captured. The failed invasion became

known as the Bay of Pigs. It left the Kennedy administration greatly embarrassed.

A year later, the United States and Cuba clashed again. Pictures from U.S. spy planes revealed that the Soviets were building nuclear missile bases in Cuba. Some bases already contained missiles ready to launch. These weapons could be aimed at the United States

President Kennedy demanded that the Soviets remove the missiles. In October 1962 he surrounded Cuba with U.S. Navy ships. These ships forced Soviet vessels trying to reach Cuba to turn around. A tense standoff followed. It appeared that war might break out. However, Soviet leader Nikita Khrushchev finally agreed to remove the missiles.

This standoff, which became known as the Cuban missile crisis, damaged Khrushchev's prestige in the Soviet Union and the world. Kennedy also endured criticism. Some Americans thought Kennedy had acted too boldly and nearly started a nuclear war. Others claimed he hadn't acted boldly enough. These critics believed that Kennedy should have invaded Cuba and ousted Castro.

1. Name the two Cuban crises that the Kennedy administration faced.

_____

_____

U.S.-SOVIET TENSIONS
How did the Americans and Soviets try to ease tensions?

In 1961 Kennedy faced a growing problem in Berlin. The city was still divided. East Berlin was under Communist control. West Berlin was under the control of Great Britain,

© Houghton Mifflin Harcourt Publishing Company

France, and the United States. By 1961 almost 3 million East Germans had fled into West Berlin.

Khrushchev threatened to sign a treaty with East Germany that would block all air and land routes into West Berlin. Kennedy warned the Soviet leader against such action. As a result, Khrushchev changed his plan. Instead, he built a large concrete barrier along the border between East and West Berlin. It was known as the **Berlin Wall.** It prevented any more East Germans from fleeing to West Berlin. The construction of the Berlin Wall heightened Cold War tensions and became a symbol of Communist oppression.

Despite their battles, Kennedy and Khrushchev did attempt to reach agreements. They established a **hot line** between their two nations. This special telephone hookup connected Kennedy and Khrushchev. It allowed them to talk directly when a crisis arose. The two leaders also agreed to a **Limited Test Ban Treaty.** This treaty barred nuclear testing in the atmosphere.

By the late 1960s the world feared nuclear catastrophe. The United Kingdom, France, and China also had tested nuclear weapons. Some world leaders feared what would happen as developing nations developed weapons, too. So world leaders agreed to try to limit the spread of nuclear weapons. Representatives from more than 60 countries signed the **Nuclear Non-Proliferation Treaty.** Nuclear powers agreed not to sell or give nuclear weapons to any other country. Non-nuclear powers promised not to acquire such weapons.

2. Name two ways the United States and Soviet Union worked to ease tensions between them.

_____

_____

THE SPACE RACE CONTINUES
Why did the Americans and Soviets compete in space exploration?

In the 1950s the Soviets had launched the first artificial satellite. Americans did the same shortly after. Then, in 1961 the Soviets launched a person into orbit around the earth. President Kennedy felt this was a challenge, so he pledged that the nation would put a man on the moon by the end of the decade. First, however, the United States successfully launched a man, Alan Shepard, into space. Then, America's National Aeronautics and Space Administration (NASA) constructed facilities to aid space exploration. And on July 20, 1969, astronaut Neil Armstrong stepped onto the moon. The United States had surpassed the Soviets!

3. Why was it so important for the United States to be the first to send a person to the moon?

_____

_____

Lesson 5, *continued*

Provide information for the timeline by answering questions on crises
or events that occurred during the 1960s.

1960	Alignment of Cuba with the Soviet Union	→	1. How did the domino theory influence Kennedy's foreign policy in Cuba?
1961	Bay of Pigs	→	2. What were the results of the Bay of Pigs invasion?
	Construction of the Berlin Wall	→	3. Why was the Berlin Wall built?
1962	Cuban missile crisis	→	4. What were the effects of the Cuban missile crisis?
1963	Installation of hot line	→	5. Why was the hot line installed?
	Negotiation of Limited Test Ban Treaty/Nuclear Non-Proliferation Treaty	→	6. What would the Limited Test Ban Treaty and the Nuclear Non-Proliferation Treaty eventually do?

© Houghton Mifflin Harcourt Publishing Company

The Cold War

The End of the Cold War

Key Terms and People

Richard M. Nixon 37th president of the United States

Henry Kissinger Nixon's secretary of state

realpolitik Nixon's foreign policy that attempted "realistic politics"

détente Policy aimed at easing Cold War tensions

SALT I Treaty Treaty to limit nuclear weapons

Gerald R. Ford 38th president of the United States

Jimmy Carter 39th president of the United States

Ronald Reagan 40th president of the United States

Mikhail Gorbachev Last leader of the Soviet Union

Strategic Defense Initiative A special defense system that was meant to keep Americans safe from enemy missiles

glasnost Gorbachev's policy of openness in discussing problems in the Soviet Union

perestroika Gorbachev's policy of reforming the economy in the Soviet Union

INF Treaty Treaty to reduce nuclear weapons

Before You Read

In the last lesson you learned about tensions between the United States, the Soviet Union, and other countries during the 1960s. In this lesson you will see how American foreign policy changed during the later part of the 20th century.

As You Read

Use a chart to take notes about U.S. foreign policy of each president.

NIXON'S FOREIGN POLICY TRIUMPHS
What is realpolitik?

Richard M. Nixon became president in 1969. Nixon's main foreign policy adviser was **Henry Kissinger,** who later became his secretary of state. Kissinger based his foreign policy views on a philosophy known as **realpolitik.** This meant that foreign policy should be based on consideration of power, not ideals or moral principles. Kissinger believed it was practical to ignore a country that was weak. But it was important to deal with strong nations.

Realpolitik was a change from the policy of containment. Nixon and Kissinger changed U.S. relations with

© Houghton Mifflin Harcourt Publishing Company

Guided Reading Workbook

Communist countries by trying to ease poor relations. They called their policy **détente.** This policy was aimed at ending Cold War tensions.

In 1972 Nixon visited Communist China. Before this, the United States had refused to recognize the Communist government. Three months later, Nixon went to the Soviet Union. Nixon and the Soviet leader signed the **SALT I Treaty.** This five-year agreement limited nuclear weapons. Nixon's successes in foreign affairs helped him win reelection.

Nixon had the CIA begin covert operations in Chile to stop the threat of communism in that country. He also sent military aid to Israel. Kissinger attempted to forge a peace agreement in the Middle East. Eventually, Israel signed a cease-fire with Egypt and then with Syria.

1. How did Nixon try to ease Cold War tensions?

_____

_____

FORD CONFRONTS THE COLD WAR
What did Ford do as president?

Gerald R. Ford replaced Richard Nixon as president. Like Nixon, he continued a foreign policy focused on stopping the spread of communism. He also kept Henry Kissinger on as secretary of state.

Ford continued talks with China and the Soviet Union. In 1974 he participated in a meeting in Helsinki, Finland. There, 35 countries, including the Soviet Union, signed the Helsinki Accords. These were agreements that promised greater cooperation between the nations of Europe.

Trouble continued in Southeast Asia. Fighting continued in South Vietnam, and Ford asked Congress for funds to help the South Vietnamese against the Communist North Vietnamese. Congress refused, and South Vietnam surrendered to the North in 1975. Then when Communist Cambodia seized U.S. merchant ships, Ford ordered air strikes against Cambodia.

Problems occurred in another continent for Ford: Africa. American forces took part in a civil war in Angola. The country was governed by three political organizations, and each wanted power. Angola's struggle became an international affair with the United States supporting two of the three warring factions, and the Soviet Union and China backing the third. Congress refused to get involved in another foreign war. A Marxist government took control of Angola.

2. Why did Ford want to become involved in conflicts in Vietnam and Angola?

_____

_____

A NEW DIRECTION UNDER CARTER
Why did Carter and the Soviet leader clash?

Ford ran for election in 1976 against Democrat **Jimmy Carter.** Carter ran as an outsider, or someone apart from Washington politics. Carter had a deep interest in human rights, and that influenced his foreign policy. It was this insistence on human rights that led to a breakdown in relations with the Soviet Union. He did not like the way the Soviet Union treated opponents of its government. So he delayed negotiations for a second SALT agreement.

Eventually, in 1979 Carter and Soviet premier Leonid Brezhnev signed SALT II. It was meant to limit the number of strategic weapons and nuclear-missile launchers that each side could produce. But the treaty met with opposition in the Senate. When the Soviets invaded Afghanistan in December 1979, Carter withdrew his support for the agreement. It was never ratified.

3. What was Carter's foreign policy based on?

_____

_____

REAGAN AND THE END OF THE COLD WAR
What ended the Cold War?

Ronald Reagan became president in 1980. He was fiercely opposed to communism. As president, he helped end the Cold War. He formed a relationship with **Mikhail Gorbachev,** the general secretary of the Communist Party in the Soviet Union.

Reagan increased U.S. defense spending, hoping to bankrupt the Soviets. He had plans to add nuclear warheads to the U.S. arsenal. He asked scientists to develop a special defense system. He did this as part of a **Strategic Defense Initiative,** a system designed to keep Americans safe from enemy missiles. Reagan's position made relations with the Soviets worse. They ended arms control talks.

Within the Soviet Union, Gorbachev supported *glasnost* (openness in discussing social problems) and *perestroika* (economic restructuring) in

the Soviet Union. He let private citizens own land. He also allowed more free speech and held free elections. He knew that better relations with the United States would allow the Soviets to reduce their military spending and help the economy. Reagan saw that Gorbachev's leadership was different from other leaders. He was willing to negotiate.

Talks led to the **INF Treaty** (Intermediate-Range Nuclear Forces Treaty). Reagan and Gorbachev signed the treaty in December 1987. The Senate ratified it in May 1988.

Gorbachev encouraged the people of East Germany and Eastern Europe to go their own ways. He encouraged satellite nations to move toward democracy.

Gorbachev's reforms and a weak economy led to the collapse of the Soviet Union. All the republics that were in the Soviet Union became independent nations. Then they formed a loose confederation called the Commonwealth of Independent States.

The collapse of the Soviet Union ended the Cold War. In January 1993 Russia and the United States signed the START II treaty. This treaty cut both nations' nuclear weapons by two-thirds. By now, George H.W. Bush was president. In December 1993 Russian voters installed a new parliament and approved a new constitution, parts of which resembled the U.S. Constitution.

4. What events in the Soviet Union led to the end of the Cold War?

_____

_____

Complete the chart with the foreign policies of each president. Some
items have been filled in for you.

Nixon's Foreign Policy	What It Was	How Achieved
1. China and Soviet Union		
2. Chile		the Central Intelligence Agency began covert operations
3. Middle East		

Ford's Foreign Policy	What It Was	How Achieved
4. Soviet Union and other European countries	similar to Nixon's	
5. Southeast Asia		
6. Africa		

Carter's Foreign Policy	What It Was	How Achieved
7. Soviet Union		

Reagan's Foreign Policy	What It Was	How Achieved
8. Soviet Union		

© Houghton Mifflin Harcourt Publishing Company

The Postwar Boom

Postwar America

Key Terms and People

GI Bill of Rights Law passed by Congress that provided financial and educational benefits for World War II veterans

suburb Residential town or community near a city

Harry S. Truman President after World War II

Dixiecrat Southern Democrat who left the party

Fair Deal President Truman's economic and social program

Before You Read

In the last lesson, you read about the end of the Cold War. In this lesson, you will read about the economic boom in the United States after World War II.

As You Read

Organize your notes in a chart as you identify solutions to problems in postwar America.

READJUSTMENT AND RECOVERY
How did the end of World War II affect America?

After World War II, millions of returning veterans used the **GI Bill of Rights** to get an education and to buy homes. At first, there was a terrible housing shortage. Then developers such as William Levitt built thousands of mass-produced homes in the **suburbs,** small residential communities near the cities. These new homes were numerous and affordable. Many veterans and their families moved in.

During the war, many women worked and made decisions. They did not want to give up these roles when their husbands returned. This led to a rising divorce rate.

At the end of the war, the United States changed from a wartime to a peacetime economy. Many defense workers were laid off. Returning veterans added to unemployment. When wartime price controls ended, prices shot up. Congress eventually put back economic controls on wages, prices, and rents.

The economy began to improve on its own. There was a huge demand for consumer goods. People had been too poor to buy these goods during the Depression. Many items had not been available during the war. Now Americans bought cars, appliances, and houses. The Cold War increased defense spending and employment.

1. What were three effects of the end of World War II on American society?

_____

_____

© Houghton Mifflin Harcourt Publishing Company

Lesson 1, *continued*

MEETING ECONOMIC CHALLENGES; SOCIAL UNREST PERSISTS
What were postwar problems?

President **Harry S. Truman** faced several problems immediately after the war. One was labor unrest. In 1946 steel workers, coal miners, and railroad workers went out on strike.

Truman was pro-labor, but he would not let strikes cripple the nation. He threatened to draft striking workers into the army and order them back to work. Unions gave in.

Before the economy improved, many Americans were upset with shortages, rising inflation, and strikes. Voters became more conservative. In the 1946 election, conservative Republicans gained control of Congress.

Racial violence erupted in the South. African American veterans demanded their rights. Truman met with African American leaders. They asked for a federal antilynching law, an end to the poll tax, and a permanent civil rights commission.

Congress would not pass any of the civil rights measures. So Truman acted on his own. In 1948 he issued an executive order to desegregate the armed forces. He also ordered an end to discrimination in hiring government employees.

Meanwhile, the Supreme Court said African Americans could not be kept from living in certain neighborhoods. These acts marked the beginning of a federal commitment to deal with racial issues.

Truman was nominated for president in 1948. Because of his civil rights views, there was a split in the Democratic Party. Many Southern Democrats, or **Dixiecrats,** were against civil rights. They formed the States' Rights

Democratic Party. Some Democratic Party liberals at the far left side were unhappy too. They formed a more liberal Progressive Party.

Opinion polls showed that Truman was losing. So he fought harder. He asked the Republican-controlled Congress to pass laws for public housing, aid to education, a higher minimum wage, and more Social Security. Congress did nothing. So he took his ideas to the people, criticizing the "do-nothing" Congress. He won a narrow victory. Democrats took control of Congress.

Truman tried to pass reforms. He called his program the **Fair Deal.** Health insurance and a crop-subsidy program for farmers met with defeat by Congress. However, Congress passed an increase in the minimum wage, extension of Social Security, and financial aid for cities.

2. What were some issues Truman fought for?

_____

_____

REPUBLICANS TAKE THE MIDDLE ROAD
Why did Eisenhower win?

Truman did not run for reelection in 1952. Major issues of that campaign were the stalemate in the Korean War and anti-Communist hysteria and McCarthyism. The Republicans nominated war hero General Dwight D. Eisenhower, popularly known as "Ike." He easily beat Democrat Adlai Stevenson.

Eisenhower followed middle-of-the-road policies and avoided controversy. However, two major civil rights events occurred while he was in office. In 1954 the Supreme Court ruled in *Brown* v.

© Houghton Mifflin Harcourt Publishing Company

Board of Education that public schools could not be segregated. Then Rosa Parks refused to give up her seat on a bus to a white man. She was arrested, which led to a boycott of the Montgomery, Alabama, bus system.

Eisenhower was a popular president. He did not lead on civil rights, but he did many other things, including balancing the budget and creating the Department of Health, Education, and Welfare. During his two terms Ike's administration raised the minimum wage, extended Social Security and unemployment benefits, increased funding for public housing, and backed the creation of interstate highways.

3. What two important civil rights actions occurred during Eisenhower's presidency?

_____

_____

Complete the chart by explaining the solutions offered to deal with postwar problems.

Problem	Solution	Who Solved
1. Millions of veterans don't have jobs as they return to civilian life		Truman administration and Congress
2. Severe housing shortage		Developers such as William Levitt
3. Rising prices and inflation		Truman administration and Congress
4. Labor strikes that threaten to cripple the nation		Truman administration
5. Discrimination and racial violence		Truman and Supreme Court
6. Low worker wages		Truman and Eisenhower administrations

© Houghton Mifflin Harcourt Publishing Company

The Postwar Boom

The American Dream in the Fifties

Key Terms and People

conglomerate Major corporation that owns smaller companies in unrelated industries

franchise Company that offers similar products or services in many locations

baby boom Soaring birthrate from 1946 to 1964

Dr. Jonas Salk Developer of a vaccine to prevent polio

consumerism Excessive concern with buying material goods

planned obsolescence Purposely making products to become outdated or wear out quickly

Before You Read

In the last lesson you read about the postwar boom in the United States. In this lesson you will read how while many Americans achieved their dreams of material comfort and prosperity, some found the cost of conformity too high.

As You Read

Use a chart to take notes on specific trends that affected Americans of the 1950s.

THE ORGANIZATION AND THE ORGANIZATION MAN
***What* changes took place in the American workplace in the 1950s?**

Businesses expanded during the 1950s as companies merged and formed larger corporations. Machines were used to complete certain jobs, so the number of blue-collar, or industrial, jobs decreased. Professional and service, or white-collar, jobs grew.

Large corporations grew even larger when they formed **conglomerates,** or major corporations that own smaller companies in unrelated industries. Other businesses expanded by franchising. A **franchise** is a company that offers

similar products or services in many locations, such as fast-food restaurants.

Some large companies offered well-paying, secure jobs to workers willing to give up their individuality. These workers were "company people" who would fit in and not rock the boat. Businesses rewarded loyalty rather than creativity. They promoted a sameness, or standardization, of people as well as products. Books such as *The Organization Man* criticized this conformity.

Union membership grew in the 1950s as unions fought for and won automatic pay raises tied to the rate of inflation. However, when newspapers reported

© Houghton Mifflin Harcourt Publishing Company

corruption and tied some unions to organized crime, support for unions fell.

1. What changes occurred in the American work force and workplace in the 1950s?

_____

_____

THE SUBURBAN LIFESTYLE
What was life like in the 1950s?

Many Americans enjoyed the benefits of the booming economy. Many worked in cities but lived in suburbs. They had the American dream of a single-family home, good schools, and a safe neighborhood with people just like them.

There was an increase in births called the **baby boom.** It was caused by the reuniting of families after the war and by growing prosperity. Medical advances also wiped out some childhood diseases. **Dr. Jonas Salk** developed a vaccine to prevent polio, which often struck children.

The baby boom created a need for more children's products, such as toys, and for schools. Congress passed legislation to fund loans for college students and to provide for improved science, math, and foreign language instruction in elementary and secondary schools.

Many parents depended on advice from a popular baby-care book by Dr. Benjamin Spock. He said it was important that mothers stay at home with their children. The role of homemaker and mother was also glorified in the media. But many women felt alone and bored at home.

By 1960, 40 percent of mothers worked outside the home. But their career opportunities usually were limited

to office support, nursing, and teaching. Even if women did the same work as men, they were paid less. Some women attended colleges, but they received little aid.

Americans had more leisure time. Suburban life encouraged conformity. Many families participated in the same social activities as their neighbors. They spent time and money on leisure activities, such as sports. They watched sports on television. They read books and magazines. Youth activities, such as scouting and Little League, became popular, too.

2. What was life like in the suburbs in the 1950s?

_____

_____

THE AUTOMOBILE CULTURE
Why were cars so important?

Easy credit for buying cars, and the low price of gasoline, led to a boom in automobile ownership. Between the 1950s and 1960s, the number of American cars on the road grew from 40 million to more than 60 million.

A car was a necessity in the suburbs because there was no public transportation. People had to drive to their jobs in the cities. They also had to drive to shop and do errands. Therefore, more and better roads were needed. In 1956 the United States began building a nationwide highway network. In turn, these roads allowed long-distance trucking. This led to a decline in the use of railroads.

Americans loved to drive. They went to drive-in restaurants and movies. They drove long distances on vacation. Motels and shopping malls were built to serve them. These new industries were

© Houghton Mifflin Harcourt Publishing Company

Lesson 2, *continued*

good for the economy. But the increase in driving also caused problems. These included stressful traffic jams and noise and air pollution. Many white people left the cities. Jobs and industries followed. This left mostly poor people in crowded inner cities.

3. How did cars change American life?

_____

_____

CONSUMERISM UNBOUND
Why did Americans turn to consumerism in the 1950s?

By the mid-1950s, nearly 60 percent of Americans were in the middle class. They had the money to buy more and more products. They measured success by their **consumerism,** or the amount of material goods they bought.

American business flooded stores with new products. Consumers bought household appliances like washing machines, dryers, and dishwashers, and recreational items such as television sets, barbecue grills, and swimming pools.

Manufacturers also tried a new marketing strategy called **planned obsolescence.** They purposely made products to become outdated or to wear out quickly. Americans began to throw away items to buy "new models." Easy credit, including the introduction of credit cards, encouraged people to buy. Private debt grew.

The 1950s were "the advertising age." Ads were everywhere including television. They tried to persuade Americans to buy things they didn't need. They appealed to people's desire for status.

4. How was consumerism encouraged in the 1950s?

_____

_____

Fill in the chart to describe how Americans were affected by various trends of the 1950s.

LIFE IN THE 1950S

Trends	Effects
1. Business expansion: conglomerates and franchises	
2. Suburban expansion: flight from the cities	
3. Population growth: the baby boom	
4. Dramatic increase in leisure time	
5. Dramatic increase in the use of the automobile	
6. The rise of consumerism	

© Houghton Mifflin Harcourt Publishing Company

The Postwar Boom

Popular Culture

Key Terms and People

mass media Means of communication that reach large audiences

Federal Communications Commission (FCC) Government agency that regulates the communications industry

beat movement Writers who made fun of the conformity and materialism of mainstream American society

rock 'n' roll Form of popular music, characterized by heavy rhythms and simple melodies, that developed from rhythm and blues in the 1950s

jazz A style of music characterized by improvisation

Before You Read

In the last lesson you read about the American dream in the 1950s. In this lesson you will read that popular culture in the 1950s reflected white, middle-class America, and a subculture challenged that conformity.

As You Read

Use your notes to create a chart on innovations and trends in the 1950s.

NEW ERA OF MASS MEDIA
What influence did TV have?

Mass media, or the means of communication that reach large audiences, include radio, television, newspapers, and magazines. Television became the most important means of communication in the 1950s. It both showed and influenced popular culture of the time.

The number of homes with televisions jumped. It went from 9 percent of all homes in 1950 to 90 percent in 1960. At first, the number of television stations was limited by the **Federal Communications Commission (FCC).** The FCC is the government agency that regulates the communications industry.

Soon, however, TV stations spread across the country. Many shows became widely popular all over the nation.

The 1950s were the "golden age" of television. Comedy shows starring Milton Berle and Lucille Ball were popular. Edward R. Murrow introduced on-the-scene reporting and interviews. There were also westerns, sports events, and original dramas, as well as children's shows such as *The Mickey Mouse Club* and *The Howdy Doody Show.*

Advertisers took advantage of this new medium. Businesses also created new products related to television. TV magazines and TV dinners, which are frozen meals to heat and eat, became popular.

© Houghton Mifflin Harcourt Publishing Company

Television reflected the mainstream values of white suburban America. These values were secure jobs, material success, well-behaved children, and conformity. Critics objected to the stereotypes of women and minorities. Women were shown as happy, ideal mothers. African Americans and Latinos hardly appeared at all. In short, TV showed an idealized white America. It ignored poverty, diversity, and problems such as racism.

As dramas and comedies moved to TV, radio changed. It began to focus on news, weather, music, and local issues. The radio industry did well. Advertising increased and so did the number of stations.

The movie industry suffered from competition by television. The number of moviegoers dropped by almost 50 percent. But Hollywood fought back. It responded by using color, stereophonic sound, and the wide screen to create spectacular movies.

1. Was the picture of America portrayed on television accurate?

_____

_____

A SUBCULTURE EMERGES
What were the beat movement and rock 'n' roll?

Television showed the suburban way of life. But two subcultures presented other points of view. One was the **beat movement.** It was centered in San Francisco, Los Angeles, and Greenwich Village in New York City. These writers, artists, and poets made fun of the conformity of mainstream American society and rebelled against consumerism.

Their followers were called beats or beatniks. They did not hold steady jobs and lived inexpensively. They read their poetry in coffeehouses. Their art and poetry had a free, open form. Major works of the beat generation include Allen Ginsberg's long poem *Howl* and Jack Kerouac's novel *On the Road.*

Many Americans were not impressed by this lifestyle. However, many college students were attracted to it.

2. How did the beat movement criticize mainstream culture?

_____

_____

AFRICAN AMERICANS AND ROCK 'N' ROLL
What role did African American artists play in the 1950s?

Some African American musicians took a new direction. They added electronic instruments to blues music to create rhythm and blues. From this came a new music that combined rhythm and blues and country and pop. It was **rock 'n' roll.** The new music was for all races because it was American music.

Rock 'n' roll had a strong rhythm, simple melodies, and lyrics that focused on the interests of teenagers, including love, cars, and the problems of being young. Teenagers bought the records of Chuck Berry, Bill Haley and the Comets, and most notably, Elvis Presley. He was the unofficial "King of Rock 'n' Roll" with 45 songs that sold over 1 million copies.

Some adults criticized rock 'n' roll. They said it would lead to teenage crime and immorality. But television and radio still brought rock 'n' roll into the mainstream.

Many great performers of the 1950s were African American, and their music

© Houghton Mifflin Harcourt Publishing Company

appealed to all races. Singers in other genres included Nat "King" Cole, Lena Horne, and Harry Belafonte. **Jazz** musicians like Miles Davis and Dizzy Gillespie also entertained audiences.

Before integration reached radio audiences, there were stations aimed specifically at African American listeners. They played popular black artists and served advertisers who wanted to reach black audiences.

3. How did African Americans influence the 1950s entertainment industry?

_____

_____

Lesson 3, *continued*

Answer questions about innovations and trends in 1950s popular culture.

1.	Television	a. Who were two popular TV comedians? Who introduced on-the-scene reporting?	b. What kinds of subjects did television tend to present?	c. What kinds of subjects did it tend to avoid?
2.	Radio	a. How did radio change to compete with television?	b. What role did it play in popularizing African American culture?	
3.	Film	How did movies change to compete with television?		
4.	The beat movement	a. Who were two famous beat writers?	b. What were the movement's chief characteristics?	
5.	Rock 'n' roll	a. Who helped to popularize rock 'n' roll? What media helped it reach the mainstream?	b. What were rock 'n' roll's chief characteristics?	

© Houghton Mifflin Harcourt Publishing Company

The Other America

Key Terms and People

urban renewal Plan to tear down rundown neighborhoods and build low-income housing

termination policy Federal government decision to end its responsibility for Native American tribes

---

Before You Read

In the last lesson you read about popular culture in the 1950s. In this lesson you will read about Americans who were not part of the American mainstream.

As You Read

Use a diagram to take notes on the solutions offered for problems faced by some Americans in the 1950s.

THE CHALLENGES OF POVERTY
What was the plight of the poor?

Prosperity reached many Americans in the 1950s. But it did not reach all Americans. In 1962 about one out of every four Americans was poor. Many of these poor people were members of minority groups.

Loss of income along with new farm technology led farm owners to hire fewer workers. Many unemployed farmworkers moved to U.S. cities. For example, many African Americans in the South moved from rural areas to cities in the North.

In the 1950s millions of middle-class white people left the cities for the suburbs. This was called "white flight." Many cities became largely African American. Businesses—and jobs—followed whites out of the cities. Cities also lost the taxes these people and businesses had paid. City governments

could no longer afford to keep up the quality of schools, public transportation, or other services. The urban poor suffered as their neighborhoods decayed.

A large number of poor people in cities lived below the poverty line. Many suburban, middle-class Americans could not believe that a country as rich as the United States had such poverty in its cities. However, Michael Harrington's 1962 book, *The Other America: Poverty in the United States,* made many Americans aware of the problem.

Many people in the city were forced to live in dirty and crowded slums. One way the government tried to solve the problem of the inner cities was called **urban renewal.** The National Housing Act of 1949 promised better living conditions for all Americans

Urban renewal was designed to tear down decaying neighborhoods and build

---

© Houghton Mifflin Harcourt Publishing Company

better housing. However, sometimes highways and shopping centers were built instead. The people who had lived in the old slums ended up moving to other slums—rather than into better housing.

1. What were some reasons for the decay of America's inner cities?

   _____

   _____

POVERTY LEADS TO ACTIVISM
How were Mexican Americans and Native Americans treated?

During World War II, there was a shortage of laborers to harvest crops. The federal government allowed *braceros,* or hired hands, to enter the United States from Mexico. They were supposed to work on American farms during the war and then go back to Mexico. However, when the war ended, many braceros stayed illegally. Many other Mexicans entered the United States illegally to find jobs.

Mexican Americans suffered prejudice and discrimination, too, even though they were citizens. When Mexican American veterans came home from the war, they wanted to be treated fairly. The fact that a Mexican American war hero was denied burial in a cemetery in his hometown showed that this did not always happen. A group of Mexican Americans formed the American GI Forum to protest such injustices. The war hero was buried in Arlington National Cemetery due to their efforts. They also gained military benefits for Hispanic veterans. Other groups, such as the Unity League of California, worked to help Mexican Americans register to vote and encouraged Mexican Americans to run for office.

Native Americans also struggled for equal rights. This struggle was complicated by federal involvement in Native American affairs. At first, the government had supported assimilation, or absorbing Native Americans into mainstream culture. That forced Native Americans to give up their own culture. In 1934 the Indian Reorganization Act changed that policy. The government now wanted Native Americans to have more control over their own affairs.

In 1944 Native Americans formed the National Congress of American Indians to work for their civil rights and for the right to keep their own customs. After World War II, Native Americans got less financial help from the government. Outsiders grabbed tribal lands for mining and development.

In 1953 the federal government decided to end its responsibility for Native American tribes. This **termination policy** stopped federal economic support. It also ended the reservation system and distributed tribal land among individual Native Americans. As part of the termination policy, the Bureau of Indian Affairs also moved thousands of Native Americans to the cities.

This termination program was a failure, however. Native Americans did not have the skills to succeed in the cities. They were cut off from medical care. They also suffered job discrimination. The termination policy was ended in 1963.

2. How did Mexican Americans and Native Americans work for equal rights after World War II?

   _____

   _____

© Houghton Mifflin Harcourt Publishing Company

Lesson 4, *continued*

Fill in causes of each problem, solutions that were offered, and effects
of those solutions. Two items have been done for you.

Problem: Decaying Cities		
1. Causes:	Solution Offered: urban renewal	2. Effects of solution:

Problem: Discrimination Against Mexican Americans		
Causes: Prejudice against Hispanics; hard feelings toward braceros who stayed to work in the United States after World War II	3. Solutions offered:	
	4. Effects of Solutions:	

Problem: Economic Hardship for Native Americans		
5. Causes:	6. Solutions offered:	7. Effects of solutions:

© Houghton Mifflin Harcourt Publishing Company

An Era of Social Change

Kennedy and the New Frontier

Key Terms and People

John F. Kennedy 35th president of the United States

New Frontier The name given to Kennedy's domestic program

mandate An overwhelming show of support by voters

Peace Corps A program that enlisted volunteers to help in poor countries

Alliance for Progress A program that supplied aid to Latin America

Warren Commission The body that investigated the assassination of President Kennedy

Before You Read

In the last lesson you read about Americans who were not part of the American mainstream. In this lesson you will read about John F. Kennedy's election, domestic agenda, and assassination.

As You Read

Complete a chart about Kennedy's New Frontier programs.

THE ELECTION OF 1960; THE CAMELOT YEARS
How did Kennedy win the election?

In 1960 President Eisenhower's second term ended. By then, many Americans were worried about the future. The economy was in a recession, and the Soviet Union was gaining strength. Some people worried that the United States was losing the Cold War.

John F. Kennedy and Richard M. Nixon faced off in the 1960 presidential election. Kennedy was a Democratic senator from Massachusetts. Nixon was Eisenhower's vice-president. Kennedy won the election by a slim margin. Two main factors led him to victory.

During a televised debate, Kennedy impressed viewers. He looked and spoke better than Nixon.

The second factor was Kennedy's

response to the arrest of Dr. Martin Luther King Jr. in October 1960. Kennedy called King's wife to express sympathy, and Robert Kennedy persuaded the judge to release King from jail. These actions won him the support of African Americans.

President Kennedy and his wife Jacqueline fascinated many Americans. The Kennedy Administration reminded some of a modern-day Camelot, the mythical court of King Arthur. Kennedy surrounded himself with advisers that one journalist called "the best and brightest."

1. What two factors helped Kennedy win the 1960 presidential election?

_____

_____

THE PROMISE OF PROGRESS
What were Kennedy's domestic plans?

President Kennedy called his domestic program the **New Frontier.** However, he had a difficult time getting Congress to support it. Conservative Republicans and southern Democrats blocked many bills, including bills to provide medical care for the aged, to rebuild cities, and to aid education.

One reason for Kennedy's difficulties was that he was elected by a small margin. As a result, he lacked a popular **mandate,** or a clear indication that the voters approved of his plans. So Kennedy rarely pushed hard for his bills.

Kennedy did succeed with some plans. To help the economy grow, his advisers pushed for the use of deficit spending, which occurs when the government spends more money than it receives in taxes. Kennedy hoped that increased spending and lower taxes would boost the economy. Congress increased defense spending and the minimum wage. It extended unemployment insurance and provided help to cities with high unemployment.

Kennedy introduced the **Peace Corps,** a program of volunteers working in poor nations around the world. Its purpose was to decrease poverty abroad. It was also meant to increase goodwill toward the United States. The Peace Corps was a huge success. People of all ages and backgrounds volunteered. By 1968 more than 35,000 volunteers had served in 60 nations around the world. The program continues today with volunteers using technology in their work in the world's countries. A second program was the **Alliance for Progress,** which gave economic and technical aid to Latin American countries.

In addition to addressing poverty abroad, President Kennedy began to focus on this and other issues at home. In 1963 he asked for a "national assault on poverty." He also wanted to deal with discrimination, so he told the Justice Department to look into racial injustices in the South. He also sent a civil rights bill and a tax cut proposal to Congress.

2. Name two successful programs of the Kennedy administration.

_____

_____

TRAGEDY IN DALLAS
Who killed President Kennedy?

On November 22, 1963, President and Mrs. Kennedy arrived in Dallas, Texas. Kennedy had come there to improve relations with the state's Democratic Party. Large crowds greeted the Kennedys as they rode along the streets of downtown Dallas. Then, rifle shots rang out. Kennedy had been shot. He died about an hour later at a nearby hospital.

The tragic news spread across the nation and the world. Americans watched on live television as Dallas police charged Lee Harvey Oswald with Kennedy's murder. On November 24, Americans watched him being transferred in jail as a gunman shot and killed Oswald. Then on the next day, Kennedy's funeral was held and the nation mourned.

The events seemed too strange to believe. Many people wondered if Oswald had acted alone, or with others. Chief Justice Earl Warren headed a commission to investigate the assassination. The **Warren Commission** determined that Oswald acted alone. In 1979 another investigation said he was part of a conspiracy. Other theories

© Houghton Mifflin Harcourt Publishing Company

Lesson 1, *continued*

exist, but none have ever been proven.

The assassination taught Americans that their system of government could survive an upset. Lyndon Johnson took office after Kennedy's death and promised to carry on his programs.

3. What did the Warren Commission determine?

_____

_____

As you read this section, take notes to answer questions about President Kennedy's attempts to solve domestic and international problems.

THE NEW FRONTIER: FULFILLED PROMISES		
Problems	**What did Kennedy believe the government could do to solve the problem?**	**What programs, laws, and accomplishments resulted from Kennedy's beliefs?**
1. Economic recession		
2. Poverty abroad		

THE NEW FRONTIER: UNFULFILLED PROMISES	
Rejected Proposals	**Later Proposals**
3. What reform proposals did Kennedy make that were rejected by a conservative Congress?	4. In 1963, what proposals did Kennedy make but never have the chance to guide through Congress?

An Era of Social Change

Johnson and the Great Society

Key Terms and People

Lyndon Baines Johnson 36th president of the United States

Economic Opportunity Act Act that created numerous antipoverty measures

Great Society Name given to Johnson's domestic agenda

Medicare and Medicaid Health benefits for the elderly and poor

Immigration Act of 1965 Established new immigration system that allowed more immigrants into the U.S.

Warren Court The Supreme Court under Chief Justice Earl Warren

reapportionment The way in which states redraw their election districts

Before You Read

In the last lesson you read about President Kennedy's domestic programs. In this lesson you will read about Lyndon Johnson's plan to reshape America.

As You Read

Use a chart to take notes on the programs of the Great Society and the decisions of the Warren Court.

LBJ'S PATH TO POWER; JOHNSON'S DOMESTIC AGENDA
How did Johnson wage a "war" on poverty?

Lyndon Baines Johnson, a Texan, first entered politics in 1937 when he filled a vacant seat in the U.S. House of Representatives. In 1948 he won a Senate seat and became Senate majority leader in 1955. Johnson was a skilled lawmaker and was successful at achieving legislative results. During the 1960 presidential campaign, John F. Kennedy thought that Johnson would make the perfect running mate. Johnson's connections in Congress and his Southern background would enhance Kennedy's presidential chances.

Johnson helped Kennedy win important states in the South.

Upon Kennedy's death, Johnson became president. Under President Johnson's leadership, Congress passed two bills that President Kennedy had proposed. One was a tax cut to help stimulate the economy. Consumers spent more money, which led to profits for businesses. This increased tax revenues and lowered the federal budget deficit. The other bill was the Civil Rights Act of 1964, which prohibited discrimination based on race, religion, national origin, and gender. This bill also gave the government the powers to enforce the law.

Johnson then launched his own

© Houghton Mifflin Harcourt Publishing Company

program—a "war on poverty." He worked with Congress to pass the **Economic Opportunity Act.** This law created the Job Corps Youth Training Program; VISTA (Volunteers in Service to America); Project Head Start, a preschool education program for underprivileged children; and the Community Action Program for poor people to take part in public-works programs.

Johnson ran for president in 1964. He easily defeated his Republican opponent, Barry Goldwater.

1. Name two programs created by the Economic Opportunity Act.

_____

_____

BUILDING THE GREAT SOCIETY
How did the Great Society change America?

President Johnson had a grand vision for America. Similar to FDR, Johnson wanted to change America. His policies were titled the **Great Society.** The programs of the Great Society were meant to deal with poverty and the needs of the poor related to healthcare, education, and housing. Programs included:

• Elementary and Secondary Education Act of 1965, which provided federal aid to public and parochial schools to buy textbooks and library materials;

• **Medicare,** which provided hospital insurance and low-cost medical insurance for Americans over 65, and **Medicaid,** which extended health insurance to people on welfare;

• funding the building of low-rent public housing units and created the cabinet-level Department of Housing and Urban Development (HUD);

• lifted restrictions on immigration through the **Immigration Act of 1965,** which opened the door for many non-European immigrants to settle in the United States;

• required efforts to ensure clean water, through the Water Quality Act of 1965;

• offered increased protection to consumers, through the Wholesome Meat Act of 1967;

• established safety standards for automobiles and tires.

2. Name one result of the Great Society.

_____

_____

REFORMS OF THE WARREN COURT
How did the Warren Court change America?

Liberal reform characterized the Great Society. The same is true for decisions made by the Supreme Court. Chief Justice Earl Warren took an active role in promoting more liberal policies. The **Warren Court** ruled school segregation unconstitutional in *Brown* v. *Board of Education.* The court also banned prayer in public schools and strengthened the right of free speech.

The Warren Court also changed the area of congressional **reapportionment.** This is the way in which states redraw their election districts. In *Baker* v. *Carr,* the Court set up the principle of "one person, one vote." It also said that federal courts had the right to tell states to reapportion districts for more equal representation.

The Warren Court strengthened the rights of people accused of crimes in several cases. These cases include:

© Houghton Mifflin Harcourt Publishing Company

Guided Reading Workbook

- *Mapp* v. *Ohio*: ruled that evidence seized illegally could not be used in state courts;
- *Gideon* v. *Wainwright*: required criminal courts to provide legal counsel to those who could not afford it;
- *Escobedo* v. *Illinois*: ruled that an accused person has the right to have a lawyer present during questioning;
- *Miranda* v. *Arizona*: all suspects must be read their rights before questioning.

There was mixed reaction to these rulings. Liberals were happy because they said it put necessary limits on the police and protected all citizens. Conservatives criticized the Court and said that the rulings helped criminal suspects and made it harder for the police to investigate crimes.

3. Name one result of the Warren Court.

_____

_____

IMPACT OF THE GREAT SOCIETY
How successful was the Great Society?

The Great Society and the Warren Court changed America. People disagree on whether these changes left the nation better or worse off than before. One point people do agree on is that Johnson extended the federal government's power more than any other president.

Johnson's antipoverty measures helped reduce the suffering of many people. However, many of Johnson's proposals did not achieve their stated goals.

While his tax cut helped the economy, the funding needed for the Great Society led to a budget deficit that continued for decades. Some Americans began to question the increased size of the federal government. They also wondered about the effectiveness of Johnson's programs. Across the country, people became disillusioned with the Great Society. This led to the rise of a new group of Republican leaders. For example, in 1966 conservative Ronald Reagan, a former Hollywood actor, became governor of California.

Also the successes and failures started to be overshadowed by the increase of Communist forces in Vietnam. Americans had a great fear of communism because of the Cold War. And Johnson, who had always wanted peace, soon would be called a "hawk" because of his decisions related to the Vietnam War.

4. How did the Great Society affect the size of the federal government?

_____

_____

© Houghton Mifflin Harcourt Publishing Company

Lesson 2, *continued*

Fill in the chart to tell what each program or law did or was intended to do. Then tell the results of each Supreme Court ruling.

Program or Law	Objectives or Results
1. Tax-cut bill of 1964	
2. Civil Rights Act of 1964	
3. Economic Opportunity Act of 1964	
4. Elementary and Secondary Education Act	
5. Medicare	
6. Medicaid	
7. Immigration Act of 1965	

Court Cases	Results
8. *Brown* v. *Board of Education*	
9. *Baker* v. *Carr*	
10. *Mapp* v. *Ohio*	
11. *Gideon* v. *Wainright*	
12. *Escobedo* v. *Illinois*	
13. *Miranda* v. *Arizona*	

© Houghton Mifflin Harcourt Publishing Company

Guided Reading Workbook

An Era of Social Change

Culture and Counterculture

Key Terms and People

counterculture Movement whose members sought to drop out of mainstream society

Haight-Ashbury Community in San Francisco that attracted many hippies

The Beatles British rock group that helped popularize rock 'n' roll

Woodstock Massive outdoor concert that demonstrated rock 'n' roll's popularity

Before You Read

In the last lesson you read about President Lyndon B. Johnson and the Great Society. In this lesson you will read about the emergence of the counterculture movement—and how the nation reacted to it.

As You Read

Use a chart to take notes on the counterculture of the 1960s.

THE COUNTERCULTURE
What characterized the counterculture?

During the 1960s many idealistic young people adopted values that differed from those of mainstream society. These Americans were part of a movement known as the **counterculture.**

The movement was made up mostly of white middle-class youths. Members of the counterculture were known as "hippies." Many hippies shared some of the beliefs of the New Left. They were disillusioned with mainstream society. They did not approve of the way American society supported materialism and technology. They also had very different ideas about war. A majority of hippies chose to turn their backs on America. They wanted to establish a new society based on peace and love.

Characteristics of the hippie culture included rock 'n' roll, unusual clothes, and the use of illegal drugs — in particular, marijuana and a new hallucinogenic drug called LSD. They typically wore jeans, tie-dyed T-shirts, and love beads. Many grew long hair, which conservative adults saw as being disrespectful. Many chose to live in large groups called communes. Many hippies moved to San Francisco's **Haight-Ashbury.** This community was popular because of the availability of drugs.

After a few years, the counterculture movement began to decline. Some aspects of the movement became violent. Many urban communes grew dangerous. The widespread use of drugs also led to the decline of the movement.

More than anything else, hippies eventually found that they could not survive outside mainstream America. They needed money to live. For many, this meant returning to mainstream society.

1. Name two characteristics of the counterculture.

_____

_____

A CHANGING CULTURE
How did the counterculture affect America?

The counterculture movement collapsed after only a few years. However, some aspects of it had a lasting effect on mainstream culture.

The rebellious nature of the movement affected the world of art. The 1960s saw the rise of popular, or pop, art. One celebrated pop artist was Andy Warhol. His work was characterized by bright, simple, commercial-looking images such as portraits of soup cans and other icons of mass culture. These images were repeated to look mass-produced. They implied that individual freedoms had been lost to a "cookie-cutter" lifestyle.

The most lasting legacy of the counterculture movement was its music. Rock 'n' roll continues to be a popular form of entertainment. Perhaps the most influential band was **The Beatles.** The British group took America by storm and helped rock music become part of mainstream America.

A dramatic example of rock 'n' roll's popularity was an event known as **Woodstock.** This was a massive outdoor rock concert in upstate New York. It occurred during the summer of 1969. More than 400,000 people attended—far more than expected. For three days, popular bands and musicians performed. Despite the crowd, however, the festival was peaceful and well organized.

Protest songs became a popular way to express political ideas. Young people sang about the ills of society, the importance of civil rights, and outrage about the Vietnam War. Bob Dylan, Joan Baez, and Pete Seeger were among those who spoke out in song.

The counterculture movement affected Americans' social attitudes as well. The movement's casual approach to relationships led to the sexual revolution. The American media began to address the subjects of sex and violence. Before this time, few Americans discussed these topics.

2. Name two areas of society affected by the counterculture.

_____

_____

THE CONSERVATIVE RESPONSE
Why did mainstream America attack the counterculture?

In the late 1960s, many mainstream Americans criticized the counterculture. They blamed the movement for the decline of traditional American values.

Some conservative groups called the movement a threat to law and order. They also accused members of the counterculture of being immoral.

Mainstream America's anger toward the counterculture affected the country's political scene. In 1968 the Republicans nominated Richard Nixon as their presidential candidate. Nixon ran on a platform of conservative values and law and order. His ideas appealed to many voters. As a result, Nixon won the election. He then set the nation on a more conservative course.

3. Cite two reasons why Americans criticized the counterculture.

_____

_____

© Houghton Mifflin Harcourt Publishing Company

Lesson 3, *continued*

Fill out the chart below by listing and describing various elements of the counterculture of the 1960s.

1. Members or participants	2. Beliefs about American society	3. Goals for society and for themselves
4. Movement center	5. Attitudes and activities	6. Violent episodes
7. Impact on art	8. Impact on music	9. Impact on mainstream America

© Houghton Mifflin Harcourt Publishing Company

An Era of Social Change

Environmental Activism

Key Terms and People

Rachel Carson Environmentalist crusader in the United States

Earth Day Annual day to celebrate the environment

environmentalist Person who actively tries to protect the environment

Environmental Protection Agency (EPA) Federal agency formed to decrease pollution

Three Mile Island Site of a nuclear plant that released radiation into the air

Before You Read

In the last lesson you learned about the counterculture movement of the 1960s and its effects on American society. In this lesson you will see how Americans addressed their environmental concerns.

As You Read

Complete a chart on issues and attitudes affecting the early environmental movement.

THE ROOTS OF ENVIRONMENTALISM
What is environmentalism?

Concern for the environment was increased by the 1962 book *Silent Spring,* written by marine biologist **Rachel Carson.** That book argued that pesticides were poisoning food and killing birds and fish. Carson cautioned that America faced a "silent spring," in which birds killed off by pesticides would no longer sing.

Carson's book was an awakening to many Americans. It alerted them to the dangers of using pesticides and made them realize that everyday actions affect the environment. President Kennedy set up a committee to investigate the situation shortly after the book's publication. It took several years, but

Carson's work helped to outlaw the use of DDT, a harmful pesticide, in 1972.

1. How did *Silent Spring* encourage environmentalism?

_____

_____

ENVIRONMENTAL CONCERNS IN THE 1970S
What were the key environmental issues of the 1970s?

On April 22, 1970, Americans celebrated **Earth Day** for the first time. Its purpose was to make Americans more aware of environmental issues, such as pollution and the overuse of resources. Earth Day became a yearly event around the world.

© Houghton Mifflin Harcourt Publishing Company

Lesson 4, *continued*

Richard Nixon was not an **environmentalist**—someone who takes an active role in protecting the environment. But he did recognize the nation's concern over the environment. In 1970 he created the **Environmental Protection Agency (EPA).** This agency had the power to regulate pollution by setting up and enforcing emissions standards and to conduct research.

Nixon also signed the 1970 Clean Air Act. This law required industry to reduce pollution from factories and automobiles. It also provided the EPA with the power to set air standards for the nation. The government was granted greater authority to enforce environmental regulations.

Congress passed other new laws to protect the environment. The Endangered Species Act sought to prevent the extinction of plants and animals. The Clean Water Act gave the EPA the authority to improve water quality in the United States.

In 1968 oil was found in Alaska. Oil companies began building a pipeline to carry the oil many miles across the state. The discovery of oil and the construction of the pipeline created many new jobs and increased state revenues.

The pipeline raised concerns about Alaska's environment and the rights of Alaska's native peoples. In 1971 Nixon signed the Alaska Native Claims Settlement Act. This law gave millions of acres of land to the state's native tribes.

In 1978 President Carter set aside 56 million more acres in Alaska as national monuments. In 1980 Congress added another 104 million acres to Alaska's protected conservation areas.

In the 1970s some people believed that nuclear energy was the energy of the future. They believed that it was cheap, plentiful, and safe.

Others opposed nuclear energy. They warned that nuclear plants were dangerous to humans and the environment. These people also feared accidents and nuclear waste.

On March 28, 1979, the concerns of opponents of nuclear energy appeared to come true. An accident caused one of the nuclear reactors on **Three Mile Island,** in Pennsylvania, to release radiation into the air. The accident made people more aware of possible dangers of nuclear energy. Afterwards, the government strengthened nuclear safety regulations and improved its inspection procedures.

Love Canal in New York was the site of another environmental disaster. Exposure to long-buried chemicals in the ground led to high rates of birth defects. The government spent a large amount of money cleaning up the toxic land.

2. What did the government do after the accident at a nuclear reactor on Three Mile Island?

_____

_____

A CONTINUING MOVEMENT
Why is there disagreement over the issue of preserving the environment?

Over time, private, nonprofit groups formed to help preserve the environment. Many worked to get environmental laws passed or to block problematic projects.

The debate over the environment continues today. The struggle is between proponents of economic growth and conservationists. Environmental regulations sometimes block economic development and cause a loss of jobs for workers. Though there is conflict, it is clear that environmental concerns have gained increasing attention and support.

© Houghton Mifflin Harcourt Publishing Company

Guided Reading Workbook

3. What might cause some people not
   to support the use of environmental   _____
   regulations?   _____

Describe how American attitudes were affected by each environmental
event or how the event affected the environment itself.

Event	Effect on Attitudes or Environment
1. Publication of Rachel Carson's *Silent Spring*	
2. Celebration of Earth Day	
3. Creation of the Environmental Protection Agency	
4. Passage of the new Clean Air Act	
5. Passage of the Alaska Native Claims Settlement Act	
6. Nuclear accident at Three Mile Island	

© Houghton Mifflin Harcourt Publishing Company

Taking on Segregation

Key Terms and People

Thurgood Marshall African American lawyer who led the legal challenge against segregation

Brown* v. *Board of Education of Topeka Supreme Court case in which segregated schools were ruled unconstitutional

Rosa Parks Woman who helped start Montgomery bus boycott

Martin Luther King Jr. Leader of the civil rights movement

Southern Christian Leadership Conference (SCLC) Civil rights organization

Student Nonviolent Coordinating Committee (SNCC) Civil rights organization formed by students

sit-in Protest tactic of occupying seats and refusing to move

Before You Read

In the last lesson you read about environmental activism. In this lesson you will read how African Americans challenged the nation's policies of segregation and racial inequality.

As You Read

Provide details for a timeline of events in the civil rights movement.

THE SEGREGATION SYSTEM
How did World War II help start the civil rights movement?

By 1950 most African Americans were still considered second-class citizens. Throughout the South, Jim Crow laws remained in place. These were laws aimed at keeping blacks separate from whites.

During the 1950s, however, a civil rights movement began. This was a movement by blacks to gain greater equality in American society.

In several ways, World War II helped set the stage for this movement. First, the demand for soldiers during the war had created a shortage of white male workers. This opened up many new jobs for African Americans.

Second, during the war, civil rights organizations challenged Jim Crow laws and campaigned for African American voting rights. In response to protests, President Franklin Roosevelt issued a presidential directive outlawing racial discrimination in all federal agencies and war-related companies.

Third, nearly 1 million African Americans had served in the armed forces. These soldiers fought for freedom in Europe. Many returned from the war ready to fight for their own freedom.

World War II had given American blacks a taste of equality and respectability. When the war ended, many African Americans were more determined than ever to improve their status.

1. What action did President Franklin Roosevelt take in response to protests against Jim Crow laws?

_____

_____

CHALLENGING SEGREGATION IN COURT

What was important in the case of *Brown* v. *Board of Education*?

Even before the civil rights movement began, African American lawyers had been challenging racial discrimination in court. Beginning in 1938 a team of lawyers led by **Thurgood Marshall** began arguing several cases before the Supreme Court.

Their biggest victory came in the 1954 case known as *Brown* v. *Board of Education of Topeka,* Kansas. In this case, the Supreme Court ruled that separate schools for whites and blacks were unequal—and thus unconstitutional.

2. What did the Supreme Court rule about separate schools in *Brown* v. *Board of Education of Topeka*?

_____

_____

REACTION TO THE *BROWN* DECISION; THE MONTGOMERY BUS BOYCOTT

Where did African Americans fight racial segregation?

Some southern communities refused to accept the *Brown* decision. In 1955 the Supreme Court handed down a

second *Brown* ruling. It ordered schools to desegregate more quickly.

The school desegregation issue reached a crisis in 1957 in Little Rock, Arkansas. The state's governor, Orval Faubus, refused to let nine African American students attend Little Rock's Central High School. President Eisenhower sent in federal troops to allow the students, later called the "Little Rock Nine," to enter the school.

School was just one place where African Americans challenged segregation. They also battled discrimination on city buses. In Montgomery, Alabama, a local law required that blacks give up their bus seats to whites. In December 1955 Montgomery resident **Rosa Parks** refused to give her seat to a white man. Parks was arrested.

After her arrest, African Americans in Montgomery organized a yearlong boycott of the city's bus system. The protesters looked for a person to lead the bus boycott. They chose Dr. **Martin Luther King Jr.,** the pastor of a Baptist church.

The boycott lasted 381 days. Finally, in late 1956 the Supreme Court ruled that segregated buses were illegal.

3. Name two places that African Americans targeted for racial desegregation.

_____

_____

THE MOVEMENT SPREADS

Where did King get his ideas?

Martin Luther King Jr. preached nonviolent resistance. He termed it "soul force." He based his ideas on the teachings of several people. From Jesus, he learned to love one's enemies. From

Lesson 1, continued

writer Henry David Thoreau, King took the idea of civil disobedience. This was the refusal to obey an unjust law. From labor organizer A. Philip Randolph, he learned how to organize huge demonstrations. From Mohandas Gandhi, King learned that a person could resist oppression without using violence.

King joined with other ministers and civil rights leaders in 1957. They formed the **Southern Christian Leadership Conference (SCLC)** for the purpose of using nonviolent protests to change public policies and attitudes toward integration. By 1960 another influential civil rights group emerged. The **Student Nonviolent Coordinating Committee (SNCC)** was formed mostly by college students. Members of this group felt that change for African

Americans was occurring too slowly.

One protest strategy that SNCC ("snick") used was the **sit-in.** During a sit-in, blacks sat at whites-only lunch counters. They refused to leave until they were served. In February 1960 African American students staged a sit-in at a lunch counter at a Woolworth's store in Greensboro, North Carolina. The students sat there as whites hit them and poured food over their heads. By late 1960 students had desegregated lunch counters in 48 cities in 11 states.

4. Name two people from whom Martin Luther King Jr. drew his ideas.

_____

_____

Lesson 1, *continued*

As you read, make notes on this timeline that answer questions about important events in the civil rights movement.

1945 **World War II ends** →	1. In what ways did World War II help set the stage for the modern civil rights movement? List at least three.	
1954 *Brown* v. *Board of Education* →	2. Who argued Brown's case?	3. What did the *Brown* ruling declare?
1955 **Supreme Court orders school desegregation** **Rosa Parks is arrested** **1956** **Supreme Court outlaws bus segregation** →	4. Why was Rosa Parks arrested?	5. How long did the Montgomery bus boycott last?
1957 **Little Rock faces school desegregation crisis** →	6. What name was given to the nine students who were the first African Americans to attend Little Rock's Central High School?	7. How did President Eisenhower respond to the Little Rock crisis?
Southern Christian Leadership Conference (SCLC) is formed →	8. What was SCLC's purpose?	
1960 **Student Nonviolent Coordinating Committee (SNCC) is formed** →	9. What did SNCC accomplish, and how?	

© Houghton Mifflin Harcourt Publishing Company

The Triumphs of a Crusade

Key Terms and People

freedom riders Civil rights activists who tried to end segregation on national buses

James Meredith African American who won enrollment to the all-white University of Mississippi

Civil Rights Act of 1964 Law that outlawed racial discrimination

Freedom Summer Name of project to win voting rights for southern blacks

Fannie Lou Hamer Prominent voting rights activist

Voting Rights Act of 1965 Act that struck down state laws intended to keep blacks from voting

Before You Read

In the last lesson you read how African Americans began challenging the nation's racist systems. In this lesson you will read how civil rights activists broke down many racial barriers and prompted landmark legislation.

As You Read

Add details to a timeline featuring steps taken to challenge segregation from 1961 to 1965.

RIDING FOR FREEDOM
Who were the freedom riders?

Freedom riders were protesters who rode buses with the goal of integrating buses and bus stations. In 1961 a bus of freedom riders was attacked in Anniston, Alabama, where a white mob burned the bus. Another instance occurred when a group of Nashville students rode into Birmingham, Alabama, where they were beaten.

Attorney General Robert Kennedy ordered a reluctant bus company to continue to carry the freedom riders. When freedom riders were attacked in Montgomery, Alabama, the federal government took stronger action.

President Kennedy sent 400 U.S. marshals to protect the freedom riders. The Interstate Commerce Commission banned segregation in all travel facilities including waiting rooms, restrooms, and lunch counters.

1. Name two ways the government tried to help the freedom riders.

   _____

   _____

STANDING FIRM
What happened in Birmingham?

Civil rights workers soon turned their attention to integrating southern

© Houghton Mifflin Harcourt Publishing Company

schools. In September 1962 a federal court allowed Air Force veteran **James Meredith** to attend the all-white University of Mississippi. However, Mississippi's governor refused to admit him. The Kennedy administration sent in U.S. marshals. They forced the governor to let in Meredith.

Another confrontation occurred in 1963 in Birmingham, Alabama. There, Martin Luther King Jr. and other civil rights leaders tried to desegregate the city. Police attacked activists with dogs and water hoses.

Many Americans witnessed the attacks on television. They were outraged by what they saw. Eventually, Birmingham officials gave in. They agreed to end segregation in the city.

On June 11, 1963, President Kennedy addressed the nation and called on Congress to pass a sweeping civil rights bill. Just hours after the president's speech, Medgar Evers, NAACP field secretary and World War II veteran, was murdered by a sniper.

2. What was the outcome of the demonstrations in Birmingham?

_____

_____

MARCHING TO WASHINGTON
What did the Civil Rights Act of 1964 do?

President Kennedy's civil rights bill outlawed discrimination based on race, religion, national origin, and gender. It also gave the government more power to push for school desegregation. Civil rights leaders wanted Congress to pass the bill, so they staged a massive march on Washington, DC.

On August 28, 1963, more than 250,000 blacks and whites marched into the nation's capital. There, they demanded the immediate passage of the bill.

Dr. Martin Luther King Jr. spoke to the crowd. He called for peace and racial harmony in his now-famous "I Have a Dream" speech.

Two weeks later, on September 15, 1963, violence again struck Birmingham. A bomb exploded at the 16th Street Baptist Church, killing four young girls. Two months later, President Kennedy was assassinated. Lyndon Johnson became president. He won passage in Congress of Kennedy's **Civil Rights Act of 1964.**

3. Name two things the Civil Rights Act of 1964 did.

_____

_____

FIGHTING FOR VOTING RIGHTS
Where did workers try to register African Americans to vote?

Civil rights activists next worked to gain voting rights for African Americans in the South. The 1964 voting project became known as **Freedom Summer.** The workers focused their efforts on Mississippi. They hoped to influence Congress to pass a voting rights act.

For some workers, the campaign to register African American voters proved deadly. In June 1964, three civil rights workers were murdered in Neshoba County, Mississippi, by local police and members of the Ku Klux Klan.

Meanwhile, civil rights activists challenged Mississippi's political structure. At the 1964 Democratic National Convention, SNCC organized the Mississippi Freedom Democratic Party (MFDP). The new party hoped to unseat Mississippi's regular party delegates at the convention.

Civil rights activist **Fannie Lou Hamer** spoke for the MFDP at the convention. She gave an emotional speech. As a result, many Americans supported the seating of the MFDP delegates. However, the Democratic Party offered only 2 of Mississippi's 68 seats to MFDP members.

In 1965 civil rights workers attempted a voting project in Selma, Alabama. They met with violent resistance. As a result, Martin Luther King Jr. led a massive march through Alabama from Selma to Montgomery. Again, violence broke out. And again, television cameras captured the scene. The rest of the nation watched in horror as police beat and tear-gassed the marchers. More marchers joined the protest, and the number increased from 300 to 25,000.

President Johnson responded by asking Congress to pass a new voting rights act. Congress passed the **Voting Rights Act of 1965.** The law eliminated state laws that had prevented African Americans from voting. As a result of the act, the percentage of registered African American voters in the South tripled.

4. Name two states where civil rights workers tried to register blacks to vote.

_____

_____

© Houghton Mifflin Harcourt Publishing Company

As you read this lesson, take notes to answer the questions about the timeline.

1961	Freedom riders travel through the South	1. What was the goal of the freedom riders?	2. What incidents of violence occurred against freedom riders in Alabama?
1962	James Meredith integrates Ole Miss		
1963	Birmingham and the University of Alabama are integrated Kennedy sends civil rights bill to Congress Medgar Evers is murdered March on Washington Birmingham church bombing kills four girls Kennedy is assassinated	3. What was the goal of the march on Washington? 5. What were 2 goals of the Freedom Summer project?	4. Who attended the march? 6. What was the goal of the Mississippi Freedom Democratic Party?
1964	Freedom Summer Three civil rights workers are murdered Civil Rights Act of 1964 is passed	7. What role did the violence shown on television play in this march?	8. What did the march encourage President Johnson to do?
1965	March from Selma to Montgomery Voting Rights Act of 1965 is passed	9. What did the Voting Rights Act eliminate?	10. How did the law affect the number of African American voters?

© Houghton Mifflin Harcourt Publishing Company

Lesson 3

Challenges and Changes in the Movement

Key Terms and People

de facto segregation Segregation by custom or practice

de jure segregation Segregation by law

Malcolm X African American civil rights leader

Nation of Islam Group headed by Elijah Muhammad

Stokely Carmichael Leader of Black Power movement

Black Power Movement that stressed black pride

Black Panthers African American group founded to combat police brutality

Kerner Commission Commission that reported on race relations in America

Civil Rights Act of 1968 Act that banned discrimination in housing

affirmative action Program aimed at hiring or including minorities

Before You Read

In the last lesson you read about the triumphs of the civil rights movement. In this lesson you will read about challenges and changes to the movement.

As You Read

Complete a chart on challenges and changes in the civil rights movement.

AFRICAN AMERICANS SEEK GREATER EQUALITY
What problems did African Americans in the North face?

The biggest problem in the North was **de facto segregation**—segregation that exists by practice and custom. De facto segregation can be harder to fight than **de jure segregation**—segregation by law. Eliminating de facto segregation requires changing people's attitudes rather than repealing laws.

De facto segregation increased as African Americans moved to northern cities after World War II. Many white people left the cities. They moved to the suburbs. By the mid-1960s, many African Americans in the North lived in decaying urban slums. There, they dealt with poor schools and high unemployment.

The terrible conditions in northern cities angered many African Americans. This anger led to many episodes of violence.

© Houghton Mifflin Harcourt Publishing Company

1. Name two problems African Americans in the North faced.

_____

_____

NEW LEADERS VOICE DISCONTENT
What did new leaders call for?

During the 1960s new African American leaders emerged. They called for more aggressive tactics in fighting racism.

One such leader was **Malcolm X.** Malcolm preached the views of Elijah Muhammad. Muhammad was the head of the **Nation of Islam,** or the Black Muslims. Malcolm declared that whites were responsible for blacks' misery. He also urged African Americans to fight back when attacked.

Eventually, Malcolm changed his policy regarding violence. He urged African Americans to use peaceful means—especially voting—to win equality. In February 1965 he was assassinated.

Another new black leader was **Stokely Carmichael.** He introduced the notion of **Black Power.** This movement encouraged African American pride and leadership.

In 1966 some African Americans formed a political party called the **Black Panthers.** The party was created to fight police brutality. They urged violent resistance against whites. Many whites and moderate African Americans feared the group.

2. Name two new civil rights leaders.

_____

_____

KING IS ASSASSINATED
Who was killed in 1968?

In April 1968 a gunman shot and killed Martin Luther King Jr. in Memphis, Tennessee. Many leaders called for peace. But anger over King's death led many African Americans to riot. Cities across the nation erupted in violence.

A bullet claimed the life of yet another leader in 1968. In June, a man shot and killed Senator Robert Kennedy. Kennedy was a strong supporter of civil rights. The assassin was a Jordanian immigrant. He allegedly was angry about Kennedy's support of Israel. Kennedy had been seeking the Democratic nomination for president when he was killed.

3. Name two of the nation's leaders killed in 1968.

_____

_____

THE MOVEMENT CONTINUES
What did the civil rights movement accomplish?

Shortly after taking office, President Johnson formed a group known as the **Kerner Commission.** The commission's job was to study the cause of urban violence. In March 1968 the commission issued its report. It named one main cause for violence in the cities: white racism. The report called for the nation to create new jobs, construct new housing, and end de facto segregation. However, the Johnson administration ignored many of the recommendations because of white opposition.

What, then, did the civil rights movement achieve? The movement claimed many triumphs. It led to the passage of important civil rights acts.

Lesson 3, *continued*

This included the **Civil Rights Act of 1968.** This law banned discrimination in housing.

The movement also led to the banning of segregation in education, transportation, and employment. It also helped African Americans gain their full voting rights.

The civil rights movement was successful in changing many discriminatory laws. Yet challenges for the movement changed, including the difficult task of changing people's attitudes and behavior.

The government continued steps to help African Americans and other disadvantaged groups. During the late 1960s federal officials began to promote **affirmative action.** Affirmative action programs involve making special efforts to hire or enroll minorities.

4. Name one goal the civil rights movement achieved and one challenge that remained.

_____

_____

© Houghton Mifflin Harcourt Publishing Company

As you read this lesson, make notes to answer the questions.

CHALLENGES AND CHANGES IN THE CIVIL RIGHTS MOVEMENT
1. What is the main difference between de facto segregation and de jure segregation?
2. How did the teachings of Elijah Muhammad, the head of the Nation of Islam, affect Malcolm X?
3. How did the early views of Malcolm X differ from his later ideas?
4. What concept did Stokely Carmichael introduce in the civil rights movement, and what did it stand for?
5. What ideas did the Black Panthers encourage? How did many whites and moderate African Americans respond?

6. What gains were made by the civil rights movement? Identify three.		
a.	b.	c.

© Houghton Mifflin Harcourt Publishing Company

Civil Rights

Hispanic and Native Americans Seek Equality

Key Terms and People

César Chávez Leader of the farm workers movement

United Farm Workers Organizing Committee Union that fought for farm workers' rights

Rodolfo "Corky" Gonzales Leader in the Chicano movement who founded the Crusade for Justice, which promoted Mexican American nationalism

La Raza Unida Hispanic American political party

American Indian Movement (AIM) Group that fought for greater reform for Native Americans

Before You Read

In the last lesson you read about challenges and changes in the civil rights movement. In this lesson you will read about how Hispanic Americans and Native Americans fought for greater equality.

As You Read

Compile your notes in a chart on the issues facing Hispanic Americans and Native Americans during the 1960s.

THE HISPANIC AMERICAN PRESENCE GROWS
Who are Hispanic Americans?

Hispanic Americans are Americans of Latin American or Spanish descent. During the 1960s the Hispanic American population in the United States tripled—from 3 million to more than 9 million.

Mexican Americans, the largest Hispanic American group, have lived mostly in the Southwest and California. Many were descendants of Mexicans who stayed on the land that Mexico surrendered to the United States in 1848. Others were the children and grandchildren of the Mexicans who

arrived after Mexico's 1910 revolution. Still others came as temporary laborers during the 1940s and 1950s. In the 1960s close to half a million Mexicans immigrated, most in search of higher-paying jobs.

About a million Puerto Ricans have lived in the United States since the 1960s. Most Puerto Ricans have settled in the Northeast, especially in New York City.

Many Cubans also settled in the United States during the 1960s. They had fled Cuba after the Cuban Revolution in 1959. Large Cuban communities formed in New York City, Miami, and in the state of New Jersey.

© Houghton Mifflin Harcourt Publishing Company

Thousands of Salvadorans, Guatemalans, Nicaraguans, and Colombians immigrated to the United States after the 1960s. They came to escape political persecution and poverty at home. Wherever they settled, many Hispanic Americans experienced poor living conditions and discrimination.

1. Name two groups that make up the Hispanic American community.

_____

_____

HISPANIC AMERICANS FIGHT FOR CHANGE
Which groups fought for change?

In the 1960s Hispanic Americans began to demand equal rights and respect. One such group was Mexican American farm workers. These men and women worked on California's fruit and vegetable farms. They often worked long hours for little pay.

César Chávez was the group's leader. Chávez believed that the farm workers should organize into a union. In 1962 he helped establish the National Farm Workers Association. In 1966 Chávez merged this group with a Filipino agricultural union. Together, they formed the **United Farm Workers Organizing Committee** (UFWOC).

California's grape growers refused to recognize the farm workers union. As a result, Chávez called for a nationwide boycott of grapes. His plan worked. In 1970 the grape growers finally signed contracts with the UFWOC. The new contracts guaranteed union workers higher pay and granted them other benefits.

Hispanic Americans also wanted greater recognition of their culture. Puerto Ricans demanded that schools offer classes taught in their native language. In 1968 Congress passed the Bilingual Education Act. This law funded bilingual and cultural programs for students who did not speak English.

Some young Mexican Americans began to express a form of cultural loyalty similar to the Black Power movement. They called themselves Chicanos or Chicanas, a shortened form of *Mexicanos.* In the past, the term *Chicano* had been an insult. Now, Chicanos wore the name proudly.

One leading figure in the Chicano movement was **Rodolfo "Corky" Gonzales.** In 1966 he founded the Crusade for Justice, a group that promoted Mexican American nationalism. The group provided legal aid, promoted Mexican culture, and offered bilingual classes.

Hispanic Americans began organizing politically during the 1960s. Some worked within the two-party system. Others created an independent Hispanic American political movement. José Angel Gutiérrez, for example, started **La Raza Unida** (the United People Party). The party ran Hispanic American candidates and won positions in city government offices.

2. Name two organizations that fought to promote the cause of Hispanic Americans.

_____

_____

NATIVE AMERICANS STRUGGLE FOR EQUALITY
What problems did Native Americans face?

Native Americans, like Hispanic Americans, are a diverse group. However, despite their diversity, most

Lesson 4, *continued*

Native American groups have faced similar problems. These problems include poverty, high unemployment rates, chronic health problems, and shorter average lifespans.

During the 1950s the Eisenhower administration tried to solve some of these problems. The government thought that introducing Native Americans to more aspects of mainstream culture would help them. As a result, the government moved Native Americans from their reservations to the cities.

The plan failed. Most Native Americans who moved to the cities remained very poor. In addition, many Native Americans refused to mix with mainstream American society.

Native Americans wanted greater opportunity to control their own lives. In 1961 representatives from 61 Native American groups met to discuss their concerns. They demanded the right to choose their own way of life.

In 1968 President Johnson responded to their demands. He created the

National Council on Indian Opportunity. The council's goal was to make sure that government programs reflected the needs and desires of Native Americans.

Many young Native Americans were not satisfied with the government's new policies. They wanted greater reform. They also wanted it more quickly. As a result, some young Native Americans formed the **American Indian Movement (AIM).** This organization demanded greater rights for Native Americans. At times, the group used violence to make its point.

Meanwhile, Native Americans won greater rights through the court system. Throughout the 1960s and 1970s, they won legal battles that gave them greater education and land rights.

3. Name two problems that Native Americans faced.

_____

_____

© Houghton Mifflin Harcourt Publishing Company

As you read, make notes concerning how Hispanic Americans and
Native Americans worked for change.

HISPANIC AMERICANS BRING ABOUT CHANGE		
How did these people bring about changes that benefited Hispanic Americans?		
1. César Chávez	2. Rodolfo "Corky" Gonzales	3. José Angel Gutiérrez
NATIVE AMERICANS BRING ABOUT CHANGE		
4. How did the Eisenhower administration fail to solve problems of Native Americans during the 1950s, and what happened as a result?		
5. What did President Johnson do to respond to the demands of Native Americans in 1968? What was the response of some Native Americans?		
6. What did Native Americans do in order to accomplish their goals for change?		

© Houghton Mifflin Harcourt Publishing Company

Civil Rights

Women Fight for Equality

Key Terms and People

feminism Belief that women should be equal to men in all areas

Betty Friedan Author of *The Feminine Mystique*

National Organization for Women (NOW) Organization that worked for women's rights

Gloria Steinem Journalist who tried to help women gain political power

Equal Rights Amendment (ERA) Amendment to the U.S. Constitution that would prohibit discrimination against women

Phyllis Schlafly Equal Rights Amendment opponent

Before You Read

In the last section you read how Latinos and Native Americans fought for greater rights. In this section you will read how the nation's women also attempted to improve their status in society.

As You Read

Complete a chart on key events of the women's movement.

A NEW WOMEN'S MOVEMENT ARISES
How did the women's movement emerge?

The theory behind the women's movement of the 1960s was **feminism.** This was the belief that women should have economic, political, and social equality with men.

The women's movement arose during the 1960s for several reasons. First, a growing number of women entered the work force. In the workplace, many women received less pay than men— even for the same job. Many women saw this as unfair.

Second, women had become actively involved in both the civil rights and antiwar movements. These movements

led women to take action on behalf of their own rights. In addition, many men in these groups refused to give women leadership roles. As a result, many women became more aware of their inferior status.

In 1963 **Betty Friedan** published *The Feminine Mystique*. This book expressed the discontent that many women were feeling. Friedan's book helped to unite a number of women throughout the nation.

1. Name two factors that helped launch the women's movement.

_____

_____

THE MOVEMENT EXPERIENCES GAINS AND LOSSES
What were the movement's successes and failures?

In 1966 several women including Betty Friedan formed the **National Organization for Women (NOW).** The group's goal was to more actively pursue women's goals. NOW pushed for more child-care facilities. It also called for more educational opportunities.

The organization also pressured the federal government to enforce a ban on gender discrimination in hiring. The government responded by declaring that male-only job ads were illegal.

Women also attempted to gain political strength. In 1971 journalist **Gloria Steinem** helped found the National Women's Political Caucus. This group encouraged women to run for political office.

In 1972 Congress passed a ban on gender discrimination in higher education. As a result, several all-male colleges opened their doors to women. In 1973 the Supreme Court's decision in the case *Roe* v. *Wade* granted women the right to choose an abortion.

The women's movement also met with some failure, such as with the **Equal Rights Amendment (ERA).** The ERA was a proposed amendment to the U.S. Constitution. It would have outlawed government discrimination on the basis of sex. One prominent ERA opponent was **Phyllis Schlafly.** Schlafly felt that the ERA would lead to undesirable consequences such as women being drafted into the military or men not taking responsibility for the support of families.

In addition, the women's movement angered many of the nation's conservatives. In response, these conservatives joined together to form a movement known as the New Right. This movement emphasized traditional social, cultural, and moral values. Throughout the 1970s the New Right gained support for its social conservatism.

In 1977 the ERA was close to being passed. It had won approval from 35 of the 38 states needed for ratification, but the New Right gained strength. By 1982—the deadline for ratification—not enough states had approved the amendment. The ERA went down to defeat.

But the influence of the women's movement could be seen in the workplace as more women started careers instead of staying home with their children. In 1970, 8 percent of all medical school graduates and 5 percent of law school graduates were women. By 1998 those numbers had risen to 42 and 44 percent, respectively. Women also made political gains as many ran for and were elected to office.

2. Name one success and one failure of the women's movement.

   _____

   _____

As you read about the rise of a new women's movement, take notes to explain how each of the following helped to create or advance the movement.

1. Experiences in the workplace
2. Experiences in social activism
3. Betty Friedan and *The Feminine Mystique*
4. National Organization for Women (NOW)
5. Gloria Steinem

The Equal Rights Amendment would have guaranteed equal rights under the law, regardless of gender. Who opposed this amendment? Why?

6. Who?
7. Why?

© Houghton Mifflin Harcourt Publishing Company

Civil Rights

The Struggle Continues

Key Terms and People

L. Douglas Wilder Nation's first elected African American governor

Colin Powell General in U.S. Army; U.S. secretary of state, 2001–2005

Condoleezza Rice First female African American secretary of state

Barack Obama 44th president of the United States; first African American president

Sonia Sotomayor First Hispanic justice of the U.S. Supreme Court

Madeleine Albright First woman secretary of state

pay equity Situation in which women and men receive equal pay for equal work

Stonewall riots Violent demonstrations by the LGBT community against police raid at the Stonewall Inn; considered the beginning of the LGBT rights movement

Americans with Disabilities Act (ADA) 1990 law banning discrimination against persons with disabilities

Before You Read

In the last lesson you read about the efforts of women to achieve equality. In this lesson you will learn about other groups and their continuing efforts to secure civil rights.

As You Read

Use a chart to list the civil rights victories and ongoing needs of different groups of Americans.

THE FIGHT FOR RIGHTS CONTINUES
What gains have minority groups experienced?

Members of many minority groups achieved greater political power during the 1980s. Hundreds of communities elected African Americans to public office. In 1990 **L. Douglas Wilder** of Virginia became the first African American elected governor in the United States.

Since the 1990s, several African Americans have held key positions in the federal government. For example, both **Colin Powell** and **Condoleezza Rice** served as secretary of state under President George W. Bush. In 2008 **Barack Obama** made history as the first African American to be elected president.

In spite of political gains, African Americans have not done as well economically as whites. Statistics show a substantial income and employment gap between African Americans and whites. In addition, although more African Americans attend college today than in the 1960s, the percentage of

© Houghton Mifflin Harcourt Publishing Company

those who graduate is only about half that of white Americans.

During the 1980s Hispanic Americans became the fastest-growing minority in the United States. By 1990 they constituted almost 9 percent of the population. It was estimated that Hispanic Americans would soon outnumber African Americans as the nation's largest minority group.

Like African Americans, Hispanic Americans gained political power during the 1980s. In 2009 **Sonia Sotomayor** became the first Hispanic justice of the U.S. Supreme Court.

Immigration reform remains one of the most important issues in the discussion of Hispanic civil rights. Meanwhile, advocacy organizations such as the League of United Latin American Citizens (LULAC) work for equal rights and opportunities for Hispanic Americans.

While Native Americans organized schools to teach young people about their past and fought for the return of ancestral lands, they also faced cuts in federal aid. Some opened casinos on their reservations. While generating income, casinos have not solved the long-term problems of Native Americans.

One issue still facing many Native American groups is lack of federal recognition. This recognition entitles the groups to receive funding and special protections from the government. Hundreds of groups from all around the country have applied for recognition but are still waiting.

Unlike other minority groups, Asian Americans did not conduct their own civil rights movement. Yet they shared in the benefits other groups gained. The laws that ended the ban on interracial marriage and protected voting rights helped Asian Americans.

Asian Americans have largely thrived economically and socially. They have low crime, school dropout, and divorce rates. Yet the Asian American community still has challenges. Some people with Southeast Asian backgrounds have experienced poverty, and some have lower education levels than other immigrants.

1. In what ways are Native Americans still struggling in spite of civil rights reforms?

_____

_____

THE EQUAL RIGHTS STRUGGLE
How are women still fighting for equality?

The failure of the Equal Rights Amendment in 1982 was a setback for the women's rights movement but not the end. Since the 1980s, women have continued to campaign to improve their political and economic situations.

In the November 1992 election, there were 47 women in the House of Representatives and 6 in the Senate. By 2009 those numbers had risen to 73 in the House and 17 in the Senate. In 2007 Nancy Pelosi of California became the first female Speaker of the House. Several women had also served in key cabinet positions. Among them was **Madeleine Albright,** the first female secretary of state, appointed by President Bill Clinton in 1997. Four women—Sandra Day O'Connor, Ruth Bader Ginsburg, Sonia Sotomayor, and Elena Kagan—have sat on the Supreme Court.

Economically, women still face challenges. By the early 2000s, about 60 percent of American women worked outside the home, making up 47 percent

© Houghton Mifflin Harcourt Publishing Company

of the work force. Yet women average only about 77 cents for every dollar men earn. In the nation's most top-level jobs, men vastly outnumber women.

Women's organizations and unions have proposed a system of **pay equity,** where salaries are based on job requirements rather than traditional pay scales in which men received higher wages than women. Still, the issues of unequal pay and unequal representation remain.

2. What are political and economic issues in which women have not yet achieved equality?

_____

_____

CIVIL RIGHTS FOR ALL
Which other groups are involved in the cause of civil rights?

Among the groups that fought for civil rights was the LGBT (lesbian, gay, bisexual, and transgender) community. Members of the community were targets of discrimination and harassment.

In 1969 New York City police officers raided the Stonewall Inn, a popular LGBT gathering spot. Angry patrons clashed with the police. The confrontation sparked several days of riots in the neighborhood. The **Stonewall riots** are credited as the beginning of the LGBT rights movement.

After years of protesting the U.S. military's policies regarding gay soldiers, the "Don't Ask, Don't Tell" policy was repealed in September 2011. For the first time, military service was open to LGBT individuals. In 2015 the U.S. Supreme Court found that the Constitution guarantees the right to same-sex marriage.

Another group that has had to campaign for their rights are Americans with disabilities, a group that includes more than 56.7 million people. For decades, disability rights activists have struggled to gain the civil rights granted to other groups.

The most significant legislation protecting the rights of people with disabilities was the **Americans with Disabilities Act (ADA),** signed by President George H. W. Bush in 1990. The ADA addresses the rights of people with disabilities in employment, public services, public accommodations, and telecommunications. The act outlawed discrimination and required state and local government, public transportation, and businesses to be made accessible to Americans with disabilities.

The ADA has improved opportunities for people with disabilities, but their struggle is not over. Finding rewarding work is still a challenge for many.

Students are another group concerned about their civil rights. In recent years, students have been punished or suspended for comments made about classes, teachers, or other students online. The Supreme Court ruled that disruptive or indecent speech by students is not a right protected by the Constitution but upheld students' rights to expression and privacy. Most recent cases have addressed the issue of students' online activity and whether schools have the right to monitor activity that takes place away from school grounds. Such debates will likely become more common.

As debates over immigration have heated up in recent years, some groups have begun campaigns to protect the civil rights of recent arrivals to the country. In 1980 Congress passed the Refugee Act, which made it easier for immigrants fleeing political turmoil or violence to settle in the country. By the

Lesson 6, *continued*

mid-1990s, however, the government had imposed new restrictions on immigration. The Immigration Reform and Control Act of 1986, for example, required that all immigrants seeking jobs prove their immigration status. More recently, some states have passed laws that allow officials to question anyone suspected of being in the country illegally, requiring them to present papers on demand. Civil rights advocates point to this requirement as a violation of immigrants' rights as Americans. The debate over reform is likely to last many years.

3. In addition to racial or ethnic minorities and women, which groups have worked to secure the protection of their rights under law?

_____

_____

As you read, identify the civil rights victories and ongoing concerns of each group.

1. African Americans	2. Hispanic Americans	3. Native Americans
4. Asian Americans	5. Women	6. The LGBT community
7. Americans with disabilities	8. Students	9. Immigrants

© Houghton Mifflin Harcourt Publishing Company

Guided Reading Workbook

The Vietnam War

Moving Toward Conflict

Key Terms and People

Ho Chi Minh Leader of North Vietnam

Vietminh Communist group led by Ho Chi Minh

domino theory Eisenhower's explanation for stopping communism

Dien Bien Phu Major French outpost captured by the Vietminh

Geneva Accords Peace agreement that split Vietnam in two

Ngo Dinh Diem Leader of South Vietnam

Vietcong Communist rebel group in South Vietnam

Ho Chi Minh Trail Network of paths running between North and South Vietnam

Tonkin Gulf Resolution Resolution that allowed President Johnson to fight in Vietnam

Before You Read

In the last lesson you read about the ongoing efforts to maintain and protect Americans' civil rights. In this lesson you will read how the United States became involved in Vietnam.

As You Read

Complete a timeline with details on how the United States became involved in a war in Vietnam.

AMERICA SUPPORTS FRANCE IN VIETNAM
Why did the U.S. get involved?

Vietnam is a long, thin country on a peninsula in Southeast Asia. From the late 1800s until World War II, France ruled Vietnam. The French treated the Vietnamese badly. As a result, the Vietnamese often rebelled. The Communist Party in Vietnam organized many of the rebellions. The group's leader was **Ho Chi Minh.**

In 1941 Japan conquered Vietnam. That year, the Vietnamese Communists combined with other groups to form an organization called the **Vietminh.** The Vietminh's goal was to achieve independence for Vietnam. In 1945 Japan was defeated in World War II. As a result, the Japanese left Vietnam. The Vietminh claimed independence for Vietnam.

However, France wanted to retake control of Vietnam. French troops moved back into the country in 1946. They conquered the southern half of Vietnam. The Vietminh took control of the North. For the next eight years, the two sides fought for control of the entire country.

© Houghton Mifflin Harcourt Publishing Company

The United States supported France during the war by sending economic aid for military expenses. America considered the Vietminh to be Communists. The United States, like other Western nations, was determined to stop the spread of communism. President Eisenhower explained his country's policy with what became known as the **domino theory.** Eisenhower compared many of the world's smaller nations to dominoes. If one nation fell to communism, the rest also would fall.

The Vietminh defeated the French. The final blow came in 1954. That year, the Vietminh conquered the large French outpost at **Dien Bien Phu.**

Several countries met with the French and the Vietminh to negotiate a peace agreement. The agreement was known as the **Geneva Accords.** It temporarily split Vietnam in half along the 17th parallel, a line of latitude north of the equator. The Vietminh controlled North Vietnam. The anti-Communist Nationalists controlled South Vietnam. The peace agreement called for an election to unify the country in 1956.

1. For what reason did the United States support France in the war?

_____

_____

THE UNITED STATES STEPS IN
Who were the Vietcong?

Ho Chi Minh ruled North Vietnam. **Ngo Dinh Diem** led South Vietnam. When it came time for the all-country elections, Diem refused to take part. He feared that Ho would win. And then all of Vietnam would become Communist.

The United States supported Diem's decision. The U.S. government provided aid to Diem. America hoped that Diem could turn South Vietnam into a strong, independent nation. Diem, however, turned out to be a terrible ruler. His administration was corrupt. He also refused to allow opposing views.

By 1957 a rebel group had formed in the South. The group was known as the **Vietcong.** It fought against Diem's rule. Ho Chi Minh supported the Vietcong from the North. He supplied arms to the group along a network of paths that ran between North and South Vietnam. Together, these paths became known as the **Ho Chi Minh Trail.**

John Kennedy became president after Eisenhower. Kennedy continued America's policy of supporting South Vietnam. He, like Eisenhower, did not want to see the Communists take over Vietnam.

Meanwhile, Diem's government grew more unstable. The Vietcong rebels were gaining greater support among the peasants. The Kennedy administration decided that Diem had to step down. In 1963 military leaders overthrew Diem. Against Kennedy's wishes, they executed Diem.

Two months later, Kennedy himself was assassinated. Lyndon Johnson became president. The growing crisis in Vietnam was now his.

2. Who were the Vietcong fighting?

_____

_____

PRESIDENT JOHNSON EXPANDS THE CONFLICT
What was the Tonkin Gulf Resolution?

South Vietnam did not improve after Diem's death. A string of military leaders tried to rule the country. Each one failed to bring stability. Johnson,

© Houghton Mifflin Harcourt Publishing Company

Guided Reading Workbook

Lesson 1, *continued*

however, continued to support South Vietnam. The president was determined to not "lose" Vietnam to the Communists.

In August 1964 Johnson received reports of an incident in the Gulf of Tonkin off North Vietnam. A North Vietnamese patrol boat allegedly had fired torpedoes at a U.S. destroyer. President Johnson responded by bombing North Vietnam.

He also asked Congress for special military powers to stop any future North Vietnamese attacks on U.S. forces. As a result, Congress passed the **Tonkin Gulf Resolution.** The resolution granted Johnson broad military powers in Vietnam. In February 1965 President Johnson used his new power. He launched "Operation Rolling Thunder," a major bombing attack on North Vietnam's cities.

3. What incident in the Gulf of Tonkin prompted President Johnson to bomb North Vietnam?

_____

_____

© Houghton Mifflin Harcourt Publishing Company

Lesson 1, *continued*

As you read this lesson, take notes to answer questions about how the
United States slowly became involved in a war in Vietnam.

1941 The Vietminh is formed →	1. What did the Vietminh declare as its main goal?	
1945 Japan is forced out of Vietnam →	2. What did Ho Chi Minh declare after Japan was forced out?	
1946 French troops return to southern Vietnam →	3. How did Ho Chi Minh respond to the return of the French?	
1950 U.S. begins its involvement in the Vietnam struggle →	4. Whom did the U.S. support?	5. What aid did the U.S. provide?
	6. Why did the U.S. get involved in the struggle?	
1954 Eisenhower introduces domino theory →	7. What did Eisenhower compare to a row of dominoes?	
Vietminh overruns Dien Bien Phu →	8. What did this Vietminh victory cause the French to do?	
Geneva Accords are reached →	9. How did the Geneva Accords change Vietnam?	
1956 Elections are canceled →	10. Who canceled the Vietnamese elections? Why?	
1957 Vietcong begins attacks on Diem government		
1963 Diem is overthrown	11. What authority did the Tonkin Gulf Resolution grant to the U.S. president?	
1964 U.S. Congress adopts Tonkin Gulf Resolution →		
1965 Operation Rolling Thunder is launched →	12. What was Operation Rolling Thunder?	

© Houghton Mifflin Harcourt Publishing Company

The Vietnam War

U.S. Involvement and Escalation

Key Terms and People

Robert McNamara Secretary of defense under Johnson

Dean Rusk Secretary of state under Johnson

William Westmoreland Commander of U.S. troops in Vietnam

Army of the Republic of Vietnam (ARVN) South Vietnamese military forces

napalm Gasoline-based explosive

Agent Orange Chemical that destroyed jungle land

search-and-destroy mission Tactic in which U.S. troops destroyed Vietnamese villages

credibility gap Situation in which the U.S. public no longer believed the Johnson administration

Before You Read

In the last lesson you read how the United States became involved in Vietnam. In this lesson you will read about the war America fought in Vietnam.

As You Read

Use a chart to take notes on the key military tactics and weapons used by the Vietcong and the Americans.

JOHNSON INCREASES U.S. INVOLVEMENT
Who **supported Johnson's decision to send U.S. troops to Vietnam?**

In 1965 Johnson began sending U.S. troops to Vietnam to fight the Vietcong. Some of Johnson's advisers had opposed this move. They argued it was too dangerous.

But most of the president's advisers supported sending in troops. They included Secretary of Defense **Robert McNamara** and Secretary of State **Dean Rusk.** These men believed that America had to help defeat communism in Vietnam. Otherwise,

the Communists might try to take over other countries.

Much of the public also agreed with Johnson's decision. Many Americans believed in stopping the spread of communism.

By the end of 1965, the United States had sent more than 180,000 troops to Vietnam. The American commander in South Vietnam was General **William Westmoreland.** Westmoreland was not impressed by the **Army of the Republic of Vietnam (ARVN)** as a fighting force. He asked for even more troops. By 1967 almost 500,000 American soldiers were fighting in Vietnam.

© Houghton Mifflin Harcourt Publishing Company

1. Name two groups that supported Johnson's decision to use troops in Vietnam.

_____

_____

FIGHTING IN THE JUNGLE
Why did the war drag on?

The United States believed that its superior weaponry would lead to a quick victory over the Vietcong. However, several factors turned the war into a bloody stalemate.

The first factor was the Vietcong's fighting style. The Vietcong did not have advanced weapons. As a result, they used hit-and-run ambush tactics. The Vietcong struck quickly in small groups. They then disappeared into the jungle or an elaborate system of tunnels. They knew how to blend in with civilians. They also placed countless booby traps and mines.

The second factor was the Vietcong's refusal to surrender. They were willing to fight at any cost. General Westmoreland's strategy for defeating the Vietcong was to destroy their morale through a war of attrition, gradually wearing them down through constant attack. Though the Vietcong suffered many battlefield deaths, they continued to fight on.

The third factor was the American troops' inability to win the support of the Vietnamese peasants. In fighting the Vietcong, U.S. troops ended up hurting the peasants as well. For example, U.S. planes dropped **napalm,** a gasoline-based bomb that set fire to the jungle. They did this to expose Vietcong tunnels and hideouts. They also sprayed **Agent Orange.** This was a leaf-killing chemical that destroyed the landscape. Both of these weapons harmed villagers and ruined villages.

American soldiers also turned the peasants against them by conducting **search-and-destroy missions.** During these missions, soldiers destroyed villages they believed supported the Vietcong.

The frustrations of fighting the war caused the morale of American soldiers to sink. Soldiers endured great hardships, especially prisoners of war captured by the North Vietnamese.

2. Name two reasons why the U.S. failed to score a quick victory against the Vietcong.

_____

_____

THE EARLY WAR AT HOME
How did the war affect Johnson's domestic programs?

The number of U.S. troops in Vietnam continued to increase. So did the cost of the war. As a result, the nation's economy began to suffer. In order to pay for the war, President Johnson had to cut spending for his Great Society programs.

By 1967 many Americans still supported the war. However, the images of the war on television began to change that. The Johnson administration told the American people that the war was going well. But television told the opposite story. Each night, Americans watched the brutal scenes of the war on their television screens. This led to a **credibility gap** in the Johnson administration. A growing number of people no longer believed what the president was saying.

3. How did the war affect Johnson's Great Society?

_____

_____

© Houghton Mifflin Harcourt Publishing Company

Guided Reading Workbook

Lesson 2, *continued*

As you read about the escalation of the war, take notes to answer the questions.

1. What role did each of the following play in the decision to escalate U.S. military involvement in Vietnam?
Lyndon B. Johnson
Robert McNamara
Dean Rusk
William Westmoreland
U.S. Congress
American public opinion

U.S. MILITARY STRATEGIES RESULT IN A BLOODY STALEMATE

2. What military advantages did the Americans have over the Vietcong?	3. What military advantages did the Vietcong have over the Americans?
4. What military strategies did the Americans use against the Vietcong?	5. What military strategies did the Vietcong use against the Americans?

PUBLIC SUPPORT FOR THE WAR BEGINS TO WAVER AS A "CREDIBILITY GAP" GROWS

6. What role did each of the following play in this change of public support?
The U.S. economy
Television

© Houghton Mifflin Harcourt Publishing Company

Guided Reading Workbook

A Nation Divided

Key Terms and People

draft System for calling people to military service

New Left Name given to the youth movement of the 1960s

Students for a Democratic Society (SDS) Prominent group of the New Left

Free Speech Movement New Left group that attacked business and government

dove American individual who called for America to withdraw from Vietnam

hawk American individual who supported the war effort

Before You Read

In the last lesson you read about America's war effort in Vietnam. In this lesson you will read about how the United States became divided over the war in Vietnam.

As You Read

Complete a chart on student organizations, issues, and demonstrations of the New Left.

THE WORKING CLASS GOES TO WAR
Who fought the war?

Most soldiers who fought in Vietnam were called into combat under the country's Selective Service System, or **draft.** Because the war was growing unpopular, thousands of men tried to avoid the draft. Some men sought out doctors who would give them medical exemptions. Others moved to a different community where there was a more lenient draft board. Some joined the National Guard or Coast Guard to avoid combat.

One of the most common ways to avoid the draft was to attend college. Most men enrolled in a university could put off their military service.

Many university students during the

1960s were white and financially well-off. As a result, a large number who fought in Vietnam were lower-class whites or minorities. Nearly 80 percent of American soldiers came from lower economic levels. Thus, Vietnam was known as a working-class war.

Early on, a high number of African Americans served and died in Vietnam. During the first several years of the war, 20 percent of American soldiers killed were black. Blacks, however, made up only about 10 percent of the U.S. population. This situation prompted protests from many civil rights leaders, including Martin Luther King Jr. Many African American soldiers also endured racism within their units.

The U.S. military in the 1960s did not allow women to serve in combat.

© Houghton Mifflin Harcourt Publishing Company

However, nearly 10,000 women served in Vietnam as army or navy nurses. Thousands more volunteered in the American Red Cross and the United Services Organization (USO). This organization provided entertainment to the troops.

1. Name two groups of Americans who did most of the fighting early on in Vietnam.

   _____

   _____

THE ROOTS OF OPPOSITION
What were the New Left groups?

By the 1960s American college students had become politically active. The growing youth movement of the 1960s was known as the **New Left.** The group took its name from the "old" left of the 1930s. That movement had tried to push the nation toward socialism. The New Left did not call for socialism. However, it did demand sweeping changes in American society.

One of the better-known New Left groups was **Students for a Democratic Society (SDS).** This organization called for greater individual freedom in America.

Another New Left group was the **Free Speech Movement** (FSM). This group was formed at the University of California at Berkeley. It grew out of a fight between students and administrators over free speech on campus. FSM criticized business and government institutions.

The strategies of the SDS and FSM eventually spread to colleges throughout the country. There, students protested mostly campus issues. Soon, however, students around the nation found one issue they could protest together: the Vietnam War.

2. Name two New Left groups.

   _____

   _____

THE PROTEST MOVEMENT EMERGES
How did the hawks and doves differ?

Across America, college students rose up in protest against the war. They did so for various reasons. The most common reason was that the conflict in Vietnam was a civil war between the North and South. Thus, the United States had no business being there. Others believed that the war kept America from focusing on other parts of the world. Still others saw the war as morally unjust.

In April 1965 SDS helped organize a march on Washington, DC. About 20,000 protesters participated. In November 1965 a protest rally in Washington drew about 30,000 protesters. Then, in February 1966 the Johnson administration changed deferments for college students. Students were required to be in good academic standing in order to avoid the draft. Campuses around the country erupted in protest. Student leaders in SDS called for civil disobedience at military recruitment centers and advised students to flee to Canada or Sweden.

Eventually, the antiwar movement reached beyond college campuses. Small numbers of returning veterans protested. Musicians took up the antiwar cause. Many protest songs became popular.

By 1967 Americans were divided into two main groups. Those who wanted the United States to withdraw from the war were called **doves.** Those who supported the war were called **hawks.** Other Americans took no stand on the war. However, they criticized doves for protesting a war in which U.S. troops were fighting and dying.

In spite of the many antiwar protests, a majority of American citizens in 1967 still supported the war. One poll showed that 70 percent of people believed the war protests were "acts of disloyalty." Some hawks felt that President Johnson was not increasing military power fast enough.

3. Briefly explain the positions of the hawks and doves.

_____

_____

As you read this lesson, take notes to answer the questions.

AVOIDING THE WAR
1. What were some of the ways that young American men avoided military service in Vietnam?
2. In what sense was the Vietnam War a "working-class" war? How did it become one?

OPPOSING THE WAR
3. What organizations and groups of Americans tended to oppose the war?
4. What were some of the reasons that "doves" opposed the war?
5. In what ways did they show their opposition to the war?

DEFENDING THE WAR
6. By 1967 how did most Americans feel about U.S. involvement in the Vietnam War?
7. Why did "hawks" criticize the Johnson administration's policies in Vietnam?

© Houghton Mifflin Harcourt Publishing Company

The Vietnam War

Lesson 4

1968: A Tumultuous Year

Key Terms and People

Tet offensive Series of Vietcong attacks during the 1968 Tet holiday

Clark Clifford A Lyndon Johnson adviser who became his secretary of defense

Robert Kennedy A Democratic candidate for president in 1968

Eugene McCarthy A Democratic presidential candidate who ran on an antiwar platform

Hubert Humphrey The 1968 Democratic nominee for president

George Wallace A third-party candidate in the 1968 presidential election

Before You Read

In the last lesson you read how the Vietnam War divided America. In this lesson you will read about the shocking events that made 1968 one of the most explosive years of the decade.

As You Read

Take notes to complete a cause-and-effect chart on the major events of 1968.

THE TET OFFENSIVE TURNS THE WAR
How did the Tet offensive affect America?

January 30 was the Vietnamese equivalent of New Year's Eve. It was the beginning of festivities known as Tet. During the Tet holiday in 1968, a weeklong truce was called. Many peasants crowded into South Vietnam's cities to celebrate the holiday.

However, many of the peasants turned out to be Vietcong rebels. The rebels launched a massive attack on nearly 100 towns and cities in South Vietnam. They also attacked 12 U.S. air bases. The attacks were known as the **Tet offensive.** The offensive lasted for about a month. Finally, U.S. and South

Vietnamese forces regained control of the cities.

General Westmoreland declared that the Tet offensive was a major defeat for the Vietcong. From a military standpoint, he was right. The Vietcong lost about 32,000 soldiers during the attacks. The United States and South Vietnam lost 3,000 soldiers.

However, the Tet offensive shattered America's confidence in the war. The enemy now seemed everywhere. Many Americans began to think that the war was unwinnable. The Tet offensive also shocked many in the White House. **Clark Clifford** was the president's new secretary of defense. After Tet, Clifford decided that America could not win the war.

© Houghton Mifflin Harcourt Publishing Company

Guided Reading Workbook

The Tet offensive also hurt President Johnson's popularity. By the end of February 1968, nearly 60 percent of the public disapproved of Johnson's handling of the war. In addition, nearly half the country said it had been a mistake to send troops to Vietnam.

1. How did the Tet offensive affect Johnson's popularity?

    _____

    _____

DAYS OF LOSS AND RAGE
Which events shocked the nation?

Even before the Tet offensive, an antiwar group in the Democratic Party had taken steps to unseat Johnson. The group looked for someone to challenge Johnson in the 1968 primary election. They asked **Robert Kennedy,** a senator from New York. Kennedy declined. However, Minnesota senator **Eugene McCarthy** agreed. He would run against Johnson on a platform to end the Vietnam War.

McCarthy surprised many people by nearly beating Johnson in the New Hampshire Democratic primary. Suddenly, Johnson appeared politically weak. As a result, Robert Kennedy declared himself a presidential candidate. The Democratic Party was now badly divided.

President Johnson decided to address the nation on television. He announced that he would seek peace in Vietnam. Then he declared that he would not seek reelection as president. The country was shocked.

In the days and months ahead, several more incidents stunned the nation. On April 4, a gunman killed civil rights leader Martin Luther King Jr. Violence ripped through more than 100 U.S. cities

as enraged followers of King burned buildings and destroyed neighborhoods. Two months later, an assassin shot and killed Robert Kennedy.

Meanwhile, antiwar protests continued to rock college campuses. During the first six months of 1968, almost 40,000 students on more than 100 campuses held demonstrations. Many of the demonstrations continued to target U.S. involvement in the Vietnam War. But other protests concerned campus and social issues. In one protest at Columbia University, students protesting the university's policies took over several buildings. Police arrested nearly 900 protesters.

2. Name two events that shocked Americans in 1968.

    _____

    _____

A TURBULENT RACE FOR PRESIDENT
What happened in Chicago?

In August 1968 the Democrats met in Chicago for their presidential convention. There, they would choose a presidential candidate. In reality, Democratic leaders had already decided on the candidate: Vice-President **Hubert Humphrey.** This angered many antiwar activists. They favored McCarthy.

About 10,000 antiwar protesters came to Chicago. Some protesters wanted to pressure the Democrats to create an antiwar platform. Others wanted to voice their opposition to Humphrey. Still others wanted to create violence to discredit the Democratic Party.

Violence eventually erupted at a downtown park away from the convention hall. There, police moved in on thousands of demonstrators. They

© Houghton Mifflin Harcourt Publishing Company

sprayed the protesters with Mace. They also beat them with nightsticks. Many protesters fled. Others fought back.

The violence in Chicago highlighted the Democrats' division. The Republicans were more unified. They nominated former vice-president Richard Nixon for president.

Nixon campaigned on a platform of law and order. He also assured the American people that he would end the Vietnam War. Nixon's campaign was helped by the entry of a third-party

candidate, **George Wallace.** Wallace was a former governor of Alabama. He took many democratic votes away from Humphrey. In November, Nixon won the election. It was now up to him to resolve the Vietnam crisis.

3. Name two reasons that protesters came to Chicago for the Democratic convention.

_____

_____

As you read this lesson, note some results or effects of the events of 1968.

Events of 1968	Effects
1. Tet offensive	
2. Johnson's poor showing in the New Hampshire primary	
3. Assassination of Dr. Martin Luther King Jr.	
4. Unrest on college campuses	
5. Disorder at the Democratic National Convention	
6. 1968 presidential election	

© Houghton Mifflin Harcourt Publishing Company

The End of the War and Its Legacy

Key Terms and People

Richard Nixon President of the United States, elected 1968

Henry Kissinger Nixon adviser who helped negotiate an end to the war

Vietnamization President Nixon's plan for ending America's involvement in the war

silent majority Those mainstream Americans who supported Nixon's policies

My Lai Site of massacre of Vietnamese civilians by American soldiers

Kent State University Site of protest where the National Guard killed four students

Pentagon Papers Government documents that showed the government had no real plan for leaving Vietnam

War Powers Act Act that forbids the president from mobilizing troops without congressional approval

Before You Read

In the last lesson you read about the explosive events that occurred in 1968. In this lesson you will read how the Vietnam War ended and what effect the war had on America.

As You Read

Complete a chart identifying the effects of the Vietnam War on the United States.

PRESIDENT NIXON AND VIETNAMIZATION
How did Vietnamization work?

Richard Nixon pledged to end American involvement in the Vietnam War. With National Security Advisor **Henry Kissinger,** he came up with a plan to end the war. Their plan was known as **Vietnamization.** It called for both the gradual withdrawal of U.S. troops and for the South Vietnamese to do more of the fighting. Nixon intended to maintain "peace with honor," meaning U.S. dignity in leaving the war. By August 1969 the first 25,000 U.S. troops had returned home. Over the next three years, the number of American troops in Vietnam dropped from more than 500,000 to less than 25,000.

Nixon, however, did not want to lose the war. So as he pulled American troops out, he ordered a massive bombing attack against North Vietnam. Nixon also ordered that bombs be dropped on the neighboring countries of Laos and Cambodia. These countries held a number of Vietcong bases.

© Houghton Mifflin Harcourt Publishing Company

Guided Reading Workbook

Lesson 5, *continued*

1. Name both aspects of the Vietnamization plan.

_____

_____

TROUBLE CONTINUES ON THE HOME FRONT
Which events weakened support for the war?

To win support for his war policies, Nixon appealed to what he called the **silent majority.** These were mainstream Americans who quietly supported the president's strategy. Many Americans did support the president. However, the war continued to divide the country.

In November 1969 Americans learned of a shocking event. U.S. troops had massacred more than 100 unarmed Vietnamese in the village of **My Lai.** In April 1970 the country heard more upsetting news. President Nixon announced that U.S. troops had invaded Cambodia. They had tried to destroy Vietcong supply lines there. Upon hearing of the invasion, colleges exploded in protest.

A protest at **Kent State University** in Ohio turned tragic. To restore order on the campus, the local mayor called in the National Guard. Some students began throwing rocks at the guards. The guards fired into a crowd of protesters. Four students were killed.

Nixon's invasion of Cambodia cost him public support. It also cost him political support. Members of Congress were angry that he had invaded Cambodia without telling them. As a result, Congress repealed the Tonkin Gulf Resolution. This had given the president the freedom to conduct war policy in Vietnam on his own.

Support for the war declined even further in June 1971. That month, a former Defense Department worker leaked what became known as the **Pentagon Papers.** These documents showed that the past U.S. presidents had never drawn up any plans to withdraw from Vietnam.

2. Name two incidents that weakened support for the war.

_____

_____

THE LONG WAR ENDS
Who won the war?

In 1972 there was a presidential election. To win reelection, Nixon believed he had to end the Vietnam War. Nixon called on Henry Kissinger, his adviser for national security affairs. Kissinger negotiated a peace settlement with the North Vietnamese. In October 1972 Kissinger announced that peace was close at hand. A month later, Nixon was reelected president.

However, the promised peace in Vietnam did not come. South Vietnam objected to the proposed peace settlement. As a result, the peace talks broke down. Nixon responded by ordering a ferocious bombing campaign against the two largest cities in North Vietnam. In what became known as the "Christmas bombings," U.S. planes dropped 100,000 bombs in the days around Christmas.

Eventually, the peace talks resumed. In January 1973 the warring parties signed a peace agreement. By the end of March, the last U.S. troops had left. For America, the Vietnam War was over.

Shortly after America left, the peace agreement collapsed. North and South

© Houghton Mifflin Harcourt Publishing Company

Lesson 5, *continued*

Vietnam resumed fighting. In April 1975 North Vietnamese troops captured the South's capital, Saigon. Soon after, South Vietnam surrendered to North Vietnam.

3. What happened to South Vietnam after America left?

_____

_____

THE WAR LEAVES A PAINFUL LEGACY
How did the war affect America?

The Vietnam War cost both sides many lives. In all, about 58,000 Americans died in Vietnam. Another 303,000 were wounded. Vietnamese deaths topped 2 million.

While families welcomed home their sons and daughters, the nation as a whole gave a cold reception to returning Vietnam veterans. Many veterans faced hostility from Americans still bitter about the war.

After the war, Southeast Asia continued to experience violence and unrest. The Communists imprisoned hundreds of thousands of South Vietnamese. In Cambodia, a Communist group known as the Khmer Rouge took power in 1975. They attempted to transform the country into a peasant society. In doing so, they killed many government officials and intellectuals. The group is believed to have killed as many as 1 million Cambodians.

In the United States, the war resulted in several policy changes. First, the government abolished the draft. In November 1973 Congress passed the **War Powers Act.** This law prevented the president from committing troops in a foreign conflict without approval from Congress.

In a larger sense, the war made Americans less willing to become involved in foreign wars. The war also left many Americans with a feeling of mistrust toward their government.

4. Name two ways in which the war affected Americans.

_____

_____

Lesson 5, *continued*

As you read about President Nixon's Vietnam policy and the end of the war, write short answers to the following questions.

1. What was "peace with honor"?	2. How did Americans at home respond to the My Lai massacre?
3. When did President Nixon announce the invasion of Cambodia, and how did some people respond?	4. Where were four students killed by National Guard soldiers during a campus war protest?
5. Why did Congress repeal the Tonkin Gulf Resolution?	6. What were the Pentagon Papers?
7. How did Nixon respond when peace talks broke down soon after his reelection?	8. Why weren't Vietnam veterans cheered and honored when they returned home?
9. Who took power in Cambodia, and what did they do?	10. What are two policy changes that occurred as a result of the Vietnam War?

© Houghton Mifflin Harcourt Publishing Company

Transitions and Conservatism

The Nixon Administration

Key Terms and People

Richard M. Nixon 37th president

New Federalism Plan to give federal power back to the states

revenue sharing Plan for the federal government to share money with state and local governments

Family Assistance Plan (FAP) Nixon's welfare reform proposal to give direct relief to poor families

southern strategy Nixon's effort to attract southern votes by opposing desegregation

stagflation Situation that occurs when unemployment and inflation rise at the same time

OPEC (Organization of the Petroleum Exporting Countries) Organization of nations that export oil

Before You Read

In the last lesson you read about the end of the Vietnam War. In this lesson you will learn about President Nixon and his attempts to move the country in a more conservative direction.

As You Read

Use a chart to take notes on policies of Richard Nixon.

NIXON'S NEW CONSERVATISM
How did Nixon pursue conservative policies?

President **Richard M. Nixon** wanted to turn the United States in a more conservative direction. He tried to decrease the power of the federal government. Nixon's plan was called **New Federalism.** Its goal was to give federal power to the states.

Nixon introduced **revenue sharing.** The federal government usually told state and local governments how to spend their federal money. Under revenue sharing, state and local officials could spend their federal dollars however they saw fit with few limits.

Nixon also wanted to reform the welfare system because he believed it had grown unwieldy and inefficient. He supported the **Family Assistance Plan (FAP).** Under this plan, every family of four with no income would receive a payment of $1,600 to $4,000 more a year. But this plan failed to pass Congress.

When Nixon first took office, he cooperated with Congress. But he soon refused to spend money that Congress wanted to spend on programs that he did not like. Federal courts ruled that

Nixon's action was unconstitutional. They ordered that Nixon spend the money on the programs.

Nixon also followed "law and order" policies to stop riots and antiwar protests. He used the Central Intelligence Agency (CIA) and the Internal Revenue Service (IRS) to harass people. He created an "enemies list" and had the CIA and IRS target people on this list. The list included liberals and other opponents of his policies.

1. What conservative programs did Nixon support?

_____

_____

NIXON'S SOUTHERN STRATEGY
What was the southern strategy?

Nixon wanted to make sure he would get reelected in 1972. To achieve this, he used what he called a **southern strategy** to win the support of southerners who were unhappy with desegregation policies.

To attract white voters, Nixon tried to slow school desegregation. He violated the *Brown* v. *Board of Education* ruling. But the Supreme Court ordered the administration to follow the ruling, which he did. Nixon also opposed the extension of the Voting Rights Act of 1965. But Congress extended the act.

Nixon believed that the Supreme Court under Chief Justice Earl Warren was too liberal. During his presidency, four justices, including Warren, left the Court. Nixon took this opportunity to appoint more conservative justices.

2. How did Nixon hope to win southern support?

_____

_____

CONFRONTING A STAGNANT ECONOMY
What is stagflation?

One of the biggest problems facing Nixon was a weak economy. Between 1967 and 1973 inflation and unemployment increased. This situation is known as **stagflation.**

Inflation increased because the government had spent more on social programs and the war in Vietnam. Also, international trade competition and many new workers caused unemployment.

To combat stagflation, Nixon wanted to raise taxes and cut the budget. Congress refused. Nixon tried to reduce the amount of money in circulation by urging that interest rates be raised. That caused a recession. Nixon also froze workers' wages and businesses' prices and fees for 90 days. That helped inflation but kept the recession going.

The economy also struggled because of the nation's need for foreign oil. The United States received much of its oil from the Middle East. Many of these countries belonged to a cartel called **OPEC (Organization of the Petroleum Exporting Countries).** During the 1960s OPEC gradually raised oil prices. Then, in 1973 a war broke out, with Israel against Egypt and Syria. The United States sent military aid to Israel. OPEC nations sided with Egypt and Syria. They stopped selling oil to the United States. Motorists faced long lines at gas stations. Some factories and schools closed. When OPEC started selling oil to the United States again, the price had quadrupled.

3. How did OPEC affect the U.S. economy?

_____

_____

© Houghton Mifflin Harcourt Publishing Company

Complete the chart by describing President Nixon's policies toward the issues facing him.

Issues	Policies
1. Size and power of the federal government	
2. Inefficiency of the welfare system	
3. Liberalism of people opposed to Nixon's policies	
4. Nixon's reelection	
5. Liberalism of Supreme Court justices	
6. Stagflation and recession	

© Houghton Mifflin Harcourt Publishing Company

Transitions and Conservatism

Watergate: Nixon's Downfall

Key Terms and People

impeachment The constitutional process for removing a president from office

Watergate Scandal that forced Nixon to resign

H. R. Haldeman Adviser to Nixon

John Ehrlichman Adviser to Nixon

John Mitchell Attorney general and director of Nixon's reelection campaign

Committee to Re-elect the President Nixon's campaign committee

John Sirica Judge in the trial of the Watergate burglars

Saturday Night Massacre Nixon's firing of Justice Department officials, including the special prosecutor investigating Watergate

Before You Read

In the last lesson you read about President Nixon's approach to politics. In this lesson you will learn about the Watergate scandal.

As You Read

Use a timeline to take notes on the events of the Watergate scandal.

PRESIDENT NIXON AND HIS WHITE HOUSE
What was Watergate?

In 1974 the House Judiciary Committee voted to recommend the **impeachment** of, or the bringing of formal charges against, President Nixon. The cause was the **Watergate** scandal, an attempt to cover up a burglary of the Democratic National Committee (DNC) headquarters.

By the time Nixon became president, the executive branch had become powerful, and Nixon expanded the power. He confided in a small group of loyal advisers. These advisers included **H. R. Haldeman,** chief of staff; **John Ehrlichman,** chief domestic adviser; and **John Mitchell,** the attorney general.

These men helped Nixon get reelected. They also shared Nixon's desire for power and secrecy. This would lead them to cover up their role in Watergate.

1. What was the Watergate scandal?

_____

_____

THE DRIVE TOWARD REELECTION
What was the CRP?

Nixon always feared losing elections. So his campaign team looked for any advantages to help him win reelection. The team hired five men to break in to Democratic Party offices in the Watergate complex in Washington, DC.

© Houghton Mifflin Harcourt Publishing Company

Guided Reading Workbook

They were caught photographing files and placing wiretaps on phones. The press found that the group's leader, James McCord, was a former CIA agent. He was also an official of the **Committee to Re-elect the President** (CRP). John Mitchell, who had been attorney general, was CRP's director.

Nixon and his staff tried to hide the link to the White House. Workers shredded evidence. Nixon asked the CIA to urge the FBI to stop looking into the burglary.

The Watergate burglary was not a big issue in the election. Only two reporters kept on the story. Their articles linked administration members to the burglary. The White House denied any connections.

2. Why did the CRP order the burglary of the DNC headquarters?

_____

_____

THE COVER-UP UNRAVELS
How did Nixon get caught?

Nixon was reelected by a landslide over George S. McGovern. Soon after, the cover-up began to unravel. In January 1973 the Watergate burglars went to trial. The trial's presiding judge, **John Sirica,** did not think that the burglars acted alone. Then in March 1973 James McCord sent a letter to Sirica, stating that he had lied under oath. He also hinted that some of Nixon's administration was involved.

Soon, public interest in the burglary increased. In April 1973 Nixon fired White House counsel John Dean. Three top aides resigned. The president then went on television and denied any cover-up. He said that he was appointing Elliot Richardson to investigate Watergate.

In May 1973 the Senate began its own investigation. In the hearings, John Dean said that Nixon knew about the cover-up. Later, aide Alexander Butterfield revealed that White House meetings had been tape-recorded. The Senate committee wanted the tapes, but Nixon refused.

Special prosecutor Archibald Cox took the president to court in October 1973 to get the tapes. Nixon refused and ordered Richardson to fire Cox. In what became known as the **Saturday Night Massacre,** Richardson refused and resigned. The deputy attorney general also refused and was fired. Solicitor General Robert Bork finally fired Cox. But Cox's replacement, Leon Jaworski, wanted those tapes, too.

3. What did Nixon do during the investigation?

_____

_____

THE FALL OF A PRESIDENT
How did Nixon's presidency end?

In March 1974 a grand jury charged seven Nixon aides with obstruction of justice and perjury. Nixon released about 1,250 pages of edited transcripts of taped meetings, but not the unedited tapes. He defended his actions by saying that releasing the tapes would reveal secrets that would endanger national security. The Supreme Court rejected his argument and, in July 1974 ordered him to release them, because evidence of possible criminal activity could not be withheld, even by a president.

Three days later, a House committee voted to impeach Nixon. If the full House approved, he would have a Senate trial. If found guilty, he would be

© Houghton Mifflin Harcourt Publishing Company

removed from office. When the tapes were released, they proved that Nixon had known about the burglary and was part of the cover-up. On August 8, 1974, before the impeachment could happen, Nixon resigned.

Watergate, coupled with the Vietnam War, made people distrust and become disillusioned with public officials.

4. Why did President Nixon resign?

_____

_____

Name _____ Class _____ Date _____

Answer the questions shown on the following timeline.

1972 **June**	Break-in at DNC campaign office	→ 1. How were the burglars connected to President Nixon?
Nov.	Nixon wins reelection	
1973 **Jan.**	Burglars go on trial	→ 2. Who was the judge? What did he believe?
Mar.	Top aides of Nixon are implicated	→ 3. How were Mitchell and Dean connected to Nixon?
April	Dean is fired; Haldeman and Ehrlichman resign	→ 4. How were Haldeman and Ehrlichman connected to Nixon?
May	Senate opens Watergate hearings	→ 5. What did the following men tell the Senate about Nixon? a. Dean b. Butterfield
Oct.	Saturday Night Massacre	→ 6. Who was fired or forced to resign in the "massacre"?
1974 **April**	Edited transcripts of tapes are released	→ 7. What reason did Nixon give for releasing transcripts instead of the tapes?
July	Supreme Court orders surrender of tapes	
Aug.	House committee adopts impeachment articles. Unedited tapes are released Nixon resigns	→ 8. What did the tapes reveal?

© Houghton Mifflin Harcourt Publishing Company

Transitions and Conservatism

Lesson 3

The Ford and Carter Years

Key Terms and People

Gerald R. Ford 38th president

Jimmy Carter 39th president

National Energy Act Law that aimed to conserve energy

human rights Rights and freedoms that all people should enjoy

Camp David Accords Agreements between Israel and Egypt

Ayatollah Ruhollah Khomeini Iranian religious leader who led the revolution against the shah of Iran

Before You Read

In the last lesson you learned about Watergate. In this lesson you will read about the presidencies of Gerald Ford and Jimmy Carter.

As You Read

Use a chart to take notes on the major events of the Ford and Carter administrations.

FORD TRAVELS A ROUGH ROAD
What did Ford do as president?

Gerald R. Ford replaced Richard Nixon as president. Upon taking office, Ford urged Americans to put the Watergate scandal behind them. The new president granted Nixon a full pardon, explaining that a long-drawn-out trial would increase the strain on the nation. For many Americans, however, Ford's actions contributed to feelings of anger and disillusionment with the presidency.

The economy was worse by the time Ford took office. He promoted a program to slow inflation by encouraging energy conservation, but it failed. He fought for higher interest rates, which caused a recession. Then he approved a stimulus package of spending increases and tax cuts. By 1976, things were a little

better. However, Ford was constantly at war with the Democratic Congress. He vetoed more than 50 pieces of legislation. He wanted to reduce government spending and curb government regulation because he hoped these reforms could reduce prices by increasing competition.

1. What did Ford do about the economy?

_____

_____

CARTER ENTERS THE WHITE HOUSE
How did Carter try to fix the economy?

Ford ran for election in 1976 against Democrat **Jimmy Carter.** Carter

© Houghton Mifflin Harcourt Publishing Company

Guided Reading Workbook

promised he would never lie to Americans. He won the election.

Carter used radio and television "fireside chats" to stay in touch with the people. But he did not try to reach out to Congress, and angered both congressional Republicans and Democrats.

Carter thought the energy crisis was the nation's most important priority. He blamed the problem on American reliance on imported oil. He presented Congress with more than 100 energy conservation proposals. The **National Energy Act** was passed. It placed a tax on gas-guzzling cars and removed price controls on oil.

But in 1979 Middle East violence caused another fuel shortage. High prices made inflation worse. Carter tried several measures, but inflation kept rising.

There were other economic problems, too. Automation and foreign competition meant fewer manufacturing jobs. The growth of the service sector meant many high-paying service jobs required more education or skills than manufacturing jobs.

While Carter was not successful in improving the economy, he had an exceptional civil rights record. He put more African Americans and women in his administration than ever before.

2. What was one way Carter tried to solve the nation's economic problems?

    _____

    _____

CULTURAL SHIFTS IN THE 1970S; A HUMAN RIGHTS FOREIGN POLICY
How did human rights affect Carter's foreign policy?

Television during the 1970s reflected life in the United States. Shows dealt with social issues such as racial and economic divisions between groups. African Americans were main characters in shows. Young, single women were also portrayed.

The 1970s was a time for advances in computer technology. By 1974 there were personal computers in homes. Microsoft was formed in 1975, and in 1977 Apple was founded. Computers became smaller, cheaper, and more powerful.

President Carter tried to follow moral principles in his foreign policy. He believed the United States should promote **human rights.** Human rights are freedoms and liberties like those listed in the Declaration of Independence and the Bill of Rights.

Carter cut aid to countries that violated their people's rights. He supported a treaty with Panama to give control of the Panama Canal to that country.

3. What was Carter's foreign policy based on?

    _____

    _____

TRIUMPH AND CRISIS IN THE MIDDLE EAST
What did Carter do about the Middle East?

In 1978 Carter held a meeting with the leaders of Egypt and Israel. The two nations had been enemies for years. After 12 days of talks, Carter and the two leaders reached agreements known as the **Camp David Accords.** Israel agreed to withdraw from the Sinai Peninsula. Egypt recognized Israel's right to exist.

In 1979 Muslim rebels and their leader **Ayatollah Ruhollah Khomeini**

© Houghton Mifflin Harcourt Publishing Company

overthrew the shah of Iran. In October 1979 Carter allowed the shah to enter the United States for cancer treatment. The rebels became angry, and on November 4, 1979, took control of the U.S. embassy in Iran. They took 52 Americans hostage. They wanted the United States to send the shah back to Iran in return for the hostages.

Carter refused. A long standoff followed. It took 444 days for the hostages to be released.

4. Name one success and one defeat in the Middle East for Carter.

_____

_____

Complete the chart by identifying the actions of presidents Ford and Carter related to the issues listed.

Gerald Ford	Actions
1. Ending Watergate scandal	
2. Troubled economy	
3. Congress hostile to Ford's agenda	

Jimmy Carter	Actions
4. Distrust of politicians	
5. Energy crisis	
6. Discrimination	
7. Human rights issues	
8. Panama Canal	
9. Middle East tensions	

© Houghton Mifflin Harcourt Publishing Company

Transitions and Conservatism

A Conservative Movement Emerges

Key Terms and People

entitlement program Program that guarantees benefits to particular groups

New Right Alliance of conservative groups to support conservative ideas

affirmative action Programs that required special consideration for racial and ethnic minorities and women

reverse discrimination Favoring one group over another on the basis of race or gender even though they might not be necessarily better qualified

conservative coalition Alliance of business interests, religious people, and dissatisfied middle-class voters to support conservative candidates

Moral Majority Organization formed to fight for traditional values

Ronald Reagan 40th president

Geraldine Ferraro Democratic vice-presidential candidate in 1984

George Bush Reagan's vice-president; elected 41st president in 1988

Before You Read

In the last lesson you read about the policies of presidents Ford and Carter. In this lesson you will learn about the growth of the conservative movement leading up to 1980.

As You Read

Use a chart to take notes on the issues that interested conservatives.

THE CONSERVATIVE MOVEMENT BUILDS
Why did conservatism grow?

American conservatism had been gaining support since Barry Goldwater's run for the presidency in 1964. Many people were questioning the power of the federal government. They wanted state governments, businesses, and individuals to have more freedom from the federal government.

Many Americans resented the cost of **entitlement programs.** These are programs that guaranteed benefits to

particular groups. By 1980 nearly $300 billion a year was being spent on these programs. Many Americans were unhappy paying taxes to support these benefits.

Some people also became frustrated with the government's civil rights policies. The Civil Rights Act of 1964 was meant to end racial discrimination. But over the years, some court decisions extended the act. Some people opposed laws that increased minority opportunities in employment or education. During the 1970s right-wing, grassroots groups

© Houghton Mifflin Harcourt Publishing Company

emerged to support single issues. Together these groups were known as the **New Right.** Among the causes they supported were opposition to abortion and school busing, blocking the Equal Rights Amendment, and supporting school prayer.

Many in the New Right were critical of **affirmative action.** This was the policy that required employers to give special consideration to women, African Americans, and other minority groups.

The New Right called this **reverse discrimination,** favoring one group over another on the basis of race or gender even though they might not be better qualified.

Right-wing groups tended to vote for the same candidates. These voters formed the **conservative coalition.** This was an alliance of intellectuals, business leaders, middle-class voters, disaffected Democrats, and fundamentalist Christian groups. The *National Review,* founded in 1955 by conservative William F. Buckley Jr., was a magazine devoted to developing conservative policies and bringing them to the public.

Members of the conservative coalition shared some basic positions. They opposed big government, entitlement programs, and many civil rights programs. They also believed in a return to traditional moral standards.

Religious groups, especially evangelical Christians, played an important role in the conservative coalition. Some of these groups were guided by television preachers such as Jerry Falwell and Pat Robertson. Falwell formed the **Moral Majority,** which interpreted the Bible literally. The group also believed in absolute standards of right and wrong. The Moral Majority criticized a decline in national morality.

1. What basic positions did members of the conservative coalition share?

_____

_____

CONSERVATIVES WIN POLITICAL POWER
Why was Reagan popular?

The conservatives found a strong presidential candidate in **Ronald Reagan.** He won the 1980 nomination and chose George Bush as his running mate.

Reagan had been a movie actor. He won political fame with a speech for Barry Goldwater during the 1964 presidential campaign. In 1966 Reagan was elected governor of California. He was reelected in 1970.

In the 1980 election, Reagan ran on a number of issues. Supreme Court decisions on abortion, pornography, the teaching of evolution, and prayer in public schools all upset conservative voters. Reagan also had a strong anti-Communist policy. High inflation and the Iranian hostage crisis caused people to vote for Reagan.

Reagan was an extremely effective candidate, partly due to his acting experience. He was known for simplifying issues and giving clear-cut answers. People called him the Great Communicator. He was also committed to military and economic strength. During a debate between Reagan and Carter, Reagan attacked Carter's handling of the energy crisis and terrorism. Carter said Reagan was too conservative for the United States and warned of cuts that would happen to social programs.

A little more than half of Americans voted in 1980. Reagan won the election by a narrow majority. The election also gave Republicans control of the Senate.

2. Why was Reagan called the Great Communicator?

_____

_____

CONSERVATIVE VICTORIES IN 1984 AND 1988
Who won the elections of 1984 and 1988?

By 1984 Reagan had the support of conservative voters who approved of his policies. These voters included businesspeople, southerners, westerners, and Reagan Democrats. Also, the economy was strong. With so much support, Reagan easily won the 1984 election. He defeated Democrat Walter Mondale. Mondale chose Representative **Geraldine Ferraro** of New York as his running mate. Ferraro became the first woman on a major party's presidential ticket.

In 1988 Vice-President **George Bush** ran for the presidency. He won the Republican nomination. The Democrats nominated Massachusetts governor Michael Dukakis.

During the campaign, Bush built on Reagan's legacy of low taxes by saying, "Read my lips: no new taxes." Most Americans saw little reason for change. They were economically comfortable and believed it was because of Reagan and Bush. George Bush won the election with 53 percent of the popular vote and 426 electoral votes.

3. What did the presidential elections of 1984 and 1988 show about the mood of the country?

_____

_____

© Houghton Mifflin Harcourt Publishing Company

Lesson 4, *continued*

Complete the chart about the conservative movement that swept the country. Note the individuals, groups, and institutions that fueled it. Then identify four factors that contributed to Ronald Reagan's victory.

1. Individuals of the conservative movement	2. Groups and institutions of the conservative movement

3. Issues and interests of conservatives

FOUR SOCIAL ISSUES THAT CONTRIBUTED TO RONALD REAGAN'S VICTORY	
4.	5.
6.	7.

© Houghton Mifflin Harcourt Publishing Company

Guided Reading Workbook

Transitions and Conservatism

Reagan and Bush Confront Domestic Concerns

Key Terms and People

Reaganomics Reagan's economic policies

supply-side economics Economic theory that tax cuts will increase jobs and government revenues

Sandra Day O'Connor First woman Supreme Court justice

deregulation The cutting back of federal regulation of industry

Environmental Protection Agency (EPA) Agency established in 1970 to fight pollution and conserve natural resources

AIDS (acquired immune deficiency syndrome) A disease caused by a virus that destroys the body's immune system

Before You Read

In the last lesson you saw how conservative power grew before the presidential election of 1980. In this lesson you will read about the conservative policies of presidents Ronald Reagan and George H.W. Bush.

As You Read

Use a chart to take notes on changes occurring during the 1980s.

"REAGANOMICS" TAKES OVER
What was Reaganomics?

Reagan tried to reduce the size and power of the federal government. He asked for deep cuts in government spending on social programs. In general, programs affecting the poor rather than the middle class were cut. Reagan also convinced Congress to lower taxes. This approach was called **Reaganomics.**

Reaganomics depended on **supply-side economics.** This theory said that cutting taxes would motivate people to work, save, and invest. More investment would create more jobs. More workers would

mean more taxpayers, which would cause government revenues to increase. Reagan's tax cuts mainly benefited the wealthy because of the president's belief in the "trickle-down" theory. According to this theory, some of the money acquired by the wealth would ultimately reach other citizens.

Reagan also increased military spending. Between 1981 and 1984, the Defense Department budget almost doubled. This was one reason that the nation's deficit grew.

For a while, the economy sank into a recession. The economy rebounded

© Houghton Mifflin Harcourt Publishing Company

once interest rates and inflation rates dropped.

Economic downturns hit the savings and loan (S&L) industry hard. More than 1,000 S&Ls closed their doors. Taxpayers lost more than $120 million.

Government revenues did not increase as much as Reagan hoped. So the federal government ran up huge budget deficits. During Reagan's first term, the size of the government debt had almost doubled.

1. What was the main idea of Reaganomics?

   _____

   _____

REAGAN'S POLICY GOALS
What kind of justices did Reagan and Bush nominate?

Reagan was able to make the Supreme Court more conservative through his appointments. He nominated Antonin Scalia, Anthony M. Kennedy, and **Sandra Day O'Connor** to the Supreme Court. O'Connor was the first woman appointed to the Court. Reagan also nominated Justice William Rehnquist to the position of Chief Justice.

President George Bush later made the Court more conservative when he nominated David H. Souter and Clarence Thomas. In many decisions, the Court moved away from the more liberal rulings of the previous 40 years. The Court restricted a woman's right to an abortion, put limits on civil rights laws, and narrowed the rights of arrested persons.

Reagan tried to reduce the power of government through **deregulation.** He cut back on government rules related to industry and removed price controls on oil and gas. He deregulated the airline industry and ended government regulation of the savings and loan

industry. Positive effects included increased competition and lower prices.

Reagan also reduced environmental regulation. He cut the budget of the **Environmental Protection Agency (EPA).** He ignored requests from Canada to reduce acid rain. Reagan appointed opponents of environmental regulation to oversee the environment. James Watt, Reagan's secretary of the interior, took many actions that were questioned by environmentalists. He sold millions of acres of public lands to private developers, allowed drilling for oil and gas in the continental shelf, encouraged timber cutting in national forests, and eased restrictions on coal mining.

2. What was the result of Reagan's and Bush's appointments to the Supreme Court?

   _____

   _____

SOCIAL CONCERNS
What problems did Americans face in the 1980s?

A scary health issue that arose in the 1980s was **AIDS (acquired immune deficiency syndrome).** The disease is caused by a virus that destroys the immune system that protects people from illness. Most of the early victims of AIDS were either homosexual men or intravenous drug users who shared needles. Many people also contracted AIDS through contaminated blood transfusions. AIDS began spreading throughout the world possibly as early as the 1960s. The United States began a campaign to treat AIDS around the world.

Another issue that concerned Americans was abortion. In the 1973 *Roe* v. *Wade* decision, the Supreme

Court said women had the right to have an abortion. Opponents of legalized abortion described themselves as "pro-life." Supporters of legalized abortion called themselves "pro-choice." In 1989 the Supreme Court ruled in *Webster* v. *Reproductive Health Care Services* that individual states could place their own restrictions on abortion.

Battles over abortion rights often competed for attention with concerns over rising drug abuse. The Reagan administration declared a war on drugs. Reagan supported laws to catch drug users and drug dealers.

Education remained an important issue. In 1983 a report entitled *A Nation at Risk* criticized the nation's schools. The report showed that American students' test scores lagged behind those of students in other nations. The findings started a debate about the quality of education. The commission recommended increased homework, longer school days and school year, and increased pay for teachers. It also asked for a greater emphasis on basic subjects such as English, math, and science.

The nation's cities were also in crisis. Many poor people remained in cities, as wealthier people moved to the suburbs. Businesses moved, too, taking jobs and tax money with them. Poor people in cities often had little hope of finding jobs. They also faced crumbling buildings, lack of health services, and many social problems. Many city dwellers become homeless.

In 1981 NASA hoped to revive interest in space with its new space shuttle program. Two firsts were achieved in 1983. Sally Ride became the first American woman in space, and Guion S. Bluford became the first

African American in space. Disaster struck in 1986 with the explosion of the space shuttle *Challenger*. Teacher Christa McAuliffe was among the crewmembers killed. Space shuttle flights stopped for two years.

3. Identify three issues that concerned Americans during the 1980s.

_____

_____

BUSH'S DOMESTIC POLICIES
Who won the elections of 1984 and 1988?

George H.W. Bush vowed to continue to address the nation's domestic problems. He also promised to support volunteers, who he called "a thousand points of light."

Bush could not address all his plans. The federal deficit had risen dramatically. Bush had promised citizens no new taxes, and this limited the amount of money available to address social issues. Bush did introduce a plan to offer parents greater say in choosing schools.

Bush also signed two important laws. These landmark laws were the Americans with Disabilities Act (ADA) and the Clean Air Act Amendments.

Bush had impressive foreign policy successes, but they were overshadowed by his minimal domestic successes. Republican leadership of the nation came to an end when Bush lost his bid for reelection.

4. Why was Bush not able to address all his plans?

_____

_____

© Houghton Mifflin Harcourt Publishing Company

Lesson 5, *continued*

Describe the result of each action during the 1980s.

Action		Result(s)
1. Government spending on social programs cut and income taxes lowered	→	Result(s):
2. Military spending increased	→	Result(s):
3. Conservative judges to the Supreme Court and other federal courts named	→	Result(s):
4. The Environmental Protection Agency budget cut and business-oriented EPA administrators named	→	Result(s):
5. American students' test scores lag behind those of other nations	→	Result(s):
6. Wealthier people leave cities for the suburbs	→	Result(s):

© Houghton Mifflin Harcourt Publishing Company

Guided Reading Workbook

Transitions and Conservatism

Foreign Policy Under Reagan and Bush

Key Terms and People

apartheid Policy of racial segregation throughout South African society

Tiananmen Square Place in Beijing where Chinese protesters demonstrated against the Communist government

Sandinistas Communist rebel group that took power in Nicaragua

Contras Rebel forces supported by Ronald Reagan to overthrow the Sandinistas

Operation Desert Storm The 1991 U.S. attack on Iraq to force the Iraqis out of Kuwait

Before You Read

In the last lesson you learned about some of the social issues Americans faced in the 1980s. In this lesson you will see how American foreign policy changed under presidents Reagan and Bush.

As You Read

Use a chart to take notes about U.S. foreign policy in different regions of the world.

FOREIGN POLICY IN ASIA AND AFRICA
What conflicts existed in Asia and Africa during the 1970s and 1980s?

The South African government mandated **apartheid** for decades. Apartheid gave the minority white population special privileges, while nonwhites were kept from good jobs, schools, and housing. They could not vote, own land, or travel freely. President Reagan's position was not to intervene. Some saw his policy as helpful to the white regime. Then in 1986 Congress overrode a veto by Reagan and imposed trade limits and sanctions on South Africa. When Bush became president, he

supported these sanctions. Eventually, apartheid ended. In 1994 South Africa had a new constitution and democratic elections.

Students in China demanded freedom of speech. In April 1989 protesters held marches to voice their demands. The marches grew into large demonstrations in Beijing's **Tiananmen Square.** The Chinese military crushed the protesters. Soldiers killed hundreds of them and arrested others. People all over the world watched these actions. The United States and other nations condemned the actions of the Chinese government and imposed economic sanctions. President Bush was criticized, however, for

© Houghton Mifflin Harcourt Publishing Company

Guided Reading Workbook

Lesson 6, *continued*

meeting with the government. People said that he was more interested in economics than in human rights. The pro-democracy movement had collapsed in China.

1. How were the situations in South Africa and China similar?

_____

_____

CENTRAL AMERICAN AND CARIBBEAN POLICY
How did the United States act toward its neighbors?

In 1979 *Sandinista* rebels overthrew the Nicaraguan government. President Carter sent aid, as did the Soviet Union and Cuba. In 1981 President Reagan charged that the Sandinista government was Communist. He supported the *Contras,* a group trying to defeat the Sandinistas. After years of conflict, a peace agreement was signed and free elections were held in 1990.

Reagan sent U.S. troops to Grenada in 1983. He feared its government had ties with Cuba. The U.S. troops overthrew the pro-Cuban government. They set up a pro-American government in its place.

In 1989 President Bush sent more than 20,000 U.S. troops to Panama. He wanted to overthrow Panamanian dictator Manuel Noriega. He also wanted to arrest him for drug trafficking. Noriega was taken by the American military. They took him to Miami. He was tried, convicted, and sentenced to 40 years in prison.

2. How did the United States influence affairs in Grenada?

_____

_____

MIDDLE EAST TROUBLE SPOTS
How did the United States act toward the Middle East?

In 1983 terrorists linked to Iran took some Americans hostage in Lebanon. Reagan condemned Iran. He called on U.S. allies not to sell Iran weapons for its war against Iraq.

Three years later, the American people found out that Reagan was breaking his own policy. He had approved the sale of arms to Iran in hopes that Iran would free the hostages in Lebanon. Also, some of the profits from the sale were sent to the Contras in Nicaragua. These illegal activities were called the Iran-Contra scandal.

In the summer of 1987, Congress investigated Iran-Contra. Some of Reagan's staff were convicted of crimes in the scandal. In 1992 President Bush pardoned some of these people.

In 1990 Iraq invaded Kuwait. On January 16, 1991, with the support of Congress and the United Nations, President Bush launched **Operation Desert Storm** to fight Iraq and to free Kuwait.

The United States and its allies staged air strikes against Iraq. On February 23 they also launched a ground attack. On February 28 President Bush announced a cease-fire. The Persian Gulf War was over. Kuwait was freed.

3. What was the purpose of Operation Desert Storm?

_____

_____

© Houghton Mifflin Harcourt Publishing Company

Complete the chart by explaining the actions taken by the United States and the outcome for each situation.

Situation	U.S. Action	Outcome of Situation
1. Apartheid in South Africa		
2. Tiananmen Square demonstrations		
3. Overthrow of Nicaraguan government		
4. Fear that Grenada's government had ties with Cuba		
5. Troops in Panama		
6. Terrorists linked to Iran		
7. Operation Desert Storm to fight Iraq and free Kuwait		

© Houghton Mifflin Harcourt Publishing Company

Into a New Millennium

The Clinton Years

Key Terms and People

William Jefferson Clinton Governor of Arkansas who became the 42nd president

H. Ross Perot Texas billionaire who was a third-party candidate in 1992 election

Hillary Rodham Clinton First Lady and health care reformer

Newt Gingrich Speaker of the House of Representatives

Contract with America Republican plan for political reform

service sector The part of the economy where businesses provide services rather than material goods

downsize To reduce the number of workers on staff

Bill Gates Extremely successful owner of Microsoft, a computer software company

Steve Jobs Computer industry executive who founded Apple Inc.

Michael Dell Successful entrepreneur who started a computer company as a teenager

NAFTA Trade agreement between Canada, Mexico, and the United States

outsourcing relocating or transferring jobs to another labor market

Before You Read

In the last lesson you learned about policies under presidents Reagan and Bush. In this lesson you will read about the presidency of Bill Clinton.

As You Read

Complete a chart on the policies of President Clinton and the changing domestic and global economy.

CLINTON WINS THE PRESIDENCY
What **was the important issue in the 1992 election?**

Governor **William Jefferson Clinton** of Arkansas was the first member of the baby-boom generation to win the presidency. He defeated President George H. W. Bush and Texas billionaire **H. Ross Perot** in the election.

Bush's popularity, which was high after the Persian Gulf War, fell as the economy went into a recession. Clinton convinced voters he would move the Democratic Party to the political center by embracing both liberal and conservative programs.

Clinton tried to reform the program for health care insurance. He appointed

First Lady **Hillary Rodham Clinton** to head the team creating the plan. Congress never voted on it after Republicans attacked its promotion of "big government." Clinton was more successful in passing a law requiring that firearm buyers wait five days before completing the purchase. He and Republicans in Congress also reformed the welfare system by placing limits on how long people could receive benefits. This led states to move millions of people from welfare to jobs.

Clinton also had success in reducing the federal budget deficit. Clinton worked with Congress to pass a bill that cut spending, lowered taxes, and had programs that would help children and improve health care. Then the federal budget had a surplus, and the economy boomed.

1. Why did George Bush's popularity fall after the Persian Gulf War?

_____

_____

CLINTON'S FOREIGN POLICY
What were President Clinton's foreign policy goals?

Major goals for Clinton included having strong relations with Russia and China. Russia and the United States cooperated on economic and arms-control issues, but Russia did not like U.S. involvement in Yugoslavia's civil war. The United States was equally bothered with Russian attacks on rebels in Chechnya. Relations with China centered on increased trade.

Clinton was willing to use troops to stop overseas conflicts. He sent troops to prevent military rulers from taking over Haiti. In Yugoslavia, Serbs began "ethnic cleansing," first in Bosnia and

then in Kosovo. The United States and NATO launched air strikes against the Serbs, forcing them to back down.

With Africa, however, Clinton was reluctant to intervene. After several U.S. servicemen's bodies were dragged through the streets in Somalia, the United States was hesitant to get involved in other conflicts. The U.S. did nothing to prevent the ethnic genocide in Rwanda in 1994.

President Clinton also took part in peace talks between Israel and Palestine. He helped convince Israel and Jordan to end fighting. However, no solution was found to end the region's conflicts.

2. Why did President Clinton use troops in some overseas conflicts?

_____

_____

PARTISAN POLITICS AND IMPEACHMENT
Why was President Clinton impeached?

President Clinton developed political troubles beginning in 1994. **Newt Gingrich,** who later became Speaker of the House, led the Republicans and launched a campaign to turn voters against Clinton. He used a document called the **Contract with America.** The document consisted of items Republicans promised to do if they won congressional control. And that is exactly what happened. In 1994 Republicans controlled both houses.

Clinton won reelection in 1996, and he and Republican leaders promised to work together. However, Clinton had more serious problems than Congress. First, he was accused of being involved in a land deal to fund his 1984 governor's campaign. Then, he was accused of

© Houghton Mifflin Harcourt Publishing Company

Guided Reading Workbook

lying under oath in questioning about an improper relationship with a young White House intern. The House approved two articles of impeachment, charging Clinton with perjury, even though a majority of Americans approved of Clinton's job performance. The Senate trial in 1999 failed to convict Clinton, and he remained in office.

3. Why was President Clinton impeached?

_____

_____

THE ECONOMY DURING THE CLINTON YEARS
What changed for American workers?

There was good news and bad news about the economy between 1993 and 1999. Millions of new jobs were created. By 2000 the unemployment rate had fallen to its lowest since 1970.

The nation's economy changed from a manufacturing to a service economy. Jobs in the **service sector,** the part of the economy that provides services to people, increased. These jobs include teachers, medical professionals, lawyers, engineers, store clerks, and wait staff. The largest growth came in jobs that paid low wages, such as retail sales and fast food.

Many companies **downsized,** which is reducing staff to cut costs and increase profits. They hired temporary workers who got lower wages and few benefits.

Manufacturing jobs declined sharply, leading to a drop in union membership. Workers with high-paying jobs saw no need to join unions. Workers with low-paying jobs were too worried about losing their jobs to join unions.

By the late 1990s computer entrepreneurs made fortunes. **Bill Gates** founded Microsoft, a computer software company. **Steve Jobs** started Apple Inc. and revolutionized personal computers. **Michael Dell** became wealthy selling computers directly to customers.

As the Internet grew, so too did the need for workers with advanced training and specialized technical skills. High-tech online businesses, called dotcoms, grew rapidly. However, by 2000 online retailing became less profitable for all but about 38 percent of companies. Many went out of business.

Clinton believed that free trade was essential to U.S. prosperity and world economics. In 1994 the **North American Free Trade Agreement (NAFTA)** became law. It provided for free trade between the United States, Mexico, and Canada. The United States and other nations signed a world trade agreement, the General Agreement on Tariffs and Trade (GATT). GATT lowered tariffs. It also set up the World Trade Organization (WTO) to settle trade disputes.

Many people believed that GATT would be good for the U.S. economy. But many American workers feared they would lose their jobs to countries that produced the same goods at a lower cost. This practice is called **outsourcing,** and many U.S. businesses did move their operations to countries such as Mexico.

4. What were three workplace changes in the U.S. during the 1990s?

_____

_____

CRIME AND TERRORISM IN THE 1990S
Where did terrorists attack?

Crime fell during the 1990s, but terrorism and violence raised

© Houghton Mifflin Harcourt Publishing Company

Americans' fears. In 1993 Islamic terrorists set off a bomb in the World Trade Center in New York City to protest U.S. support for Israel. In 1995 American terrorist Timothy McVeigh exploded a bomb at the federal building in Oklahoma City. The bomb killed 168 men, women, and children.

School violence also plagued the nation. In 1999, two students at Columbine High School in Colorado killed 12 students and a teacher and wounded 23 classmates before killing themselves.

Attacks against Americans also occurred in other countries. In 1996 a bomb killed 19 U.S. service members and wounded about 500 people in Saudi Arabia. In 1998, two U.S. embassies in East Africa were attacked. In 2000 a suicide bomber attacked a U.S. Navy destroyer while it was in Yemen.

5. What building was attacked by Islamic terrorists in 1993?

_____

_____

© Houghton Mifflin Harcourt Publishing Company

Guided Reading Workbook

Answer the questions to identify achievements of President Clinton's domestic and foreign policies and to identify trends in the domestic and global economy during his presidency.

THE CLINTON ADMINISTRATION	
1. What did Clinton achieve in domestic policy?	2. What did Clinton achieve in foreign policy?
THE CHANGING DOMESTIC AND GLOBAL ECONOMY	
3. What trends led to explosive growth in the service sector?	
4. What trends led to explosive growth in temporary work? How were workers affected?	
5. What trends led to a sharp decline in manufacturing jobs? How were workers affected?	
6. What trends led to explosive growth in the high-tech industry?	
7. What trends affected international trade and competition? How did those trends affect U.S. businesses and workers?	

© Houghton Mifflin Harcourt Publishing Company

Into a New Millennium

The Bush Administration

Key Terms and People

Al Gore Clinton's vice-president; Democratic candidate in 2000 election

George W. Bush 43rd president of U.S.

Osama bin Laden Saudi Arabian millionaire who directed terrorist attacks of 9/11/2001

al-Qaeda A global militant Islamist organization based in Afghanistan

Taliban Strict fundamentalist Islamic regime

USA PATRIOT Act Law that gave the government the power to conduct search and surveillance of suspected terrorists

weapons of mass destruction (WMD) biological, chemical, and nuclear weapons

Sarbanes-Oxley Act Act that established a regulatory board to oversee the accounting industry and its involvement with corporations

Great Recession A severe decline in economic activity

housing bubble Widespread overpricing of residential real estate

Troubled Asset Relief Program (TARP) Authorized $700 billion to stabilize the banking and automobile industries

Before You Read

In the last lesson you learned about the Clinton presidency. In this lesson you will read about the presidency of George W. Bush.

As You Read

Use a chart to take notes on the people and events that affected President George W. Bush during his two terms in office.

THE RACE FOR THE WHITE HOUSE; SEPTEMBER 11 AND THE AFTERMATH

How did George W. Bush confront terrorism?

The 2000 presidential candidates were Democratic Vice-President **Al Gore** and Republican Texas governor **George W. Bush.** There was confusion on election night over who won the state of Florida. Gore had won the popular vote. But the winner of Florida would win a majority of the electoral votes and the election.

Both sides sent lawyers to Florida to try to secure victory. Bush held a slim lead. A manual recounting of the votes began. Then the battle moved to the courts. On December 12 the U.S. Supreme Court ruled 5–4 to stop the recount. As a result, Bush won Florida and the presidency. However, many people disagreed with the decision.

© Houghton Mifflin Harcourt Publishing Company

On September 11, 2001, Arab terrorists hijacked jets and used them to destroy targets. Two planes hit and leveled the twin towers of the World Trade Center in New York City, its tallest buildings and the symbolic center of American finance. A third plane hit the Pentagon building outside Washington, DC. A fourth plane crashed near Pittsburgh, Pennsylvania, but not before passengers fought the hijackers, perhaps keeping the plane from hitting the White House or the U.S. Capitol. Altogether, these acts killed around 3,000 people.

Firefighters, police officers, rescue workers, and volunteers attempted to find survivors, and many of them perished as well. From around the country, people sent donations to New York City, which was named "ground zero."

After the terrorist attacks, the government declared that **Osama bin Laden,** a Saudi Arabian millionaire, had directed the attacks. He and his terrorists were part of the **al-Qaeda** network, a global militant Islamist organization. A strict fundamentalist Islamic regime called the **Taliban** rules al-Qaeda.

President Bush put together an international alliance to fight terrorism. The Taliban would not surrender bin Laden, so coalition forces led by the United States began military action in Afghanistan. These forces broke up the terrorist network in Afghanistan but did not capture bin Laden.

The September 11 attacks made Americans afraid that terrorism would continue in the United States. So Congress created the **USA PATRIOT Act.** This law allowed the government to conduct searches and surveillance of suspected terrorists, measures that some people said violated the First, Fourth, Fifth, Sixth, and Seventh Amendments to the Constitution. Security at airports also became the government's responsibility.

1. What action did President Bush take in the war on terrorism?

_____

_____

BUSH'S FOREIGN POLICY
What events led to the war in Iraq?

The Bush administration said that Iraqi dictator Saddam Hussein supported al-Qaeda terrorists. Demands by the United Nations for Iraq to stop the production of biological, chemical, and nuclear weapons, called **weapons of mass destruction (WMD),** were minimally followed by Hussein. Bush believed that Hussein was helping terrorists and might supply them with WMD. So the United States and Great Britain ended diplomacy with Iraq and invaded that country in 2003. Iraq's forces were defeated, and Saddam Hussein was captured. When U.S. forces searched for WMD in Iraq, however, none were found. Many Americans then questioned the war. Events in Iraq led to a decline in Bush's popularity.

Iran was of concern to Americans, too. The UN said Iran had to stop enriching uranium, which leads to nuclear weapons, and threatened to impose sanctions if Iran continued this activity.

2. Why did Bush expand the war on terrorism to Iraq?

_____

_____

© Houghton Mifflin Harcourt Publishing Company

Guided Reading Workbook

Lesson 2, *continued*

BUSH'S DOMESTIC GOALS; CONFRONTING ECONOMIC PROBLEMS
What happened to the economy during President Bush's presidency?

Education reform was a major goal for President Bush. He passed a law calling for required testing of basic skills and specific grades. The law also required school test scores to show improvement.

Bush wanted to partially privatize Social Security; however, this proposal was not approved. On social issues, Bush was a conservative who promoted limiting abortion and supporting capital punishment. Although many people were unhappy with Bush as president, he was reelected in 2004.

Problems continued for Bush as people wanted an end to the war and as it became known that American citizens had been spied on for no reason. In addition, people became aware that his administration had allowed torture to be used on terrorist suspects. Not surprisingly, in 2006 the Democrats regained control of Congress.

Bush had problems with the economy, too. When he took office, the country had a national surplus. When he left office, the country had a large deficit. Two wars had increased military spending. Terrorism threats had negative effects, and Bush's tax cuts were accused of benefiting the rich and doing little to create jobs.

Corporate scandals plagued the country during the early 2000s, so Congress passed the **Sarbanes-Oxley Act.** It set up a regulatory board to check on the accounting industry and its involvement with corporations. Then, in late 2007 the U.S. had a financial crisis. Poor decisions by some large banks caused them to collapse. There was an economic slowdown. By 2008 the country was in a **Great Recession,** a decline in economic activity. It was the worst decline since the Great Depression. Investment banks had been allowed to operate with little government oversight, and they faced bankruptcy. In addition, government policies had encouraged homeownership. A boom in housing construction came about because there were low mortgage interest rates. Many people borrowed money to buy overpriced homes. This overpricing of residential real estate was called the **housing bubble.** Many families could not pay their mortgages and were in debt. Some banks stopped lending, so businesses had a hard time getting credit to invest in inventory or pay their employees. Unemployment rose and incomes fell. Then the housing bubble burst, and housing prices dropped. Many homeowners owed more on their mortgages than their houses were worth. For people who had lost their jobs, they were unable to pay their mortgages, and it was hard to sell their homes. Banks foreclosed on the homes of thousands of Americans.

Stock prices dropped during the Great Recession, so pensions and savings lost billions in value. Also, the U.S. national debt rose. Bush tried to prevent more damage. He signed the **Troubled Asset Relief Program (TARP)** to provide money to stabilize the banking and automobile industries. Critics said the act was a "bailout" funded by taxpayers. Supporters said it was necessary to keep the banking system from crashing any further.

3. What were some causes of the Great Recession?

_____

_____

© Houghton Mifflin Harcourt Publishing Company

Describe how each person, thing, or event affected the United States
and/or President George W. Bush's presidency.

1. Al Gore
2. Terrorist Attacks of September 11, 2001
3. Osama bin Laden, al-Qaeda, and Taliban
4. USA PATRIOT Act
5. Saddam Hussein
6. Great Recession

© Houghton Mifflin Harcourt Publishing Company

Obama's Presidency

Key Terms and People

Barack H. Obama 44th president; the first African American president

Joe Biden Senator from Delaware; vice-president under Barack Obama

John McCain Senator from Arizona; Vietnam War hero; Republican candidate for president in 2008

Sarah Palin Governor of Alaska; running mate of John McCain

American Recovery and Reinvestment Act (ARRA) Economic stimulus package to combat the recession

Patient Protection and Affordable Care Act (PPACA) Health care reform act

Benghazi City in Libya where U.S. diplomatic compound was attacked by Islamic militants

tea party A libertarian, conservative movement

Before You Read

In the last lesson you learned about the presidency of George W. Bush. In this lesson you will read about the presidency of Barack Obama.

As You Read

Use a chart to take notes on the presidency of Barack Obama.

THE 2008 ELECTION
***What* factors helped the Democrats to win the 2008 presidential election?**

The continuing war in Iraq and a failing economy contributed to President Bush's unpopularity. The Democratic Party nominated **Barack H. Obama,** U.S. senator from Illinois, as their candidate. His running mate was long-time senator from Delaware, **Joe Biden.** The Republican Party nominated Senator **John McCain** of Arizona, a Vietnam War hero. His running mate was the governor of Alaska, **Sarah Palin.** The campaign focused on the economy and foreign

policy. Americans voted for a change in direction by electing Democrat Obama. He made history as the first African American to be elected president of the United States. The Democrats also increased their majority in the House of Representatives. Nancy Pelosi, a California Democrat, became the first woman to be Speaker of the House.

1. Why were the Democrats able to win the presidency in 2008?

_____

_____

OBAMA'S DOMESTIC AGENDA
What were major elements of President Obama's domestic policy?

To fight the recession, President Obama signed the **American Recovery and Reinvestment Act (ARRA)** in early 2009. This economic stimulus package gave tax credits, including ones for college tuition and home improvements to increase energy efficiency. About 98 percent of Americans received a tax cut. Obama also signed laws to regulate financial institutions, in order to protect consumers and investors and to prevent another financial crisis. The recession ended in mid-2009.

While campaigning for president, Obama had made health care reform one of his main issues. In 2010 the **Patient Protection and Affordable Care Act (PPACA)** became law. Often referred to as Obamacare, this law extended health coverage to children of low-income families and tackled the issue of uninsured adults. It also allowed young people to stay on their parents' insurance until age 26 and said that patients cannot be denied coverage for pre-existing health conditions. Individuals are required to get some level of health coverage. The program remains controversial because some people do not think the government has the right to require health insurance. Others say that the law does not go far enough in guaranteeing health care for all.

President Obama pushed for increased use of renewable energy sources and stricter limits on businesses that produce high levels of carbon pollution. He vetoed a congressional bill approving the Keystone XL, an oil pipeline that was planned to extend from Canada to the Gulf of Mexico.

2. What makes the PPACA controversial?

_____

_____

FOREIGN POLICY CHALLENGES
What international events were problems for President Obama?

When President Obama took office in 2009, he planned to bring forces in Iraq home. That happened in December 2011. However, there were still problems in Afghanistan. U.S. troops fought the Taliban, and there were many injured. One problem was that Osama bin Laden had never been captured. For Obama, this was a priority. On May 2011 the CIA, the U.S. Army, and U.S. Navy Seals found bin Laden in Pakistan and killed him. After that, Obama said troops would start leaving Afghanistan.

Problems throughout the Middle East plagued Obama. There were issues with Israel over new homes being built in a disputed area of Jerusalem. Obama and some European leaders backed pro-democracy demonstrators against Hosni Mubarak's oppressive regime in Egypt. In **Benghazi,** Libya, Islamic militants attacked the U.S. diplomatic compound and killed the ambassador and another State Department employee. A second attack killed two CIA workers and injured others.

Other areas of concern for the Obama administration include North Korea, which threatened to reignite armed conflict with South Korea. Interactions

© Houghton Mifflin Harcourt Publishing Company

with Russia remained tense, and drone attacks continued in Pakistan.

3. What major event occurred in May 2011?

_____

_____

REELECTION AND STALEMATE
What role did partisanship play in President Obama's second term?

In the 2010 midterm elections, Republicans gained a majority in the House of Representatives. This meant Obama had difficulty getting his initiatives passed. Much of this was caused by the facts that opponents were less willing to compromise, personal attacks became common, and many people had extreme views. It seemed as if people were more likely to be on opposite sides of issues.

This increased partisanship over government's role in people's lives gave rise to the **tea party,** a libertarian conservative movement. The group took its name from the Boston Tea Party. Its goals were to lower taxes, reduce government spending on programs such

as health care, and lower the national debt and budget deficit. It opposed abortion, gay marriage, and gun control. Although the tea party movement has been described as a grassroots organization, developing from ordinary Americans, records show that wealthy corporate interests provided financial support.

Obama was reelected in 2012, winning both the popular and electoral votes. However, in 2014 the Democrats lost control of the Senate, which meant Republicans dominated Congress.

During his second term, Obama changed decades of foreign policy by normalizing diplomatic relations with Cuba. Embassies were set up in both countries and restrictions on travel to Cuba were eased. In the Middle East, Obama began negotiations with Iran regarding restrictions to its nuclear program in exchange for removal of sanctions against Iran.

4. What led to the formation of the tea party and what were its goals?

_____

_____

Complete the chart by answering the questions about President
Obama's presidency.

THE 2008 PRESIDENTIAL ELECTION		
1. a. Who was the Democratic presidential candidate?	2. a. Who was the Republican presidential candidate?	3. a. What did the campaign focus on?
b. Who was the vice-presidential candidate on the Democratic ticket?	b. Who was the vice-presidential candidate on the Republican ticket?	b. What happened in the presidential election and the majority of congressional elections in 2008?

PRESIDENT OBAMA'S DOMESTIC AND FOREIGN POLICIES	
4. What did Obama achieve in domestic policy during his two terms in office?	5. What were challenges Obama faced in foreign policy during his two terms? What did he achieve?

PRESIDENT OBAMA'S SECOND TERM
6. How did partisanship affect President Obama's second term?

© Houghton Mifflin Harcourt Publishing Company

Guided Reading Workbook

Technology Shapes Life

Key Terms and People

Internet Worldwide computer network

telecommute The ability of people to work out of their homes

geographic information system (GIS) A computer system that collects and analyzes spatial or geographical data

Telecommunications Act of 1996 Controversial law to reform the communications industry

intellectual property A legal term that refers to creations of the mind

genetic engineering Method of changing the genes of living cells

Before You Read

In the last lesson you learned about President Obama's terms in office. In this lesson you will learn how technology has changed Americans' lives.

As You Read

Use a chart to take notes on the technological changes described in this lesson and how these changes have affected life in the United States.

THE COMMUNICATIONS REVOLUTION
How **have new technologies affected communications?**

From the 1960s to the 1980s, few computer networks existed. The National Science Foundation created a network for its own use, NSFNET. Then the Digital Revolution began and thousands of industries were using computers for their businesses. Americans bought personal computers for their homes. NSFNET grew into the **Internet,** an international network linking computers and allowing almost instant transmittal of text, images, and sound. By 2014 about 43.6 percent of the world population used the Internet.

Advances in computers and communications have had an impact on society and business similar to the Industrial Revolution of the late 1800s. Computers allow employees to perform their jobs more quickly and easily, which has meant greater worker productivity and increased output.

New technologies have enabled companies to connect worldwide. Cell phones, the Internet, wireless connectivity, and overnight shipping make it possible for many Americans to **telecommute,** or work from a location of their choice instead of going to an office every day. Email and videoconferences

© Houghton Mifflin Harcourt Publishing Company

Guided Reading Workbook

Lesson 4, *continued*

make it possible for workers in different cities and countries to communicate easily. Some businesses and governments use **geographic information system (GIS)** technology. A GIS is a computer system that collects and analyzes many kinds of spatial or geographical data.

Companies have capitalized on technology, selling products for personal use. Consumers buy smartphones, laptop computers, and tablets.

Computer technology has changed how people live. People shop online, spending tens of billions of dollars in electronic transactions, or e-commerce. Also, Americans spend hours sending instant messages, "texting," and posting on social networking sites. Schools use the Internet for learning. Many universities offer classes and complete degree programs over the Internet. Now education is possible for anyone who can connect to the Internet. Computer users also have access to applications, or "apps" for their tablets and smartphones.

The changes in communications caused the growth of many communications companies. Congress passed the **Telecommunications Act of 1996** to make sure people would receive good service. The law allowed telephone and cable companies to enter each other's industries. One of the results of the law was an increase in mergers. This cut the number of competing companies.

The communications industry liked the Telecommunications Act. But some people believed that the law allowed a small number of people to control the media. Civil rights activists thought the Communications Decency Act (passed as part of the Telecommunications Act) limited free speech. Parts of these laws were struck down in court. Since the

early 2000s, the issue of network neutrality has created considerable controversy. In 2015 supporters of net neutrality were happy when the FCC prevented service providers or the government from restricting access to, or content delivered on, the Internet.

Since the Internet grew, protecting **intellectual property** rights, or creations of the mind, have become more difficult. It is easy for computer users to avoid giving payment to those who created something. For example, musicians have gone to court to keep their unreleased songs from playing on the Internet.

Computer technology has created many challenges. The Internet is a source of useful information, but it is also a center for spreading pornographic and anonymous hate material. Digital networks have led to "cybercrime." Hackers engage in criminal activities such as stealing Social Security numbers and other personal information. There is also a growing concern over "cyberterrorism."

While many people have access to technology, it remains out of reach for many poor people. This may cause these families to fall further behind because they may lack necessary computer skills.

In addition, some people worry that too much reliance on digital devices may lead to an inability to communicate face-to-face. Also, some people film everything they see, even things that are inappropriate.

1. How has technology made a difference for businesses and their workers?

    _____

    _____

© Houghton Mifflin Harcourt Publishing Company

SCIENTIFIC ADVANCES ENRICH LIVES

How does technology affect daily life?

In addition to telecommunications, great progress was made in robotics, space exploration, and medicine. Visual imaging and artificial intelligence were combined to provide applications in industry, medicine, and education. Flight simulators helped train pilots. Doctors have used virtual reality to take a computerized tour of different parts of a patient's body to check for medical problems. Surgeons have operated long distance.

Astronomers and engineers have expanded our view of the universe. NASA's *Pathfinder* and *Sojourner* transmitted live pictures from the surface of Mars. Other rovers have gone to Mars, and as of 2015, two were still active. Shuttle missions did scientific research and assembly, transport, and repair of orbiting objects. NASA worked on building the *International Space Station (ISS),* which promised to offer scientists a zero-gravity laboratory for research in medicine, architecture, and long-term living in space.

The Hubble Space Telescope has been used to show views of space, including planets outside our solar system. The final mission of NASA's 30-year shuttle program ended in 2011 with the *Atlantis.*

Enormous progress was made in the field of biotechnology. The Human Genome Project and Celera announced in 2000 that they had mapped the genes of the human body. Molecular biologists hoped this genetic map of DNA would help them to develop new treatments for inherited diseases. DNA has also been used to prove both the guilt and innocence of people accused of crimes. But the applications of this new information, or "biotechnology," were controversial. Many people were concerned about animals that were cloned from single cells. The use of **genetic engineering,** the artificial changing of the molecular biology of organisms' cells to alter an organism, caused public concern. Scientists used genetic engineering to alter food crops like corn and rice. The FDA says these foods are safe, and scientists agree. Others say the long-term effects are unknown.

People suffering from some diseases such as cancer have benefited from technology such as improved diagnostic methods, gene therapy, genetically engineered antibodies, and the use of stem cells, which is controversial. AIDS patients have been treated with combination therapies so that deaths from AIDS have been reduced. Advances in magnetic resonance imaging (MRI), which produces cross-sectional images of any part of the body, have made the procedure faster and less expensive. A remarkable technology, 3D bioprinting, places living cells in a structure that is built up by a 3D printer, layer by layer. This allows technicians to build new tissues to repair organs such as kidneys, livers, and hearts. Plastic surgeons have also successfully completed face transplants to help patients whose faces have been ruined by diseases or accidents.

2. What were some important technological advances in the United States?

_____

_____

© Houghton Mifflin Harcourt Publishing Company

Guided Reading Workbook

Complete the chart. List technological advances related to each area.
Explain how one of the advances in each area has affected life in the
United States.

1. Communications	
2. Education	
3. Commerce	
4. Health care	
5. Space exploration	
6. Genetic engineering	

© Houghton Mifflin Harcourt Publishing Company

Guided Reading Workbook

The Changing Face of America

Key Terms and People

urban flight Movement of people away from cities

gentrification The rehabilitation of old neighborhoods and displacement of lower-income people

Proposition 187 California law which cut benefits to illegal immigrants

Before You Read

In the last lesson you learned about the ways technology affects modern life. In this lesson you will read about the changes facing Americans at the start of the 21st century.

As You Read

Use a chart to take notes on changes in the United States.

URBAN CHALLENGES
Why did people move to suburbs?

After World War II through the 1980s, the United States experienced a pattern of **urban flight,** where Americans left cities and moved to the suburbs.

Urban flight was caused by overcrowded cities. This overcrowding contributed to increased crime rates and poor housing. As a result, city dwellers who could afford to move relocated to the suburbs for better schools and safer neighborhoods. Even some industries relocated to suburban areas. Cities lost taxes, and downtown shopping districts lost business to suburban malls. In the 1990s the 31 poorest U.S. communities were in cities.

By the mid-1990s people began to return to the city because property values declined. In a process known as **gentrification,** people bought and rehabilitated old houses, industrial sites,

and neighborhoods. Young single adults in particular were drawn to city life. As downtown neighborhoods came back, lower-income residents were displaced by rising housing costs.

While some smaller cities and towns had less problems with gentrification, they nevertheless began to revitalize their downtown areas by developing "main street" programs. These programs created jobs while the areas were being rehabilitated, and also later when new businesses moved into the area. As people moved downtown, more money became available for services.

Many suburban workers commuted to the city for work. Some workers telecommuted, using new communications technology to work from home. In addition, many minorities moved to the suburbs. So suburbs competed for business and industry. They offered tax breaks to get businesses to locate there and

© Houghton Mifflin Harcourt Publishing Company

then saw their tax revenues decline as a result.

Some urban areas have had difficulty because of natural disasters. In 2005 New Orleans had major floods and destruction due to Hurricane Katrina. This storm devastated other parts of Louisiana as well as parts of Alabama and Mississippi. Hurricane Sandy hit northern cities in New Jersey and New York in 2012. Some cities also have to face blizzards and earthquakes. These natural disasters do damage to the environment, overburden local governments, destroy property values, and affect population distribution.

1. How did urban flight change the nation's cities?

   _____

   _____

THE AGING OF AMERICA
How will aging affect America?

The U.S. Census Bureau documents that in 2010, Americans were older than ever before. The median age, 37.2 years, was two years older than the median age in 2000. The rising median age points to several trends. First, the country's birthrate has slowed. The huge baby-boom generation has reached retirement age. The number of seniors has increased since medical advances and healthier lifestyles keep people alive longer. The graying of America has put pressure on programs for the elderly. In 1955 these programs were only 6 percent of the national budget. By 2015 they are more than one-third of that budget. Programs that provide care for the elderly and disabled people are Medicare and Social Security. Social Security was designed to rely on continued funding from younger

workers. In the past, when younger workers outnumbered retirees and when most workers didn't live long after retirement, the system worked. In 1996, three workers made Social Security contributions to support every retired person. But experts expect that by 2030, there will be only two workers to support each retired person. Social Security will begin to pay out more than it takes in. As a result, some people want to reform the Social Security system.

2. How does the increase in the number of elderly people affect Social Security and Medicare?

   _____

   _____

IMMIGRATION AND POPULATION
How has immigration affected America?

The U.S. population has grown from 204 million to more than 309 million between 1970 and 2010. Immigration is responsible for much of that growth.

Over the years, the pattern of immigration to the United States has changed. The large numbers of immigrants who entered the country before and just after 1900 came from Europe. In contrast, since the 1960s the majority of immigrants have come from Asia and the Western Hemisphere, mostly from Mexico.

A major "push" factor in why so many people come from Mexico is the devaluing of the Mexican peso, which has caused a decline in Mexico's economy. Almost a million Mexicans are out of work, so they head to the U.S. for jobs. "Push" factors in Central America include civil wars and drug gang violence that have left people homeless. They flee to the U.S. for

Lesson 5, *continued*

safety. Thousands of legal and illegal immigrants come to the U.S. every day.

Census Bureau data show that patterns of immigration are changing the country's ethnic and racial makeup. By 2001, for example, California had become a majority-minority state, with Asian Americans, Latinos, African Americans, and Native Americans making up more than half its population. By 2010 Hawaii, New Mexico, and Texas had also become majority-minority states. Some other states, including Arizona, Florida, Maryland, and New York, are close to majority-minority status.

The large number of immigrants has led to debate over immigration policies. Many Americans believe that the country can't absorb more immigrants. By the early 1990s, many illegal immigrants arrived from Latin America, Canada, Poland, China, and Ireland. They took jobs such as farm work that many Americans turn down. By 2013 an estimated 11.4 million illegal immigrants resided in the U.S.

Hostility toward illegal immigration has increased in states such as California and Arizona. **Proposition 187** was passed in California in 1994. It cut all education and nonemergency health benefits to illegal immigrants. By March 1998 it was ruled unconstitutional. In 2010 Arizona passed a law that enhanced local and state police power to enforce federal immigration laws.

These efforts to control immigration inspired political participation among Hispanic voters, who saw themselves as targets.

As more immigrants make their way to the U.S. and the nation's ethnic makeup changes, immigration debates will continue.

Native Americans continued to struggle. The end of the 20th century saw most Native Americans leading very difficult lives. In 2007 about 25 percent of Native Americans lived below the poverty line. Throughout the 1990s, Native Americans strived to improve their lives through building casinos and using the courts to gain greater recognition for their tribal ancestry and land rights.

Although immigration is still an issue and Native Americans have problems, the U.S. is definitely a multicultural nation. Changes in art, music, dance, religion, literature, food, customs, and other areas reflect the changes in society. Examples of multicultural influence on American society can be found in the foods people enjoy, the languages people speak, and the religious holidays people celebrate.

3. How is immigration changing the United States?

_____

_____

© Houghton Mifflin Harcourt Publishing Company

Lesson 5, *continued*

Write three facts or statistics concerning each of the following
important trends in the late 20th and early 21st centuries.
Then answer the questions about challenges.

URBAN FLIGHT	1.
	2.
	3.
BABY BOOMERS	4.
	5.
	6.
IMMIGRATION	7.
	8.
	9.

10. What is one challenge the U.S. will face related to urban and suburban life?

11. What is one challenge the U.S. will face related to its aging population?

12. What is one challenge the U.S. will face related to its immigration policy?

The United States in the 21st Century

National Security and Public Safety

Key Terms and People

drone Unmanned aerial vehicle operated by a pilot on the ground

National Security Agency (NSA) Intelligence-gathering organization with the U.S. government

racial profiling The act of suspecting or targeting a person simply on the basis of his or her race or ethnic background

human trafficking The illegal movement of people for the purposes of forced labor or exploitation

Before You Read

In the last lesson you learned about the changes facing Americans at the start of the 21st century. In this lesson you will read about ways that the U.S. government works to keep the public safe.

As You Read

Complete a chart about safety and security issues.

TERRORISM AND SECURITY
What is the difference between foreign and domestic terrorism?

The FBI describes terrorism as violent acts intended to intimidate a civilian population, to influence the policy of a government by intimidation, or to affect the conduct of a government by mass destruction, assassination, or kidnapping.

In the United States, the most deadly act of terrorism happened on September 11, 2001. More than 3,000 people died in New York City, Washington, DC, and rural Pennsylvania. The Department of Homeland Security was created to keep terrorists from striking the United States. Congress also passed the USA PATRIOT Act, expanding the government's powers to use search warrants, tap phones, and detain suspects. Some Americans felt that the USA PATRIOT Act violated their constitutional rights to privacy and freedom. Congress agreed to let parts of the act expire, but there have been repeated extensions of the law for security reasons.

Since the September 11 attacks, there have been other terrorist threats and attacks. Air travel makes it easier for people from other countries to bring violence to the United States. Radicals can inspire violence through videos and recruit others on websites and social media. Radical Islamist writings and videos have inspired horrific terrorist acts. In April 2014 brothers Tamerlan and Dzhokhar Tsarnaev, immigrants to the United States from Russia and Kyrgyzstan, detonated bombs killing 3 and injuring more than 260 people at the Boston Marathon.

© Houghton Mifflin Harcourt Publishing Company

Domestic terrorism is a problem in the United States as well. Americans have committed crimes to intimidate others or influence government policy. Some terrorists wage attacks through beatings and murder to intimidate those they find objectionable. Such groups include the Aryan Nations, Stormfront, and the Ku Klux Klan. These groups claim white supremacy and may be anti-Semitic, anti-gay, anti-immigrant, anti-Muslim, and anti-gun control. Hate groups target an entire class of people, and there are believed to be over 700 of these groups. Extremists who do not belong to a group also are a threat. Whether they are organized in groups or acting alone, foreign and domestic terrorists threaten the security and safety of Americans.

1. How did the acts of September 11, 2001, change the United States?

_____

_____

SURVEILLANCE AND PRIVACY
How is surveillance both an advantage and a disadvantage?

Intelligence agencies and law enforcement rely on technology to keep track of the activities of terrorists. However, this technology is also used to keep track of regular citizens.

Technology makes surveillance of day-to-day activities possible. Closed-circuit television is used at airports, banks, and convenience stores. This may help deter or solve crimes.

Unmanned aerial vehicles called **drones** carry cameras, which make them useful for surveillance. They are used for movie-making, detecting forest fires, or inspecting power lines. Police departments may fly drones to check on crowded public events. The Department of Homeland Security uses them to find immigrants crossing illegally from Mexico into Texas.

Another surveillance tool is the smartphone camera. Some uses of smartphone cameras are a crime, such as using stolen images for blackmail. However, photos from smartphones also have helped solve crimes.

The federal government is able to access information on its citizens through the **National Security Agency (NSA).** This intelligence-gathering organization was founded during the Cold War. Its monitoring today has increased because of the threat of terrorism. However, some of its actions have come under media scrutiny. Top-secret internal NSA documents showed that the agency collected telephone information on millions of people throughout the world. Many of these people were not suspected of criminal activities. Edward Snowden, a contractor for the NSA, admitted to downloading classified documents and making them available to journalists. Some Americans called him a heroic whistleblower for revealing government wrongdoing; others said he was a traitor for endangering national security. He was charged with two counts of espionage and theft of government property.

In 2015 Congress passed a new bill that eliminated the NSA's bulk phone-records collection program. This was in response to a federal appeals court ruling.

While the NSA and other government agencies gather vital information that may save lives and property, some people question the high cost to individual rights.

2. What are some benefits of drones and smartphone cameras?

_____

_____

© Houghton Mifflin Harcourt Publishing Company

CRIME AND PUBLIC SAFETY
How has law enforcement changed?

Many states have "three strikes" laws that say that any person found guilty of two previous crimes receives a stiff sentence of 20 to 30 years after conviction for a third. While this may serve to deter crime, it also adds to racial bias because many prison sentences involve African Americans.

The United States jails the largest percentage of people in the world. Some people say prison keeps people from committing additional crimes. Others say that it turns many nonviolent offenders into hardened criminals.

Putting people in prison for drug crimes such as marijuana use may be changing. Colorado, Alaska, Oregon, Washington State, and the District of Columbia have either legalized the use of marijuana by adults or loosened their marijuana laws.

In recent years, some police have been accused of inappropriate responses to public disturbances. Many of their actions have been recorded by smartphones or videos. In places such as Ferguson, Missouri, and New York City, young African American men have been shot and killed or treated in a harsh manner that has led to their deaths.

These incidents have brought into question ways police relate to minorities. Civil rights advocates have said that there is **racial profiling** by law enforcement. This is the act of suspecting or targeting a person simply on the basis of his or her race or ethnic background. A study of police records from the first five months of 2015 showed that U.S. police killed 399 people. Of that amount, 45 were unarmed and two-thirds of those were black or Hispanic. In response to these incidents, many police officers now are required to wear body cameras.

Another issue facing Americans is gun violence. More than 11,200 people were killed by gunfire in 2013. Almost 3,000 children and teens were killed by gunfire in 2014.

Supporters of gun ownership point to the Second Amendment and argue that gun-control laws violate its intent. Others say that the amendment was created to protect the state's right to maintain military units. However, the U.S. Supreme Court has ruled that individuals do have the right to own firearms.

A crime that has grown in recent years is **human trafficking.** This occurs when people are brought into the U.S. against their will and in violation of the law. This trafficking involves mainly women and children. A major cause of human trafficking is poverty. Some parents sell their children in the hope that their children will have a better life in the United States. They may not know the children will be abused. Adults who need jobs are often offered work, but then find themselves trapped in physical labor or prostitution. Most human trafficking involves victims from South Asia, Southeast Asia, and Central America. However, some runaway teenagers from the United States also have been forced into sexual slavery. California, Texas, and Florida focus on enforcing laws against trafficking. Unfortunately, this is a crime that may continue for a long time. With global trade, there is a need for cheap labor. This encourages illegal immigration, which leads to trafficking.

3. Why is racial profiling unfair?

_____

_____

© Houghton Mifflin Harcourt Publishing Company

Complete the chart by writing one or two short phrases to answer each question on security and safety issues.

WHAT IS THE PURPOSE?	
1. Why do terrorists use violence?	
2. Why do radicals use videos, websites, and social media?	
3. Why do hate groups use beatings and murders?	
4. Why do Intelligence agencies use closed-circuit television?	
5. Why do law enforcement agencies use drones?	
6. Why does the NSA engage in intelligence gathering?	
7. Why did Congress pass the USA PATRIOT Act?	
WHAT IS THE PROBLEM?	
8. What problems did some Americans see with the USA PATRIOT Act?	
9. Why do many Americans object to racial profiling?	
10. Why do Americans disagree on gun-control laws?	

The United States in the 21st Century

Foreign Policy in the 21st Century

Key Terms and People

national interest A country's goals and ambitions

Vladimir Putin President of Russia; former agent of the KGB

ISIS Terrorist enemy, the Islamic State of Iraq and Syria

Boko Haram West African terrorist group centered in Nigeria that is allied with ISIS

Before You Read

In the last lesson you learned about ways that the U.S. government works to keep the public safe from terrorism. In this lesson you will read about foreign policy during the 21st century.

As You Read

Use a chart to take notes on U.S. foreign policy during the 21st century.

THE UNITED STATES AS A WORLD LEADER
Why is U.S. national interest important?

The United States is the most powerful country in the world. While some people respect the United States for its freedom, prosperity, and hope, others resent the country's power and influence.

The guiding force in determining U.S. relationships with other countries is **national interest.** This relates to our goals and ambitions. National interests may be political, such as supporting the growth of democracy in new and developing countries. National interest may also involve military strength.

The United States has great involvement in world affairs through international organizations. For example, the United States is a key member of the United Nations. Since the UN is a global organization that tries to protect the interests of all nations, its efforts are often against those of the United States. While many Americans support the UN, others want the United States to withdraw from it. In 2000 the UN wrote goals to help solve world problems such as poverty, hunger, and disease. Some countries have made great progress in reaching the goals.

Another organization the United States is involved in is the North Atlantic Treaty Organization (NATO). While its focus is no longer the Soviet Union, it does intervene militarily to end violence and stop terrorists. Places where NATO has played an important role include Bosnia and Herzegovina, Kosovo, and the Middle East. It has also intervened in the civil war raging in Libya and worked to stop pirates attacking ships in Somalia.

© Houghton Mifflin Harcourt Publishing Company

Lesson 2, *continued*

When natural disasters such as floods and earthquakes occur, or when human-made disasters happen, the United States often steps in to provide humanitarian aid. Several organizations deal with global health and AIDS relief around the world. These organizations work to prevent malnutrition, cholera, and other conditions that kill millions of people annually.

The United States also helps other countries when people's human rights are being violated. The country often asks repressive governments to end human rights abuses. For example, it showed disapproval of South Africa's racist apartheid government by imposing travel restrictions.

1. What is one way that the United States demonstrates its commitment to helping people throughout the world?

_____

_____

REGIONAL POLICIES
What is the job of the Department of State?

The Department of State is concerned with international relations. It has a difficult job trying to keep the peace, protect U.S. international business interests, and support global cooperation. American foreign policies differ from region to region and from country to country.

The United States maintains friendly relations with its close neighbor Canada. Trading and tourism between the countries is beneficial to both countries. Relations with Mexico and some Central American countries, however, are often strained. This is because of the drug trade and the number of immigrants entering the United States illegally.

In 2015 a major change occurred in U.S. policy toward Cuba. President Obama and Cuban president Castro worked together to reestablish diplomatic relations after a more than 50-year separation.

Relations with Europe and the United States are strong. Many Americans trace part of their heritage to a European country. Also, trade and tourism thrives between Europe and the United States.

After the disintegration of the Soviet Union in 1991, relations with Russia eased. People hoped that the country would become democratic. However, with the rise to power of **Vladimir Putin,** this has not happened. He has imprisoned potential rivals, suppressed dissent, and stifled democratic reforms. In 2014 Putin sent Russian troops into Ukraine's Crimean Peninsula. Russia eventually annexed the region. In response to Russia's actions, the United States, the European Union, and several other countries imposed sanctions against Russia. Relations between the United States and Russia became tense.

The People's Republic of China is the most powerful country in East Asia. The U.S. policy toward China is cautious since its Communist government violates basic human rights.

Economically, China has grown. It is the world's largest exporter and holds more of the U.S. public debt than any other entity. The United States also has a huge trade deficit with China, which means we buy much more from the Chinese than they buy from us.

The United States also has a complex relationship with South Korea. U.S. forces remain there to protect it from Communist North Korea. In Southeast Asia, the United States enjoys good

© Houghton Mifflin Harcourt Publishing Company

relations with Communist Vietnam and Indonesia. However, a violent Islamist terrorist group, Jemaah Islamiyah, causes concern.

The United States has positive dealings with India as many American businesses rely on its high-tech industries. But dealings with Pakistan, also in South Asia, are shaky because Pakistan was accused of shielding Taliban fighters and allowing Osama bin Laden to hide in the country.

The Middle East presents the United States with many problems, including wars, terrorism, and lack of trust. With U.S. dependence on the region's oil, the situation remains complicated. Syria has been in the midst of a civil war, causing millions of Syrians to be displaced. Then a new terrorist enemy, the Islamic State of Iraq and Syria, or **ISIS,** came into existence. This group wants to set up a strict new Islamic state ruled by religious authorities. ISIS controls land in northern Iraq, and while the United States supports Iraq's efforts to fight ISIS, distrust of the United States is widespread.

The United States has not had formal diplomatic relations with Iran since the U.S.-supported shah was overthrown in 1979 and an Islamic theocracy began

ruling. In 2015 an agreement was proposed requiring Iran to reduce its nuclear program in exchange for easing punitive sanctions.

Israel and the United States are strongly connected economically, diplomatically, and militarily. U.S. military aid to Israel is high, and Israel has a positive view of the United States. Turkey, too, is an ally.

Africa presents several unique issues for the United States. North African countries Libya and Egypt are dominated by Islamic culture, with both countries experiencing protests in recent years. Struggles for power continue. In West Africa, Islam is also an influence. A terrorist group, **Boko Haram,** is centered in Nigeria but is active in nearby countries. This group is an ally of ISIS, and wants to establish an Islamic state. It is responsible for the kidnapping of 276 primarily Christian schoolgirls that it sold into sexual slavery.

2. How have terrorist groups impacted the Middle East and Africa?

    _____

    _____

Lesson 2, *continued*

Describe the nature of U.S. foreign policy with each of the first
five countries. Then describe problems that exist in the second set
of countries. Lastly, choose one country included in the lesson and
explain how it does or does not fit in with the national interests of
the United States.

Country	Relationship with the United States
1. Mexico	
2. Russia	
3. China	
4. Pakistan	
5. Israel	

Country	Problems
6. Syria	
7. Iraq	
8. Nigeria	

Country	How It Fits/Does Not Fit with the National Interests of the U.S.
9.	

© Houghton Mifflin Harcourt Publishing Company

Guided Reading Workbook

The United States in the 21st Century

Poverty and Social Concerns

Key Terms and People

minimum wage The lowest wage that employers can legally pay their workers

income gap Difference in income shown by the fact that the rich are getting richer, the poor are getting poorer, and the middle class is shrinking

Citizens United* v. *Federal Election Commission 2010 Supreme Court ruling that affected campaign spending by organizations

political action committee (PAC) An organization that merges campaign contributions from members and uses the merged funds to campaign for or against candidates or legislation

Before You Read

In the last lesson you learned about foreign policy in the 21st century. In this lesson you will read about how poverty and other social issues affect millions of Americans.

As You Read

Use a chart to take notes on modern social issues and their effects on Americans.

POVERTY IN AMERICA
Why is poverty a major problem in the United States?

Poverty has many causes, including illness, natural disasters, and economic downturns. Other causes are lack of skills, limited access to childcare, illiteracy, and discrimination against racial minorities.

Many employed adults are still below the poverty line. These working poor have low-wage jobs with few benefits. To help these workers, some people say that the **minimum wage** should be increased. Many Americans say this increase will help buying power. Other people say that it will hurt small businesses and result in job loss. However, when states recently raised their minimum wages, more jobs were created.

A major sign of poverty is the homeless population. About 750,000 Americans do not have access to shelter on any given night. This is a symptom of larger problems including unemployment, low-wage jobs, and high housing costs.

The **income gap** between the rich and the poor has widened during the 21st century. Causes include tax policies that favor the rich, and difficulty for people with lower incomes to afford health care, childcare, and higher education. Other causes are a global economy that puts low-wage workers in competition with workers abroad, and

© Houghton Mifflin Harcourt Publishing Company

Guided Reading Workbook

Lesson 3, *continued*

the fact that corporate CEOs receive huge salaries.

Income inequality is a major problem. It leads to slower economic growth, economic instability, high levels of debt, and fewer opportunities to advance.

1. How is the widening income gap related to poverty?

_____

_____

MONEY AND INFLUENCE
How do PACS influence politics in the United States?

Vast sums of money are spent on political campaigns. Special-interest groups use money to gain influence. In 2010 the Supreme Court ruled that the First Amendment could not restrict political expenditures by nonprofit corporations in *Citizens United* v. *Federal Election Commission.* Corporations are free to spend money on advertisements for candidates. However, they cannot donate directly to candidates. This case also influenced the growth of the **political action committee (PAC).** A PAC is an organization that merges campaign contributions from members. Then it uses the merged funds to campaign for or against candidates or legislation. This has led to Super PACs, that collect unlimited amounts of money from corporations, unions, and individuals. The power and influence of these groups is enormous.

2. Suppose a Super PAC supports a candidate's views. How is this a benefit to the candidate?

_____

_____

THE ROLE OF GOVERNMENT
What role does the government play in helping its citizens?

The federal government has addressed issues related to its people's welfare throughout its history. During the Depression, FDR passed New Deal programs that created jobs for the unemployed. Republicans argued against these programs because they did not want the government to have so much power. Then in the 1960s President Johnson proposed programs to end poverty and racism. Once again, Republicans objected.

Leaders disagree on how the government should deal with poverty. Some feel that federal programs are necessary. Others think that the government's role should be more limited.

Since the New Deal, the main way people get aid is through the Social Security Administration. This is funded by a tax paid by working Americans. Because people are living longer, more money is being paid out than is being taken in. The same is true for Medicare, which funds health care for disabled Americans and the elderly. People have suggested placing restrictions on Medicare benefits, raising the age of eligibility, or increasing the share to be paid by the elderly.

In 2010 President Obama signed the Patient Protection and Affordable Care Act in order to improve Americans' health care. Many uninsured Americans were able to get coverage.

3. What is one reason Social Security and Medicare seem to be running out of money?

_____

_____

Name _____ Class_____ Date_____

Complete the chart by summarizing the effects of each issue.

WHAT WAS THE EFFECT OF EACH ISSUE ON AMERICANS?	
1. Minimum wage	
2. Income gap	
3. *Citizens United* v. *Federal Election Commission*	
4. Super PACS	
5. Social Security/Medicare	
6. The Patient Protection and Affordable Care Act	

© Houghton Mifflin Harcourt Publishing Company

Guided Reading Workbook

The United States in the 21st Century

Lesson 4

Conservation and the Environment

Key Terms and People

global climate change A change in climate that involves high temperatures and extreme weather events, such as droughts and floods

fracking A drilling process for extracting oil and natural gas

biodiversity The entirety of a region's different species of plants and animals

Before You Read

In the last lesson you learned about how poverty and other social issues affect millions of Americans. In this lesson you will read about issues related to energy and the environment.

As You Read

Use a chart to take notes on environmental issues.

THE AMERICAN ENVIRONMENT
***How* does the government protect the environment?**

Throughout the United States, there are many natural resources and beautiful scenery. People who visit the United States from densely populated areas are delighted by open spaces and forests. However, our natural resources are not distributed evenly. Fertile farmland is not found everywhere. Rivers may flood in one part of the country, while they are dry in another part.

The country's water supply is shrinking. Droughts plague parts of the country, which makes the water situation critical. Air quality in some cities is poor. In addition, forests are being harmed by illegal logging on protected lands and some coal-mining techniques.

To deal with environmental threats, the government has passed legislation and formed conservation agencies. During the 1800s the government started

trying to conserve natural resources. It again became a focus in the 1960s and 1970s. The Clean Air Act of 1963 established a program to control air pollution. The Environmental Protection Agency (EPA) was formed in 1970 to deal with issues related to pollution and water and air quality. It also monitors emissions of toxic wastes. The Clean Water Act deals with water pollution.

There are also laws to protect plants and animals. The Endangered Species Preservation Act protects threatened species and their habitats.

In addition to federal laws, states such as California have strict environmental regulations. Not everyone is in favor of these laws. Some people feel that environmental preservation slows down industrial progress.

1. What does the EPA protect?

_____

_____

_____

© Houghton Mifflin Harcourt Publishing Company

Guided Reading Workbook

CHALLENGES FOR TODAY AND TOMORROW
Why is fracking controversial?

Dependence on fossil fuels—oil, natural gas, and coal—causes problems. Fossil fuels release gases into the atmosphere when burned. The gases trap heat and make the climate warmer. This has led to global warming and **global climate change.** This change involves high temperatures and extreme weather events such as droughts and floods. Some people believe that if these gases are reduced, then the negative effects of climate change may be reduced. Opinions differ as to whether human activity is causing climate change.

With so much use of nonrenewable fossil fuels, people are looking for other sources of these fuels. One controversial method is **fracking.** This is a drilling process for extracting oil and natural gas. While drillers are able to get oil and gas deposits that are not easily accessible, fracking's impact to the environment is a concern. One fracked well uses millions of gallons of water over its lifetime. Methane can escape from fracked wells. Some wells have exploded, leaving harmful chemicals on the land. Fracking has also been shown to cause an increase in earthquakes in areas where they were rare.

Another challenge for the environment is the lack of **biodiversity,** which is the entirety of a region's ecosystems and different species of living things. Ecosystems with biodiversity are healthier and have an easier time recovering from disruptions. Food crop biodiversity is important so that plant varieties can take over for damaged crops.

The honeybee population has been dwindling, too. This is a problem because honeybees are needed to pollinate many food crops. If honeybees continue to decline, many staple crops might be lost. Some scientists say that the decline is due to loss of habitat and food supply. Many uncultivated meadows have been lost to farming or suburbs.

2. What is most likely to happen if the honeybee population continues to decline?

_____

_____

SOME CHANGES FOR THE BETTER
What can people do to make the environment better?

Americans have made some progress in improving the environment. They recycle, use alternative energy sources, and have done away with many harmful pesticides.

Changes have occurred in relation to wetlands. Research has shown that wetlands shelter aquatic and bird species, help control pollution, and limit damage done by floods. Federal laws save wetlands from farming and development. Private organizations have also worked to preserve wetlands. More than 12 million acres of wetlands have been saved.

Dams have had benefits, too. For example, dams provide hydroelectric power, flood control, and reservoirs for reliable water supplies.

Another positive change is that Americans are buying more energy-efficient vehicles. This helps reduce air pollution and dependence on foreign oil. Electric cars, and even cars powered by solar energy, are being built.

3. How are Americans working to help the environment?

_____

_____

© Houghton Mifflin Harcourt Publishing Company

Lesson 4, *continued*

Complete the chart by writing the correct words or phrases to complete
the sentences about conservation and the environment.

1. Natural resources in the United States are not	2. Two ways forests are being harmed are by
3. The Clean Air Act was established to control	4. The Clean Water Act was established to control
5. The Endangered Species Preservation Act protects	6. Some people are not in favor of environmental preservation because they think that it slows down
7. Fossil fuels release gases into the atmosphere when	8. The change that involves high temperatures and extreme weather events is known as
9. People don't agree as to whether human activity is causing	10. An advantage to fracking is that drillers are able to get oil and natural gas deposits that are
11. In certain areas, fracking has been shown to cause an increase in	12. A region's variety of ecosystems and different living things is known as

© Houghton Mifflin Harcourt Publishing Company

The United States in the 21st Century

Education

Key Terms and People

flipped classroom A strategy that reverses the traditional approach of delivering instructional content by delivering it outside the classroom, often online

school voucher Subsidy given directly to parents for tuition at any school, public or private

Individuals with Disabilities Education Act (IDEA) Law that requires that students with a disability are provided with a Free Appropriate Public Education (FAPE) that is tailored to their individual needs

Before You Read

In the last lesson you learned about conservation and environmental issues. In this lesson you will read about issues involved with educating a diverse population.

As You Read

Use a chart to take notes on innovations or issues related to education in the 21st century.

THE CHANGING CLASSROOM
How has technology affected education?

Technology has changed education. Today, most classrooms have Internet access, and students may use tablets or smartphones rather than printed books to read content. After completing an assignment, they may receive immediate feedback. E-learning, or the use of electronic technology in education, is the standard in many U.S. schools. In a **flipped classroom,** e-learning is particularly important. Content is delivered outside the classroom, online, so time in class can be spent on research, group projects, discussion, and other interactive learning. While this strategy has raised test scores, improved graduation rates, and increased college

attendance in some schools, many students from poor families may not have access to the technology. And some students are not focused enough to complete the out-of-class learning.

1. What is a benefit of the flipped classroom?

_____

_____

CHALLENGES FOR EDUCATION
How do economic diversity and ethnic differences affect students in public schools?

Schools are paid for by local property taxes, which are based on the property values in a town or city. This means that schools in poorer areas get less money than those in richer sections. To deal with less funding, some school districts cut music, art, and other courses. They may have more students per class, or old buildings.

While 90 percent of children in the United States go to public schools, others go to private secular or religious schools or are taught at home. The parents of these children most likely pay taxes to fund public schools. Some feel they should get funding, or **school vouchers,** from the state to help with tuition costs. Supporters of vouchers say it increases competition among schools and leads to improvements in public schools. Opponents argue that vouchers take away funds from public schools. Also, some people say vouchers fund religious schools, which means taxpayers are paying for it. This is a violation of separation of church and state.

Student populations vary based on economic diversity. Family income may affect student success. Many qualify for free or reduced-price lunches. The federal government and some state governments are increasing funding to poor districts.

Student populations also vary in their ethnic backgrounds. Participation in programs for English language learners (ELL) is on the rise. In 2002–2003 the national figure for ELL students was at 8.7 percent. By 2011–2012 it had risen to 9.1 percent. However, there are differences in the numbers of ELL students according to states. In 2011–2012 California, for example, had more than 23 percent of its students needing ELL instruction, while West Virginia's rate was at 0.7 percent. So California needs more resources, such as specially trained teachers and modified materials for ELL instruction.

Children with special needs must be educated by public schools. The

Individuals with Disabilities Education Act (IDEA) requires that students with a disability be given a free education that is suited to their needs.

Educating different populations has long-term societal benefits. These students are better able to participate in American society and become self-sufficient.

The issue of how to improve public education is a challenge. Suggestions have ranged from longer school days, to more testing, to less testing. In 2002 President Bush passed an education program, No Child Left Behind. It uses results from yearly reading and math tests to hold schools accountable for student performance. If a school fails to show enough yearly progress, it could lose students to other schools or be forced to change staff. While some progress has been made, this program has problems, such as schools ignoring subjects other than reading and math. And testing special-education students with other students provides unfair results. In 2009 President Obama proposed Race to the Top. This plan focuses on rewarding schools for progress rather than punishing them for failure.

The costs for attending a college or university have risen dramatically. Between 2001 and 2012 the price for a public institution including tuition, room, and board rose 40 percent. The cost increase at private institutions was 28 percent. These increased costs make it hard for students to attend college. Many have to take out loans and work part-time jobs to afford higher education.

2. Why are school vouchers controversial?

_____

_____

Complete the chart by summarizing each innovation and problems associated with it. Then summarize each challenge and how it affects students.

INNOVATIONS IN EDUCATION	
1. E-learning	
2. Flipped classroom	
CHALLENGES IN EDUCATION	
3. Differences in property taxes	
4. Differences in ethnic backgrounds	
5. Individuals with Disabilities Education Act	
6. No Child Left Behind	
7. Rising cost of higher education	

© Houghton Mifflin Harcourt Publishing Company

The United States in the 21st Century

Globalization and Cultural Diffusion

Key Terms and People

globalization The process of international integration resulting from the interchange of worldviews, products, ideas, and other aspects of culture

free trade The policy in international markets in which governments do not restrict imports or exports

comparative advantage The idea that a nation will specialize in what it can produce at a lower opportunity cost, or trade-off, than any other nation

Kyoto Protocol An international treaty that seeks to reduce emissions of greenhouse gases

cultural diffusion The way cultural practices spread from one community to another

popular culture A collection of ideas, attitudes, and images that are part of a mainstream culture heavily influenced by and spread through the media

Before You Read

In the last lesson you learned about issues related to education. In this lesson you will read about how technology has connected the people of our country with people and cultures all over the world.

As You Read

Use a chart to take notes on how globalization developed and led to cultural diffusion.

THE GLOBAL ECONOMIC COMMUNITY

***How* has technology led to a global economy?**

Technology, communication, and expanded and improved transportation has led to **globalization.** This is the process of international integration resulting from the interchange of worldviews, products, ideas, and other aspects of culture. With these changes have come some problems. For example, multinational corporations take over and push out smaller businesses, and job loss occurs because domestic companies move their factories and hire workers abroad. However, globalization also creates jobs since new international markets increase exports, and new workers are needed to create products.

A key driver of economic globalization is technology. Computers changed industries and the role of individual workers. They made it possible for workers to share information through

© Houghton Mifflin Harcourt Publishing Company

Lesson 6, *continued*

computer networks. Devices such as laptops and cell phones allow people to work at home. Companies can outsource tasks such as support services.

Globalization and free trade go hand in hand. **Free trade** is the policy in international markets in which governments do not restrict imports or exports. Free trade is also connected to **comparative advantage,** the idea that a nation will specialize in what it can produce at a lower opportunity cost than any other nation.

Even with globalization there is conflict. Companies compete for resources, trade routes, and markets. Countries form trading blocs, which help reduce trade barriers such as tariffs among their members. For example, the United States is allied with Canada and Mexico in the North American Free Trade Agreement (NAFTA).

Economic competitors to the United States include the Organization of the Petroleum Exporting Countries (OPEC). Most OPEC countries are in Africa or the Middle East, and OPEC has a lot of control over the oil and oil prices in the world. Since the United States has increased domestic oil production, some of OPEC's influence has lessened.

The European Union (EU) is another competitive trade alliance, as well as being a strong political ally of the United States. Consisting of 28 member countries, EU citizens, goods, services, and economic capital can move freely among its countries.

1. Why is technology a key driver of economic globalization?

_____

_____

_____

CHALLENGES OF GLOBALIZATION
What are the negative impacts of globalization?

Economic globalization has helped places such as India and Bangladesh. However, new jobs in these countries often pay low wages and working conditions are poor. Children are often forced to work in conditions similar to slavery. American workers are affected by economic globalization, too. Jobs have been lost to countries with lower wages.

The environment has also been affected by globalization. Some countries have proposed plans to protect air and water, such as the **Kyoto Protocol.** Many Americans who believe global warming is caused by human activity approve of the Kyoto Protocol. Others do not think an international group should monitor U.S. industries. Although the United States signed the treaty, it has not ratified it. Some say this is because fossil fuel industries are too powerful in the United States.

Not all countries have the same laws and practices related to business, so companies must make ethical decisions. Subcontractors who subject workers to sweatshop conditions and no protection from hazardous chemicals may not be breaking laws. But buyers may refuse to purchase the company's products when they go on sale in the United States. Some other companies hire workers in countries with poor human rights records. Sometimes corruption leads to bribes.

2. A business uses subcontractors in a country where children are forced to work in dangerous conditions. When this fact is shared with the American public, how are they likely to react?

_____

_____

_____

© Houghton Mifflin Harcourt Publishing Company

Guided Reading Workbook

DIFFUSION ON A GLOBAL SCALE
How does popular culture spread?

Globalization has also affected international politics. Ideas spread through blogs and social media. Upset or discontented people use technology to lead dissent. For example, Egypt's rebellion in 2011 was organized through the Internet.

Globalization has led to **cultural diffusion,** in which people spread the ideas of their home cultures into the cultures of others. In the past, cultural diffusion happened when people traveled or immigrated to other countries. Now that the Internet allows instant connection to places and cultures around the world, cultural diffusion happens constantly.

Popular culture is the collection of ideas, attitudes, and images that are a part of mainstream culture. Pop culture, such as music and fashion, has spread quickly because of the Internet, movies, and television. People all over the world have access to the same news, music, and products. In this way, American pop culture has spread to other parts of the globe, and Americans have more access than ever before to ideas and trends from different cultures.

An example of cultural diffusion is the spread of hip-hop around the world. Hip-hop was born in New York City in the 1970s and quickly became popular throughout the United States. Movies such as *Wild Styles* introduced hip-hop to other parts of the world in the 1980s. In the 1990s companies used hip-hop music and the popularity of hip-hop culture to sell products.

As hip-hop culture spread, other countries began incorporating elements from their cultures into it. The Internet allows the hip-hop community all over the world to communicate, and video-sharing sites help spread new music from country to country.

3. How does the Internet help cultural diffusion happen constantly?

_____

_____

© Houghton Mifflin Harcourt Publishing Company

Complete the chart with the effects of each situation.

Situation		Effects
1. Computers transformed industry and the lives of workers.	→	
2. Free trade has opened up international markets.	→	
3. Technological innovations in transportation and communication have led to an expanding global economy.	→	
4. People all over the world have access to the same movies, music, and products.	→	

© Houghton Mifflin Harcourt Publishing Company